ALCOHOL: MINIMISING THE HARM

ALCOHOL: MINIMISING THE HARM

WHAT WORKS?

Edited by
Martin Plant, Eric Single
and Tim Stockwell

FREE ASSOCIATION BOOKS • LONDON / NEW YORK

Published in 1997 by
Free Association Books Ltd
57 Warren Street
London W1P 5PA
and 70 Washington Square South
New York, NY 10012-1091

ISBN: 1 85343 358 6 hbk   1 85343 359 4 pbk

A CIP catalogue record for this book is available from the
British Library.

Produced for Free Assocation Books Ltd by
Chase Production Services, Chadlington OX7 3LN
Printed in the EC by J.W. Arrowsmith Ltd, Bristol

Contents

List of Tables and Figures

Notes on Contributors

James Berson MPH. Postgraduate Student, Boston University School of Public Health, Boston, USA.

Douglas Cameron MD. Senior Lecturer (Clinical) in Substance Abuse, Department of Psychiatry, University of Leicester, UK.

Katie Dowley MPH. Projects Co-ordinator, Prevention Research Center, University of Illinois, Chicago, USA.

Benedikt Fischer Dipl.-Verw.wiss. Research associate, Addiction Research Foundation, Toronto, Ontario, Canada.

Christine Godfrey BSc. Reader, Department of Health Sciences & Clinical Evaluation, University of York, UK.

Kathryn Graham PhD. Scientist, Addiction Research Foundation, London, Ontario, Canada.

Tom Greenfield PhD. Senior Scientist, Alcohol Research Group, Western Consortium for Public Health & Department of Psychiatry, University of California, San Francisco, California, USA.

Ralph Hingson ScD. Professor, Boston University School of Public Health, Boston, USA.

Ross Homel PhD. Professor/Head, School of Justice Administration, Griffith University, Queensland, Australia.

David Musto MD. Professor of Child Psychiatry and History of Medicine, School of Medicine, Yale University, New Haven, USA.

Martin Plant PhD. Professor/Director, Alcohol & Health Research Group, Department of Psychiatry, The University of Edinburgh, UK.

Moira Plant PhD. Deputy Director, Alcohol & Health Research Group, Department of Psychiatry, The University of Edinburgh, UK.

Jürgen Rehm PhD. Director, Social Evaluation and Research Department, Addiction Research Foundation, Toronto, Canada.

Philip Rydon PhD. Research Fellow, National Centre for Research into the Prevention of Drug Abuse, Curtin University, Perth, Western Australia.

Robert F. Saltz PhD. Deputy Director/Senior Research Scientist, Prevention Research Center, Berkeley, California, USA.

Eric Single PhD. Director of Policy and Research, Canadian Centre on Substance Abuse and professor of Preventive Medicine and Biostatistics, University of Toronto, Canada.

Kathryn Stewart MS. Senior Research Scientist, Pacific Institute for Research & Evaluation, Rockville, Maryland, USA.

Tim Stockwell PhD. Professor/Director, National Centre for Research into the Prevention of Drug Abuse, Curtin University, Perth, Western Australia.

Barry M. Sweedler MA. Director, Office of Safety Recommendations, United States National Transportation Safety Board, USA.

Friedner D. Wittman PhD. President, CLEW Associates and Program Director for the Community Alcohol Prevention Planning Program, Institute for the Study of Social Change, University of California at Berkeley, California, USA.

Preface

This book presents a collection of reviews of some of the available evidence on the effectiveness of some approaches to minimising alcohol problems. The twenty contributors were not selected because they agree on 'what is to be done' about alcohol problems. Like many researchers, clinicians and other commentators in the 'alcohol field', they have varied views on this complex subject. The editors themselves have rather different perspectives on what constitutes 'harm minimisation'. This book does not, therefore, purport to be the definitive treatise on the control of alcohol-related problems, nor does it present a neat package of policies guaranteed to achieve this ambitious goal. Instead, what is offered is a selection of thoughtful and sometimes highly critical, appraisals of what has been attempted and what has, apparently, been accomplished in reducing the adverse consequences associated with the consumption of beverage alcohol. Solutions to alcohol problems have to be tailored to suit the historical, political and social context in which they occur. Some of the evidence considered below may have relevance in many contexts, while some of it may not readily or appropriately be transplanted into other settings. The debate about alcohol and its role in society is often heated and strongly influenced by ideological fervour, personal experience, professional or economic interests. It is hoped that this essentially pragmatic text will make a contribution to this ongoing debate.

Acknowledgements

The editors would like to thank Ms Gill Davies, Managing Director of Free Association Books Ltd, for her encouragement and support during the conception and production of this book. Her commitment to publishing books related to alcohol and other psychoactive drug use has a long and distinguished track record spanning over twenty years. The editors also thank the contributors for agreeing to provide reviews in areas in which they have great personal expertise and for documenting available evidence in these fields in an accessible, critical and informative manner.

Finally, the hard work of Dr Moira Plant and Ms Christine Thornton of the Alcohol & Health Research Group in the University of Edinburgh is acknowledged for providing invaluable assistance in the compilation of the final text of this book.

PART I

Introduction

1 Introduction: Harm Minimisation and Alcohol

Martin Plant, Eric Single and Tim Stockwell

Alcohol is the most widely used recreational psychoactive drug in most countries of the world. While most drinkers mainly consume alcohol in moderate quantities, some people drink heavily, inappropriately and with adverse and sometimes tragic results. 'Alcohol-related problems' constitute a major cause for concern at a local, national and international level. Such problems include ill-health, injuries, premature mortality, social, family and economic difficulties; public order offences and a host of behavioural consequences. The very popularity of alcohol makes the control of alcohol-related problems highly controversial and politicised. Often the debate about how to curb such problems is charged by ideological fervour, vested interest or prejudice. Discussions about the best approaches to reduce levels of alcohol-related problems are also frequently restricted by uncertainty about what the effects of some of the possible strategies might be.

Alcohol: Minimising the Harm is an attempt to present a pragmatic review of the effectiveness of key strategies designed to achieve a significant reduction in levels of alcohol problems. These strategies are described and critically assessed by some of the world's leading authorities on the use of alcohol and its related problems. It is emphasised that this book is not a collective statement endorsing a single, agreed, philosophical perspective. It is also not an attempt to promulgate a detailed manifesto for public policy. Neither the contributors to this book, nor even the three editors, agree with each other completely about either philosophy or public policy options. Researchers, clinicians and others in the 'alcohol field' subscribe to many viewpoints.

This book is an attempt to review in detail the available evidence about the proven effectiveness or ineffectiveness of some of the main methods whereby the adverse consequences associated with alcohol consumption may be reduced. In the view of the editors, it is appropriate to consider this evidence under the general classification of 'harm minimisation'. The terms 'harm minimisation' or 'harm reduction' have more commonly been applied in recent years to programmes which were developed to deal with problems associated with illicit drug use, particularly the spread of HIV infection from the sharing of injecting equipment by intravenous drug users. Therefore people may tend to think of harm minimisation in the context of illicit drug use. Examples of harm minimisation strategies include the provision of sterile needles and syringes for injecting drug users, the prescribing of methadone for opiate users and the dispensing of free condoms to sexually active people, such as those working in the sex industry (Plant 1990, Strang and Stimson 1990, Plant and Plant 1992, Heather et al. 1993). O'Hare (1992) has noted that harm minimisation in relation to illicit drug use was fostered by HIV infection, together with a suspicion that past policies to deal with drug use had made matters worse rather than better. In the context of alcohol, the main criterion of successful policy should simply be the reduction of harm.

The central thesis of this book is that there is a trend towards harm minimisation in alcohol problems prevention with increased attention being given to measures which focus on reducing the adverse consequences of drinking without necessarily reducing drinking per se. It is often necessary to reduce drinking to reduce alcohol-related harm. Even so, it is the reduction of high-risk drinking that is required, rather than the reduction of all drinking (Stockwell et al. 1996). 'Harm reduction' is controversial. It has been attacked on the grounds that some strategies, such as the operation of injecting-equipment exchanges, imply condoning illicit drug use or other illicit or potentially health-damaging forms of behaviour. In fact, as the editors of this book believe, harm minimisation is neutral on the virtue or shame attached to such behaviours. Its impetus stems from a practical desire simply to reduce the level of tragedy, harm, pain and misery. It is important how harm minimisation strategies are perceived by key groups of people, especially those who are vulnerable in relation to alcohol or other health-related damage. It is possible that some strategies, such as decriminalising illicit drugs or the prescription of opiates to drug-dependent people, might lead to the increase of drug use. In such cases it becomes an empirical issue as to whether focusing on reducing the harm of established users or heavy consumers puts at risk a substantial number of people who are currently non-users or moderate users. Another important feature of harm minimisation is the prominence given to the considerations of 'what works?' and the practical feasibility of implementing any specific policy.

Commenting on harm minimisation in relation to illicit drug use, O'Hare has set out the following considerations:

Evaluating the effectiveness of interventions designed to reduce the harmful effects of drug use is a difficult task, requiring the selection of a set of criteria for evaluating outcomes, and recognition of the hierarchical nature of harm reduction goals.

... Harms and benefits are classified according to a two dimensional scheme: type of consequence (health, social and economic) and level of consequence (individual, community and societal). Risks are classified according to quantitative dimensions (dosage, potency and frequency) and qualitative dimensions (access, preparation, route and style of administration, poly-use patterns, after-care, set and setting). This conceptual analysis provides a framework within which specific harm reduction interventions can be planned, implemented, evaluated and, if necessary, modified. (1992: xvi–xvii)

Harm reduction is not in conflict with the reduction of overall consumption as a measure to prevent alcohol problems. Many, probably most, researchers would agree that the overall level of alcohol-related problems generally fluctuates with general national levels of per capita alcohol consumption. Even so, rates of individual problems such as drunkenness convictions and alcohol-related liver disease or cancers do not all fluctuate simultaneously or even in the same way (Plant 1997). It is also becoming increasingly apparent that different subgroups of people have different drinking habits. Moreover, there is growing evidence pointing to the importance of *pattern* of drinking in influencing the consequences that are caused thereby (Rehm et al. 1996). In view of the widespread use of alcohol, its popularity and the major political and economic interests that support its production, distribution and consumption, it is concluded that magic solutions to alcohol-related problems are in short supply. The aetiology of drinking and of 'problem drinking' is complex and so too are solutions to alcohol-related problems. Such responses need to be both politically and practically feasible. In addition, public policy regarding alcohol-related problems has to be implemented in ways that suit national, regional or local needs, context and political culture. Some policies, including some of those described in this book, may be difficult to export to other situations.

The characteristic feature of harm minimisation which distinguishes it from other public health approaches to alcohol is that it attempts to reduce the harmful consequences of drinking in situations where the drinking can be expected to take place. The decision to drink is accepted as a fact. This does not imply approval (or disapproval) of alcohol consumption. It is simply presumed that people will be drinking in a particular situation and efforts should be made to reduce the potential harmful consequences that may occur. This will often include measures designed to encourage the consumption of alcohol at less risky levels.

Harm minimisation is also not in conflict with abstinence-oriented approaches to the prevention of alcohol problems. Just as harm minimisation does not imply approval of drinking, it also does not imply that the eventual goal of intervention might not include abstention. Indeed, in some instances, harm minimisation measures may be a first step towards reducing harmful drinking practices and eventually the cessation of drinking altogether. Harm minimisation involves a *prioritisation* of goals, in which immediate and attainable objectives take priority when dealing with high-risk drinkers who cannot be realistically expected to cease their drinking in the near future. Even so, it does not conflict with an *eventual* aim of abstention. It is simply neutral regarding the long-term goal of intervention. Much of the evidence that is considered in this book involves modifying drinking behaviour as well as the environment in which drinking occurs in order to reduce harm.

Harm minimisation does not simply refer to any alcohol policy or programme which aims at reducing harm, as this is the universal goal of all alcohol policies and programmes. The term 'harm minimisation' is restricted to those policies and programmes which attempt to reduce the harm associated with drinking without the drinker necessarily giving up his or her use of alcohol at the present time.

Whereas the contrast between harm reduction approaches for illicit drugs to a 'zero tolerance' approach is almost self-evident, the parallel differences between harm minimisation approaches for alcohol and prevailing conceptualisations of alcohol problems prevention are less obvious. Until recently, public health advocates in the field of alcohol problems prevention have tended to focus on alcohol control measures such as the nature and extent of state monopolisation of alcohol trade, the number and location of off-premise sales outlets, licensing regulations, drinking age restrictions, proscriptions against selling to intoxicated persons, advertising and sponsorship restrictions, criminal penalties for driving while intoxicated and alcohol taxation. The focus on alcohol availability is based on the assumption that controlling price, drinking age and licensing hours are likely to influence alcohol consumption and indicators of alcohol-related health and social problems (Bruun et al. 1975, Mäkelä et al. 1981, Moore and Gerstein 1981, Edwards et al. 1994). The focus in preventive education has generally been on the minimisation of drinking and the avoidance of dependence. The message for all drinkers was generally unequivocal: drinking less is better (World Health Organization 1992).

The message in harm minimisation approaches is somewhat different: *avoid problems when you drink*. This is complementary rather than contradictory to the message that drinking less is better. Indeed, some harm minimisation approaches (for example, the promotion of low alcohol content beverages) do involve drinking less. Even so, harm minimisation differs from prior alcohol prevention strategies in that it focuses on decreasing the risk and severity of adverse consequences arising from alcohol consumption without necessarily decreasing the level of consumption. It is essentially a practical rather than an idealised approach: the standard is not some ideal drinking level or situation (abstention or 'low-risk' levels), but whether or not the chances of adverse consequences have been reduced by the introduction of the prevention measure.

Each of the authors of this book was completely free to express their personal, and often very varied, perspectives on this many faceted and important theme. The editors hope that the material that is presented in this book presents a broader, more varied set of views than those concentrating solely upon the traditional public health perspective. The latter emphasises control of per capita alcohol consumption. This, as noted above, is not necessarily inconsistent with harm minimisation, but is only an example of one strategy. It was intended that this book would range much wider. The following contributions review past experience in the context of the political and practical feasibility of specific policies. Such considerations have great practical importance in relation to the realistic prospects that individual policies might be implemented.

Alcohol: Minimising the Harm offers a wide-ranging and international review. Whenever possible and appropriate, reference has been made to evidence from non-'Western' and non-industrial societies.

This book presents critical appraisals of a number of local and national approaches. These are considered against the context of the history of alcohol control policies and the ongoing polemic about the status of the 'harm minimisation' approach to the control of problems associated not only with alcohol, but also with tobacco, illicit drugs and other health-related behaviours. The contemporary issues considered are set in the context of an introduction to what is meant by 'harm minimisation' or 'harm reduction' and a historical perspective on alcohol control is provided. The second part of the book presents evidence on a number of examples of attempts to reduce the harm associated with alcohol consumption. These include fiscal and supply controls, zoning and local action, prevention where alcohol is sold and consumed, standard unit labelling of alcoholic beverage containers, the use of warning labels, driving under the influence of alcohol, US experience in the reduction of drinking and alcohol problems amongst college students, the creation of safer bars, alcohol education and local regulation and enforcement strategies. The third part of the book considers the implications of harm minimisation in relation to clinical responses for those with alcohol problems, and the measurement of harm and its implications for epidemiology. Finally, the editors consider the implications of the evidence presented and outline some future priorities for action.

References

Bruun, K., Edwards, G., Lumio, M., Mäkelä, K., Pan, L., Popham, R., Room, R., Schmidt, W., Skog, Ø-J., Sulkunen, P. and Österberg, E. (1975) *Alcohol Control Policies in Public Health Perspective*, Helsinki, Finnish Foundation for Alcohol Studies.

Edwards, G., Anderson, P., Babor, T.F., Casswell, S., Ferrence, R., Giesbrecht, N., Godfrey, C., Holder, H., Lemmens, P., Mäkelä, K., Midanik, L., Norström, T., Österberg, E., Romelsjö, A., Room, R., Simpura, J. and Skog, Ø-J. (1994) *Alcohol Policy and the Public Good*, Oxford, Oxford University Press.

Heather, N., Wodak, A. and O'Hare, P. (eds) (1993) *Psychoactive Drugs and Harm Reduction: From Faith to Science*, London, Whurr Publishers.

Mäkelä, K., Room, R., Single, E., Sulkunen, P. and Walsh, B. (1981) *Alcohol, Society and the State. 1. A Comparative Study of Alcohol Control*, Toronto, Addiction Research Foundation.

Moore, M. and Gerstein, D. (eds) (1981) *Alcohol and Public Policy: Beyond the Shadow of Prohibition*, Washington, D.C., National Academy Press.

O'Hare, P.A. (1992) 'Preface: A note on the concept of harm reduction', in O'Hare, P.A., Newcombe, R., Matthews, A., Buning, E.C. and Drucker, E. (eds) *The Reduction of Drug-Related Harm*, London, Tavistock/ Routledge, pp. xiii–xvii.

O'Hare, P.A., Newcombe, R., Matthews, A., Buning, E.C. and Drucker, E. (eds) (1992) *The Reduction of Drug-Related Harm*, London, Tavistock/ Routledge.

Plant, M.A. (ed.) (1990) *AIDS, Drugs and Prostitution*, London, Tavistock/ Routledge.

Plant, M.A. (1997) 'Trends in alcohol and illicit drug-related diseases', in Charlton, J. (ed.) *Health of Adult Britain*, London, HMSO.

Plant, M.A. and Plant, M.L. (1992) *Risk Takers: Alcohol, Drugs, Sex and Youth*, London, Tavistock/Routledge.

Rehm, J., Ashley, M., Room, R., Single, E., Bondy, S., Ferrence, R. and Giesbrecht, N. (1996) 'On the emerging paradigm of drinking patterns and their social and health consequences', *Addiction* (forthcoming).

Stockwell, T., Single, E., Hawks, D. and Rehm, J. (1996) 'Sharpening the focus of alcohol policy from aggregate consumption to harm and risk reduction', Paper presented at 22nd Annual Alcohol Epidemiology Symposium, Kettil Bruun Society, Edinburgh, 7 June.

Strang, J. and Stimson, G.V. (eds) (1990) *AIDS and Drug Misuse*, London, Tavistock/Routledge.

World Health Organization (1992) *European Alcohol Action Plan, Copenhagen*, World Health Organization Regional Office for Europe.

2 Alcohol Control in Historical Perspective

David F. Musto

The origin of alcohol-containing beverages is lost in time. Viticulture is thought to have begun in the area of modern Armenia, the site of the vineyard said to have been established by Noah immediately after the Flood. The wild grape (*Vitis vinifera silvestris*) grew there as well as in most areas of Europe and Asia that are now wine-producing regions. Beers are chiefly a result of grain harvests and presumably were well under way with the establishment of farming; they were a staple in Pharaonic Egypt. At any rate, by the time writing was invented, fermented alcoholic beverages were available and used.

Factors Favouring Alcohol Consumption

The impulse to control drinking is probably as old as the discovery of the mood-altering properties of alcohol, and the history of alcohol use takes the form of a struggle between the polarities of indulgence and abstention, between high esteem for the valuable assistance of alcohol and fear of any consumption of what some considered a poison.

Divergent attitudes towards drinking were institutionalised in the competing city-states of Athens and Sparta. Athens was characterised by the symposium, a banquet with drinking and conversation, and by the annual Dionysian festival which included plays, ceremonies and drinking in honour of the wine god. Fifth and fourth century BC Athens was noted for excessive drinking in taverns; it is said that Alcibiades taught Athenians to drink in the morning, thereby intensifying the consumption of wine (McKinlay 1951: 67). Xenophon took the Greeks to task for their drinking, but his criticism allowed for one exception: the Spartans (McKinlay 1951: 77ff.).

The legendary Lycurgus is said to have established a set of severe laws for the Spartans in the seventh century BC which included a prohibition of wine drinking for any reason other than thirst. Spartans occasionally made their serfs drink to excess so children could learn to despise the effect of wine (McKinlay 1949: 311). Plato praised the Spartans for their temperance in contrast with the Athenian laxity in drink (McKinlay 1951: 79–80).

These two remarkable and remarkably contrasting cities symbolise divergent approaches to alcohol in society: a positive attitude which looks for the best way to provide drink and regulate only the excesses which occur, or a negative attitude which seeks to reduce consumption to a minimum.

By the first millennium AD concern about controlling beer and wine had become more common. Nevertheless, wine was, and is, an essential element of Judaism and later became so in the Christian church. The Jewish Seder as well as the Christian Eucharist require wine. In addition to the Eucharist, an extra-canonical ritual use of alcohol developed in Christianity in which wine would be drunk on a particular saint's day or in memory of the deceased – at times the congregation and the priest would become drunk (Fichtenau 1991: 60–1, 149). This practice was condemned by church authorities, but altering one's state of consciousness through alcohol consumption as an offering or act of honour can still be witnessed at wakes.

Around the twelfth century the process of distillation was known at the medical school of Salerno (Forbes 1948: 58, 87–8). Distillation was employed to obtain the essence of various substances such as herbs and also to concentrate the ingredient in wine which gave it such power. For centuries this special substance was produced in small quantities, usually in secrecy, and used as a medicine. Thus began a slow but inexorable growth of distilled spirits that would explode in the sixteenth and seventeenth centuries. It was in the centuries before distilled spirits became cheap and easily available that alcohol came to be considered the most central element in life and life's preserver. A high concentration of alcohol obtainable after a number of distillations was called the water of life, *aqua vitae*, and even the fifth element, the quintessence. One fifteenth-century proof of its special and vital function was that if a piece of meat was left in water it would rot, but if left in *aqua vitae*, it would harden and last (Wilson 1975: 57).

Once spirits became easily accessible through widespread distillation, consumption rose to extraordinary levels. During this trend for distilled spirits a medical theory was propounded that drinking to drunkenness once or twice a month was in itself a healthful purging of the body (Forbes 1948: 187–8). Early medical advice provided strong argument for drinking any alcoholic beverage and little sanction for moderation. Even John Wesley, the founder of Methodism and a severe critic of distilled spirits, praised wine as 'one of the noblest cordials in nature' (Wesley 1901: 419).

Established drinking customs are a further reason for imbibing. In particular the drinking of 'healths', the toasting of companions, who in turn toast others, typically with the requirement that each glass be drained, results in a great deal of alcohol being consumed at routine social events. Similarly, if the first action of a good host is to bring out a bottle of vodka or whisky rather than the tea pot, the per capita consumption is easily raised.

Identification with some valued symbol encourages drinking that might otherwise not occur, at least not in such amounts. The rapid increase in gin consumption in England after the accession of William III in 1688 was for many a sign of loyalty to the new king from Holland – where gin had originated (Blunt 1729: 28). In the United States after the War of Independence rum fell into disrepute because its basis was molasses from the British Caribbean; allegiance was transferred to the new national drink, whiskey, made from American grain (Rorabaugh 1979: 67ff.). Youthful identification of alcohol with adulthood similarly adds an attraction that goes beyond the effect of alcohol itself.

Finally, alcohol was said to provide courage and energy, essential to workers in general and especially to soldiers and sailors. The legendary Persian discoverer of wine, Djemshid, found it so healthful that he urged everyone to drink it and made a point of giving it to his soldiers in order to make them strong (Cherrington 1924–30: I, 213). In the first half of the eighteenth century, when attacks on distilled spirits began to mount after the consequences of uncontrolled gin consumption became apparent, one of the counter-attacks was to declare that gin was necessary for the British combatants in the many wars of that time. In his *Autobiography* Benjamin Franklin describes the almost continuous drinking of strong beer in the London printing house where he was apprenticed. Franklin, at that time a teetotaller, tells how other workmen believed 'it was necessary, [they] supposed, to drink *strong* Beer that [they] might be *strong* to labor' (Franklin 1987: 1348).

The beliefs listed above for drinking are in addition to the use of alcohol as a mild social lubricant or as a savoury addition to one's meal; they are arguments for drinking whether one feels like it or not. With so many reasons for drinking, attempts at control have been difficult. Yet the negative effects of alcohol have spurred efforts at regulation or even prohibition from a very early date.

The Problems of Alcohol

Immediate personal effects of drinking alcohol are unsteadiness, garrulity, emotional alteration – hostility or cheerfulness or sleep – and, with increasing dosage, more loss of control until coma supervenes. Clearly, alcohol use can be a problem if there are responsibilities to be met. The more structured a person's life, the more alcohol interferes with work duties. Although inefficiency, falling productivity and danger when operating machinery became obvious alcohol-related hazards during the Industrial Revolution, missteps due to alcohol occurred throughout the history of its use. Attributing diseases and general deterioration of the body and mind to alcohol came early. The lifespan might be shortened by excessive alcohol and long-term illnesses, such as liver cirrhosis, and require resources that could be employed elsewhere. Acute problems, like drink-driving, affect the whole of modern society. Beyond the imbibing individual, the impact on the family and neighbours is a serious complication of alcohol's effects.

From the larger view of government, the rise of alcoholic beverages meant the diversion of time and income away from traditional paths. This could mean a loss of taxes and, if individual income barely met the necessities of life, a reduced living standard for the user. If grain supplies were close to the food demand for them, diversion into beer production or later to distillation would cause a food shortage. In contrast with the beliefs of the early Persians and some eighteenth-century English, when war or preparation for war coincided with increasing public disapproval of drinking, government officials were likely to believe that alcohol weakened soldiers and sailors, and that liquor control was a matter of national security. Restrictions applied to taverns near military bases in the United States before and during the First World War are a good example of this perception.

Several religious groups saw alcohol as an obstacle to personal salvation. The rise of Islam in the seventh century presented a dynamic and rapidly growing religious faith that forbade the use of alcoholic beverages, thereby clearly setting it apart from Judaism and Christianity. Later groups, especially from the Reformation onward, set themselves apart from the traditional acceptance of alcohol in Christianity. Among the faiths to question alcohol were the Quakers and the Methodists (Bainton 1945: 54–7). Baptists also rejected alcohol. In the United States particularly, a theology that stressed human co-operation in attaining salvation targeted alcohol as a grave danger (Ahlström 1972: 421ff.). If man had a duty to participate with God's grace in gaining salvation, then intoxication, by clouding the mind and by stimulating sinful acts, would lead the user to hell, a fate much worse than death of the body. As discussed below, this belief led to urgent, evangelical campaigns against alcohol.

A somewhat more abstract problem linked to alcohol is the observation that a nation with much drunkenness has great difficulty in reforming itself in any area. Such a concern can be found in Isaiah and other prophets who blame drinking for obstructing moral reform (Isaiah 28: 3,7). It was also apparent in the liberal efforts in Czarist Russia to curb or prohibit vodka consumption in the years shortly before the First World War. When the Czar finally agreed to end the alcohol monopoly and institute prohibition near the outbreak of the First World War, he performed one act that found favour with the Bolshevik Revolution a few years later. The revolutionaries saw the haze of alcohol consumption as a barrier to their organisation of the nation and only re-established the old system in the 1920s on the grounds that the Soviet Union could obtain no foreign loans, thus illustrating the ambivalence governments exhibit over alcohol: to tax alcohol for needed revenue or curb consumption to enhance the quality of life (White 1996: 22).

Seven decades after the Czar's condemnation of vodka, Mikhail Gorbachev undertook a Soviet attack on vodka. In 1985 he launched an anti-alcohol crusade that tried quickly to change the long-standing acceptance of drink into a culture that frowned on drunkenness and even alcohol itself. A national temperance society was formed that soon boasted of more then ten million members while the legal production of vodka was drastically reduced. However, long lines formed outside liquor stores, popular resentment burgeoned and the production of illicit alcohol grew enormously. Within five years the plan had foundered. In a curious parallel, the 1914 and 1985 campaigns failed, among other reasons, because their authors believed that a change in attitude toward such a fundamental custom as drinking could be ordered into existence by the central authority (White 1996: 59ff.).

Civil Alcohol Control

Nations which have not attempted to reduce alcohol consumption have usually moved over the centuries to a regulated system which aims to provide good quality alcoholic beverages at clean, safe sites and at a reasonable price. The path to this idealised situation has been traversed slowly and with repeated obstacles. In a significant way, attempts to control alcohol distribution have paralleled efforts to realise governmental centralisation and to influence citizens' lifestyles. Of course, this goal has never fully been met. Governments still have great difficulty in affecting lifestyle, as witnessed in the campaigns to discourage drug use or alter practices that might lead to the spread of AIDS.

Governments have also concerned themselves with the quality of alcoholic beverage manufacture and sale: Was it pure? Were correct measures used? Was the price reasonable? Consumers have long been protected by penalties against adulteration, as in 1492 when the Scottish Parliament approved the death penalty for such a violation of trust (Cherrington 1924–30: V, 2383). The locations where beverages were sold also came under the inspection of magistrates. By the late eighteenth century in England alehouses and their proprietors had come under close scrutiny and their numbers had been reduced (Clark 1983: 256–7). Similarly, in Massachusetts in 1645, town officials were required to see to it that only 'fitt men' be allowed to operate a public house (Shurtleff 1853: 279–80). In these ways, the provision of alcoholic beverages was regularised in both the government's and consumers' interests. Through these reforms, the negative side of alcohol distribution – dirty, unsafe and inconvenient tippling houses, poorly or dangerously manufactured beverages, and exorbitant prices – was ameliorated.

When the problems associated with alcohol dominated its image, the effort to curtail use employed some of the same measures noted above, but extended them to make alcohol less available. More than three decades before John Adams became the second President of the United States, he tried to reduce the bad behaviour of imbibers in eighteenth-century Braintree, Massachusetts, by lobbying for limits to the number of places where alcohol could be bought (Adams 1961: 128–30). Early in this century when the prohibition movement had not yet succeeded in the United States, numerous localities adopted stringent rules concerning a bartender's qualifications and the appearance of a bar (Clark 1976: 96ff.). These rules could be contradictory: some cities required that windows facing the street be opaque up to a height where passersby could not see the drinking, while other cities required clear windows so no one could drink in private.

Taxes represent one of the most direct ways to influence alcohol purchases and also to raise revenue. In times of indifference or approval of alcohol, these taxes have been regulated so that they do not reduce consumption, but maximise revenue. If a tax had a negative effect, in these circumstances, a correction was usually made. Protection of domestic production has led to high tariffs on foreign beverages, as when England placed a duty on French brandy in 1677 to protect the growing English distilled spirits industry (Dowell 1888: 163). Designating a specific group to monopolise alcohol production, such as the English brewing and distilling guilds, helped governments rationalise the market and simplify tax collection. The belief that extremely high tax rates can drastically reduce use underlay the English 1729 Act levying high licence and duty on gin. The high taxes led to extensive circumvention of the law, and the Act was repealed in 1733 (Clark 1988: 63–84). Alexander Hamilton took another approach when he was advocating adoption of the US Constitution: discussing the tariff powers of the proposed new government, Hamilton, who would become the first Secretary of the Treasury, gave as an example a high tariff on foreign distilled spirits. If citizens continued to buy, the government would realise a healthy revenue, and if the public reduced its consumption, the health and efficiency of the citizenry would be improved (Hamilton 1937: 75). Taxes also provide a way for governments to distinguish among various beverage forms. In the United States, for example, the excise tax on alcohol is higher for distilled spirits than that for beer or wine.

In the struggle to overcome the 'gin epidemic' in London during the first half of the eighteenth century, several tax schemes were tried in conjunction with licence requirements and other restrictions. Repeal of the 1729 Act brought back some of the conditions that led to the statute. A much stronger act was passed in 1736 which also failed of its purpose. In 1743 Parliament enacted a more moderate scheme, the Tippling Act. The subsequent fall in consumption, however, upset landowners who produced grain for distilling, so, to facilitate sales, modifications were added to the Act, but finally revoked in 1751 when the provisions of the Tippling Act were essentially reinstated. Due to the fine-tuning of taxation and success of the anti-spirits campaign after decades of experience with high consumption, the gin epidemic faded (George 1925: 22ff.). Without the conviction that spirits use had to be reduced, the 1751 Act might have been weakened once again to use more grain supplies. The relationship between public compliance and regulatory law is vital to the success of such laws, as the US experience with national Prohibition would again illustrate. Taxation played a part in reducing spirits consumption in the eighteenth century, but its limitations in the face of demand were clearly demonstrated.

John Adams failed in his quest for fewer taverns, but one of his complaints reminds us of a powerful but somewhat ancillary reason for closing drinking places: the use of these gathering spots for plotting. The plotting could be mere criminal activity or could extend to conspiracies against the government. Coffee shops were banned by Charles II in 1675 not because of the coffee, but because coffee drinkers hatched plans and mooted ideas that the Crown thought dangerous to domestic stability (Lilywhite 1963: 18). There may be wisdom in this fear, for taverns have been called the 'nursery' of the American War of Independence, an arena dominated by John Adams's cousin Samuel, although they were precincts John found unappealing. In addition to controlling the number of drinking houses, governments regulate business hours. During the First World War, England imposed mandatory afternoon closing hours, a regulation which only recently has been relaxed. Opening-time restrictions accompanied a decline in per capita consumption and liver cirrhosis (Smart 1974: 109–21). Some regulations specified how much one could drink. Massachusetts even regulated the speed at which beverages were drunk: in 1645 drinkers could not spend more than one half-hour drinking, and the amount could not exceed one pint of wine (Shurtleff 1853: 100).

One stratagem for dealing with time spent drinking alcohol is to alter the activity or the drink. James I of England and VI of Scotland compiled a book of sports suitable for the free hours of Sabbath days, with the goal of keeping villagers from alehouses (Hill 1961: 85). If people could not be diverted from drink, perhaps the object of thirst could be changed. The growth of tea and coffee in the seventeenth century provided drinks that did not intoxicate and still allowed for the sociability that the tavern or alehouse offered. Today, even water is packaged and surrounded with such an aura of distinction that there are 'bars' that serve only water and juices.

Age limits for drinking extend as far back as Plato who had serious concern about the dangers of alcohol. He felt one should not drink before the age of eighteen, and then only moderately until the age of forty (Plato 1926: 666a–c). The drinking age has continued to be a target of reform in the two subsequent millennia. In the United States, the drinking age has been raised to twenty-one over the last decade, chiefly as a means of reducing drink-driving accidents among youth. There is substantial evidence that this measure has reduced alcohol-related traffic deaths among those under twenty-one (National Highway Traffic Safety Administration 1990: 4–5; 1995: 37).

Another form of control, centralising the legal distribution of alcohol into a state monopoly, has characterised three Scandinavian nations – Sweden, Norway and Finland. Their goal has been to reduce alcohol consumption by high retail prices, especially on distilled spirits, and education about reasonable limits of consumption. The key to success in such a system lies in a careful balance between a legal cost high enough to discourage use but not one so high that an opportunity is created for smuggling, and private production of alcohol. The recent entry of Sweden and Finland into the European Union has raised questions as to whether there will be substantial changes in this style of restriction (Holder et al. 1995).

Religious Movements and Alcohol Control

Beyond specific strategies for curbing alcohol consumption, religious faith offers larger and deeper forces affecting the image of alcohol. It has been suggested that prohibitionist movements have their origin in the sixteenth century with the Anabaptist struggle for purity and the Calvinist reliance on civil authority to fulfil religious objectives (Bainton 1945: 52–3). As we have seen, policies of abstinence or careful moderation are not necessarily religious in origin, yet since the Reformation some churches in Western society have assumed an important role in the attempts to eliminate alcohol itself. While the Roman Catholic church has not considered alcohol to be intrinsically evil, various Protestant groups and new religious movements such as the Mormons and Seventh Day Adventists have branded alcohol an evil which no one should use unless for strictly medical reasons. Where these groups have predominated, as in the United States, their role in drives for prohibitions has been central and, at times, in the lead. Prohibition sentiment has not been continuously effective in the US; rather, it has ebbed and flowed, reaching peaks in the 1850s and the 1920s when prohibitive legislation was in force (Musto 1996). Religious groups that arose in that earlier era have maintained an abstinent stance through decades in which the remainder of American society has returned to a more carefree use of alcohol. One might include Methodism in this pattern, for the Methodist church began in an even earlier temperance crusade, the English reaction to gin drinking in the mid-eighteenth century.

The drama of American temperance movements offers a good representation of the clash between positive and negative attitudes towards alcohol that have led to extremes of high and low consumption and the role of religious and quasi-religious organisations in the conflict. The American experience began with a high level of consumption which rose from the late eighteenth century to a peak in the 1830s of 7.1 gallons of alcohol per person per year over the age of fifteen (Rorabaugh 1979: 233). The majority of this alcohol was in the form of distilled spirits, chiefly rum until the late eighteenth century and, increasingly, grain-based whiskey afterwards. The attitude towards spirits was similar to that in England and Northern Europe in general – that it promoted strength and warded off disease. Workers demanded it and the wealthy celebrated with it. This extraordinarily high level of consumption (about three times current consumption of alcohol in the United States) stimulated a medical and social response that could be called the first American temperance movement. Benjamin Rush exemplified the early stage of the movement in the late eighteenth century when he denounced distilled spirits as unhealthy and dangerous to a productive, responsible life (Rush 1784).

Early in the nineteenth century the Reverend Lyman Beecher took up leadership of the temperance movement and extended the concept of temperance from a refusal to drink spirits to a total condemnation of all alcohol, whether beer, wine or spirits. In 1826 his *Six Sermons on Intemperance* spread the uncompromising message throughout the US and abroad (Beecher 1826). The belief that total abstinence represented the desirable condition for the United States led Beecher and his like-minded colleagues to agitate for Prohibition at the state level. By 1855 about a third of Americans lived – if briefly – under legal Prohibition (Lender and Martin 1987: 206). The consequence of this achievement was not a solidly entrenched statutory Prohibition. Rather, state controls rapidly faded in most instances, and the reform spirit was absorbed by the cataclysmic Civil War and commitment to the abolition of slavery. The level of drinking, however, had fallen greatly during the temperance campaign; by the 1850s it was 1.8 gallons per adult, a fall of almost three-quarters in twenty-five years (Rorabaugh 1979: 233). Average consumption has never since exceeded 3 gallons.

Time had to pass before a second temperance movement could get under way. The emotional energy could not be re-stimulated immediately after the rejection of state Prohibition. When a new campaign did take hold, the early progress was made by women who found in the alcohol issue a means to enter the political and public sphere from which they had been so long excluded. Relegated to the 'home', women found, in the domestic damage caused by alcohol, a complete justification for activism. The Woman's Christian Temperance Union (WCTU) took its name from the crusade against alcohol, but continued further to campaign for equal legal rights for women including the vote and other goals quite unrelated to temperance (Bordin 1986: 129–54).

Then, in 1895, the Anti-Saloon League appeared and took control of the fight against alcohol (Kerr 1985). Eventually, after twenty years of zealous effort to establish local and state Prohibition, the time appeared ripe for the most dramatic achievement ever considered by the anti-alcohol forces, the possibility of national Prohibition ensured by an amendment to the US Constitution. It was an elaborate process, but reversal would be extremely difficult and, to that time, no amendment had ever been repealed.

At a peak of enthusiasm for repressing alcohol, the Eighteenth Amendment to the Constitution was adopted by both houses of Congress and by all but two of the forty-eight states. The nearly fourteen-year era of Prohibition began in January, 1920. An important point which usually gets lost in the widespread condemnation of this well-known experiment is that the consumption of alcohol did decline in the period of growing state Prohibition shortly before 1920 as well as during national Prohibition (Gusfield 1986: 198). Prohibition ended in late 1933. Per capita consumption in 1934 was slightly less than 1 gallon of alcohol per year, the lowest recorded level in American history; from there it rose until it reached a new peak in 1980 (2.8 gallons), from which point a decline of about one-sixth has taken place (Lender and Martin 1987: 206).

Prohibition failed not because it did not reduce alcohol consumption, but because it could not gain the overwhelming support of the American people, a necessary prerequisite for the successful prohibition of a drug. Bootlegging filled the pages of newspapers and a sense of futility could not be countered indefinitely by the dry forces. This was especially true after 1929 when the Great Depression settled on the nation and provided the wet forces with one of their most effective arguments, that revival of the alcohol beverage industry would create many new jobs and, furthermore, the tax revenues would provide funds to meet the needs of a desperate nation (Kyvig 1979: 166ff.).

It is customary to judge the impact of Prohibition by the amount of alcohol that was consumed – that either it did or did not reduce the amount of drinking – or by adding up the lives saved from cirrhosis deaths compared to those shot by gangsters and Prohibition agents. The most serious impact of Prohibition, however, was the half-century of resistance to dealing with alcohol problems that followed repeal. Prohibition's backlash instilled the view that reasonable efforts to control alcohol and reduce the problems associated with it were hopeless and probably the inspiration of those who wanted to reimpose draconian laws. Only in the last decade or two have the social burdens of alcohol come to be effectively readdressed by such groups as Mothers Against Drunk Drivers (MADD).

Scientific Research and Alcohol Control

Religion has been much more consistent in its attitude towards alcohol than scientific research which, at least in the US, has tended to echo the great swings in public opinion regarding the value or danger of alcohol. During the first American temperance movement, which peaked in the 1850s, the most unexpected experiments – those of Dr William Beaumont on Alexis St Martin, whose stomach had been permanently opened by a gunshot wound – revealed that the stomach lining reacted with irritation to a drink of distilled spirits, although the drinker was unaware of any discomfort (Beaumont 1833: 237, 240, 276). Beaumont added this observation to the chorus of condemnation concerning spirits by showing damage at the earliest stage of drinking. In the second period of American temperance activism, scientific data – from actuarial reports that indicated social drinkers had a higher mortality rate, to the effect on dexterity of one or two beers – and temperance literature hammered home the idea that any drinking was harmful (Fisher 1926: 123ff.).

The most dramatic example of contrary conclusions reached by respected researchers working in periods of differing public opinion with respect to alcohol consumption is the question of alcohol's effect on the foetus. During the English 'gin epidemic', complications of alcohol were described in books, pamphlets and in Methodist sermons. Priest and physiologist Stephen Hales's *A Friendly Admonition* ... was based on experiments 'purposely made, with Brandy, on the Blood and Blood-Vessels of Animals' (Hales 1735: 3). Hales listed jaundice due to obstruction of the liver, dropsy, palsy and apoplexy as the effects of chronic use of distilled spirits. He also echoed the warning issued in 1726 by the College of Physicians that alcohol could damage the foetus (Munk 1878: 53). Hales took an opposite view on the hardening of tissues caused by alcohol that to earlier writers was proof if its ability to prolong life. He was especially concerned for the foetus, infants and young children, 'for nature is then under a necessity of drawing out very slender threads of life, when the nourishment of either unborn, or born children, is hardened and spoiled by such pernicious liquors' (Hales 1735: 15). The result, he warned, would be a degeneration of future generations.

During the period leading up to national prohibition in the United States, the effect of even a small amount of alcohol on the fetus was widely discussed in medical journals (Warner and Rusett 1975: 1395–1420). The teratogenic effects of alcohol seemed to be confirmed. Then, as the mood of the nation swung towards repeal of prohibition and advocacy of prohibition was relegated to the dustbin of history, the attitude of experts also changed. By the 1940s E.M. Jellinek and colleagues rejected the idea that any 'acceptable evidence has ever been offered to show that acute alcoholic intoxication has any effect whatsoever on the human germ, or has any influence in altering heredity, or is the cause of any abnormality in the child' (Haggard and Jellinek 1942: 207).

Over the last few decades, we have witnessed growing concern over the effects of a small amount of alcohol on the fetus. In the 1970s, identification of the Fetal Alcohol Syndrome (FAS) and Fetal Alcohol Effects (FAE) led to official warnings regarding any alcohol consumption during pregnancy (United States Office for Substance Abuse Prevention 1989: 11). The fear of FAS led the United States to require a warning label on all alcohol beverage containers beginning in 1989 (United States Congress: 1988). (This is discussed further by Greenfield in Chapter 7.) Historical studies cannot answer which conclusion is correct, but they can suggest that research in such close harmony with current feelings should undergo the most rigorous scrutiny.

For the majority of the American public, scientific descriptions of alcohol's negative effects have pretty much replaced religious exhortations in current debate. These secular criticisms of alcohol go beyond warning about an individual's spiritual and physical state. Arguments typical of what may be a new 'temperance movement' now address the loss to national income resulting from the medical care required for alcohol-related disease such as cirrhosis, high blood pressure and brain damage, and accidents caused by drink-driving and impaired operation of machinery. With the assumption of central government responsibility for health care, the pressure to change unhealthy habits is increasing. In this context, scientific research will play a crucial role in determining governmental actions against what might be a cause of 'unnecessary' or self-inflicted illness.

The question facing the current movement is, How far will it go? The United States has experienced two previous attempts to control alcohol that ended in widespread prohibition. In the end, prohibition of alcohol has not succeeded, and even its successful adoptions were preludes to unanticipated backlashes against any attempt to moderate the use of alcohol. The history of anti-alcohol movements should be studied by those who are involved in the current effort. How to minimise the harm of alcohol in ways that are politically and socially viable should be the goal so that the swings from one extreme to the other are smoothed out and health and safety steadily improve.

References

Adams, J. (1961) Diary and Autobiography of John Adams, ed. L. Butterfield, Cambridge, MA, Harvard University Press.

Ahlström, S.E. (1972) A Religious History of the American People, New Haven, CT, Yale University Press.

Bainton, R.H. (1945) 'The Churches and Alcohol', Quarterly Journal of Studies on Alcohol, 6: 45–58.

Beaumont, W. (1833) Experiments and Observations on the Gastric Juice and Physiology of Digestion, Plattsburgh, NY, F.P. Allen.

Beecher, L. (1826) Six Sermons on the Nature, Occasions, Signs, Evils and Remedy of Intemperance, Boston, MA, T.R. Marvin.

Blunt, A. (1729) Geneva: A Poem, London.

Bordin, R. (1986) Frances Willard: A Biography, Chapel Hill, N.C., University of North Carolina Press.

Cherrington, E. (ed.) (1924–30) Standard Encyclopedia of the Alcohol Problem (6 Vols), Westerville, OH, American Issues Publishing Company.

Clark, N. (1976) Deliver Us from Evil: An Interpretation of American Prohibition, New York, W.W. Norton.

Clark, P. (1983) The English Alehouse: A Social History 1200–1830, London, Longman.

Clark, P. (1988) 'The "Mother Gin" Controversy in Early Eighteenth-Century England', Transactions of the Royal History Society, 38: 63–84.

Dowell, S. (1888) A History of Taxation and Taxes in England from the Earliest Times to the Year 1885, London, Longmans, Green & Company.

Fichtenau, H. (1991) Living in the Tenth Century: Mentalities and Social Order (translated by P.J. Geary), Chicago, IL, University of Chicago Press.

Fisher, I. (1926) *Prohibition at its Worst*, New York, Macmillan.

Forbes, R.J. (1948) *Short History of the Art of Distillation*, Leiden, E.J. Brill.

Franklin, B. (1987) *Writings*, New York, Library of America.

George, M.D. (1925) *London Life in the Eighteenth Century*, London, Kegan, Paul, Trench, Trubner and Co.

Gusfield, J. (1986) *Symbolic Crusade: Status Politics and the American Temperance Movement* (2nd edn), Urbana, IL, University of Illinois Press.

Haggard, H. and Jellinek, E.M. (1942) *Alcohol Explored*, New York, Doubleday, Doran and Co.

Hales, S. (1735) *A Friendly Admonition to the Drinkers of Brandy and Other Spiritous Liquors*, London, M. Downing.

Hamilton, A. (1937) *The Federalist*, New York, Modern Library.

Hill, C. (1961) *The Century of Revolution 1603–1714*, New York, W.W. Norton.

Holder, H.D., Giesbrecht, N., Horverak, Ø., Nordlund, S., Norström, T., Olsson, O., Österberg, E. and Skog, Ø-J. (1995) 'Potential consequences from possible changes to Nordic retail alcohol monopolies resulting from European Union membership', *Addiction*, 90: 1603–19.

Kerr, K.A. (1985) *Organized for Prohibition: A New History of the Anti-Saloon League*, New Haven, CT, Yale University Press.

Kyvig, D.E. (1979) *Repealing National Prohibition*, Chicago, IL, University of Chicago Press.

Lender, M.E. and Martin, J.K. (1987) *Drinking in America: A History* (New and Expanded Edition), New York, Free Press.

Lilywhite, B. (1963) *London Coffee Houses*, London, Allen and Unwin.

McKinlay, A. (1949) 'Ancient Experiences with Intoxicating Drinks: Non-Attic Greek States', *Quarterly Journal of Studies on Alcohol*, 10: 289–315.

McKinlay, A. (1951) 'Attic Temperance', *Quarterly Journal of Studies on Alcohol*, 2: 61–102.

Munk, W. (1878) *The Role of the Royal College of Physicians of London* (2nd edn), London, College of Physicians.

Musto, D.F. (1996) 'Alcohol in American History', *Scientific American*, 269: 78–83.

National Highway Traffic Safety Administration (1990) *Traffic Fatality Facts*, Washington, D.C., United States Department of Transportation.

National Highway Traffic Safety Administration (1994) *Traffic Safety Facts*, Washington, D.C., United States Department of Transportation.

Plato (1926) *Laws* (translated by R.G. Burg), Loeb Classical Library, Cambridge, MA, Harvard University Press.

Rorabaugh, W.S. (1979) *The Alcoholic Republic: An American Tradition*, New York, Oxford University Press.

Rush, Benjamin (1784) *An Enquiry into the Effects of Ardent Spirits*, Philadelphia, PA, Bradford.

Shurtleff, N.B. (1853) *Records of the Governor of the Massachusetts Bay in New England*, Boston.

Smart, R.G. (1974) 'The Effect of Licensing Restrictions During 1914–18 on Drunkenness and Liver Cirrhosis Deaths in Britain', *British Journal of Addiction*, 69: 109–21.

United States Congress (1988) *Anti-Drug Abuse Act of 1988*, Title VIII Public Law No. 100-690.

United States Office for Substance Abuse Prevention (1989) *Message and Material Review Process April 1989*, Washington, D.C., Alcohol, Drug Abuse, and Mental Health Administration.

Warner, R.H. and Rusett, H.L. (1975) 'On the Effects of Drinking and Offspring', *Journal of Studies in Alcohol*, 36: 1395–420.

Wesley, J. (1901) *The Journal of the Reverend John Wesley*, London, Wesleyan Conference Office.

White, S. (1996) *Russia Goes Dry: Alcohol, State and Society*, New York, Cambridge University Press.

Wilson, C.A. (1975) 'Burnt wine and cordial waters: The early days of distilling', *Folk Life*, 13: 34–65.

PART II

Some Examples

3 Can Tax be Used to Minimise Harm? A Health Economist's Perspective

Christine Godfrey

Governments have a long tradition of taxing the goods people want to buy to raise revenue. Alcoholic beverages have, in most countries, borne a higher rate of tax than the average. However, home produced beverages are often favoured with lower rates of tax compared to those which are mainly imported. The setting of tax levels is subject to a number of pressures including the campaigning of the beverage alcohol industry. Decisions about the comparative levels and structures across different beverages may, as a result of these pressures, seem haphazard.

The purpose of this chapter is to explore the potential for using fiscal policy to achieve harm minimisation objectives. While there is agreement that harm minimisation involves a focus on the various harms caused by alcohol, details about the precise goals are less clear. To evaluate the role of taxation requires a framework and in the first section of this chapter a view on how an economist may assess harm minimisation policies is presented. Using the economic framework, available evidence on the effectiveness of price changes to achieve policy goals are explored in the second section. Prices of alcoholic beverages comprise a number of different components. In the third section of the chapter the ability to influence price by changing taxes is explored. The final section of the chapter contains a brief discussion on the feasibility of a harm minimisation directed tax policy being applied in practice. The question is whether a rational tax policy based on the public good can win the political struggle on tax rates.

An Economist's View of Harm Minimisation

Criteria

From an economic perspective, policies are evaluated in order to assess whether their enactment would either make better (more efficient) use of society's scarce resources, that is, the overall level of welfare is greater than before, or that the policy results in more equity, that is, the distribution of well-being across the population is more fair. Both the efficiency and equity criteria are important when considering alcohol tax policy. The question may be, for example, whether an overall rise in tax levels leads to less harm (and therefore greater welfare) by, say, reducing alcohol-related traffic accidents. However, others may argue that tax increases penalise all drinkers, not just those who drink and drive, and is not equitable. In reality there may be some 'trade-off' between these two objectives if more efficient policies are also more inequitable.

Models of Evaluation

An economic evaluation framework allows some exploration of the effects of different policy choices. Within this framework the full costs and consequences of a change in policy can be compared to the alternative of the change not taking place or an alternative policy action being made. For example, the effects of a tax increase could be compared to the tax levels remaining the same or another policy such as a raising of the minimum drinking age or increasing the penalties for drinking and driving.

To judge the full societal impact of any policy it is necessary to examine the costs and benefits of the alternative policy options on the individuals, their families and the rest of society. This involves identifying, measuring and valuing all these costs and benefits. To evaluate the need for a tax increase, for example, the current balance of costs and benefits could be assessed. If the costs of alcohol exceed the benefits then there may be a case for a tax increase. Under certain assumptions, however, some costs and benefits may be assumed to balance each other and therefore do not need to be taken into account. For most commodities, for example, it would be assumed that individuals take into account the costs to themselves as well as the benefits when they decide to consume a good. If consumers are rational, in economic terms, costs and benefits for the individual are assumed to be in balance. Evaluating policies may therefore only involve considering the effects on the rest of society – in economists' terminology, the external costs and benefits. If at current levels of consumption those consuming alcohol are imposing costs on third parties then consumption levels are not economically efficient, there are net costs. Taxing individuals in order to take account of these third-party effects could result in higher overall levels of welfare. Such arguments have been used to argue that the existing levels of tax are not sufficient (Richardson and Crawley 1994).

The externality model has built-in assumptions that individuals both have sufficient information to make choices and are 'capable' of making those choices. Information about the harm caused by alcohol is not widely available. While there is considerable agreement about the harmful effects of very heavy drinking, the risks at moderate to heavy levels are subject to considerable debate. Media coverage about the benefits of light drinking on health may have caused further confusion. Also, many of the social, workplace and criminal effects of inappropriate drinking have been given far less attention in the media than health effects.

Even if epidemiological knowledge is improved, it may be difficult for individuals to make an overall assessment of their risks from their drinking patterns. Different problems have different 'risk curves' and the effect of alcohol may be interlinked with other lifestyle factors. Without sufficient information about the costs or benefits of drinking, individuals may make suboptimal consumption decisions. If they are underestimating the risks of drinking, the benefits the individual receives from drinking will be less than the full costs. A framework for evaluating policies, including tax, could then take account of some of these private costs. The government is using tax changes in this situation to 'correct' the consumption decisions to those which may have been made if the information was known. This may also be supported by individuals as a means of avoiding difficult decisions or future regret for drinking at a level which caused problems (Crain et al. 1977).

It could be argued that dependence on alcohol means that individuals cannot make free choices about consumption decisions. It could be argued that resources devoted to alcohol consumption (or at least part of this consumption) would yield more benefits or welfare if devoted to other goods or services. This would add some 'costs' to the current situation which an increase in tax may reduce. However, not all drinkers who have problems can be classified as dependent and many would argue that even those who are dependent can make choices about the level at which they consume. Some economists have also proposed a 'rational' model of addiction (Becker and Murphy 1988). These models can predict a number of features of dependent behaviour while still being based on an assumption that individuals are capable of acting in their own best interests.

These arguments suggest that there is no one 'correct' model by which tax policies could be evaluated. Different assumptions about the knowledge and rationality of consumers will lead to a different list of costs and benefits to be included in the assessment about the net effects of a tax change (Buck et al. 1996).

Measuring and Valuing the Harms of Alcohol

Alcohol has varied effects in a number of different areas: health, social, work and crime. If tax or other policies reduce alcohol-related problems then the value of the potential reduction in these problems is one of the 'benefits' from that policy change. However, this implies that changes in problem rates can be both measured and valued.

Given the different economic models, it is also important to distinguish between those harms whose costs fall on the individual drinking and those which fall on others. Third parties are clearly involved in alcohol-related accidents, violence and crime. Some other effects will be borne by third parties even though the 'problem' is with the individual. This will vary from country to country in how individuals' problems are dealt with. In the majority of countries some part of health care services, for example, are financed by taxpayers or through insurance schemes. Individuals, therefore, do not bear the full costs of health care use. Similarly, low productivity at work may be borne by work-mates or shareholders rather than being directly reflected in the earnings of the individual.

Harms also take a number of forms. Some are tangible; for example, the physical damage associated with accidents, but other harms are more intangible; for example, the pain, grief and suffering of the relatives of a drink-driving victim. Putting some value on intangible items is clearly difficult.

There are also some areas of dispute among economists; in particular, premature loss of life. For some this loss of life is simply a private cost. If individual drinkers are rational and informed, the risk of loss of life through accidents or ill health could be assumed to be taken into account by the drinker and set against the benefits of drinking. Others would argue that premature death has a value to the wider society. This could be in the form of caring externalities, that is, individuals put some value on preventing the suffering of others. Premature death can also involve a loss of labour resource for the economy and in many studies it is the loss of future earnings which is taken as the value of the loss of life. This method can be questioned. In most time-periods there is a surplus of labour because of unemployment. The value of individuals as a labour resource is also only part of their wider value.

Single et al. (1996) have outlined this and a number of other issues involving the measurement and valuation of different alcohol-related harms in an attempt to provide some guidelines to improve future economic studies. A wider bank of studies, both epidemiological and economic, are required. Only with this knowledge will it be possible to undertake a full evaluation of different policy options.

Costs of Policies

Different policies will have different costs which need to be set against any potential benefits. Tax changes may be favoured by governments and states as they involve few direct costs, the main costs of administrating the policy change being borne by the beverage alcohol and retailing industry. In some countries, however, changing tax levels may not be so simple and, clearly, if some special legal procedure is needed, this will involve resource costs. Other policies have more visible costs. For example, a public education campaign can involve considerable expenditure. Changing laws also involves a long process and increasing media involvement to publicise the change, as well as the costs of enforcement once the regulation is in place.

Tax policy also has other potential costs. These take the form of the lost benefits from reduced drinking for those who are 'rational, well-informed' drinkers imposing no costs on third parties. If their consumption is lowered because of a tax increase then they have lost some of the benefits of drinking without being compensated by a decrease in costs. If tax affects the decision to drink for light-drinking middle-aged men or post-menopausal women, then there may be an increase in health problems.

Tax policy can, therefore, be seen as a relatively blunt instrument. There will be gains from a tax increase in terms of reduced problems from the 'alcohol abusing'/problem drinker population, but also potential losses from the loss of consumption benefits to the 'non-abusing' population (Pogue and Sgnotz 1989). The difficulty lies in ascertaining how large these sections of the populations are. Alcohol problems are complex and can occur across a wide range of the consumption spectrum and are not confined to those dependent on alcohol. However, most drinkers (often the majority of a population) do not experience many problems.

Putting Eonomic Models into Practice

Economic evaluation involves comparing the costs and benefits of different policy actions. The main benefit of alcohol control policies is seen to be the reduction in the costs of problems. By definition this is a type of harm minimisation approach. The decision rule is to adopt the policy with the highest net benefits. The policy should be employed up to the point where the benefits from, say, another small increase in the tax level are equal to the costs. Any further increase would mean that the costs would start to outweigh the benefits and society would be marginally worse off. Conversely, if the tax is below the ideal rate more benefits than costs would be gained by a small increase. However, in most cases this optimum tax rate will not equate with a situation where there are no problems caused by alcohol. The harm minimisation rule in economic terms is the point where reducing problems costs more than the problems themselves.

In theory, therefore, the economic approach does provide a framework within which to evaluate tax as part of a harm minimisation approach to alcohol problems. There are, however, a number of problems in applying the framework in practice, both in deciding on the basic assumptions of the model and in measuring and valuing the costs and benefits of different policies. Furthermore, there are equity issues around the balance of costs and benefits across different drinking groups.

Do Prices Affect the Level of Problems?

Tax policy works through changing the prices of beverages and hence the cost of alcohol to individuals. The initial task that arises in judging the effectiveness of fiscal control as a harm minimisation policy is to examine the evidence for the effect of changes in prices on consumption and problems. Economists rarely have access to experimental research results, hence multivariate statistical techniques need to be applied to observational data to determine the effect of prices after controlling for the effects of other influences on consumption or problems. The majority of studies have considered the effect of prices on consumption aggregated across populations. These studies indicate whether changes in prices induced by tax increases may affect the overall level of consumption. Whether different groups of the population, especially heavy drinkers, have varying levels of price responsiveness is also of policy interest. There tends to be, however, less information on individual drinking across time which can be used to measure these effects. Finally, there are a few studies which have attempted to look at the relationship between changes in prices and changes in problem rates.

Prices and Total Alcohol Consumption

Evidence from economic studies is consistent in suggesting that price is a determinant of alcohol consumption (Leung and Phelps 1993, Österberg 1995). However, the size of the impact of price on alcohol consumption varies across countries, beverages and time. Economists measure the size of the impact of any factor in terms of elasticities. A price elasticity of -0.5 for beer, for example, would suggest that a 10 per cent increase in the price of beer would, other things remaining the same, result in a 5 per cent fall in beer consumption. The size of the price responsiveness is important in determining the potential impact of a tax change. The more price responsive a beverage, the more impact on consumption a tax change will have.

It would be expected that different beverages would in each country have different price elasticities. The more popular a drink, the more it may be regarded as a necessity, not a luxury, and price changes would be expected to have a smaller impact on consumption (that is, a lower absolute value of the negative price elasticity). This was certainly the case in the UK where a number of studies indicated a far lower price responsiveness for beer than for wine and spirits (Godfrey 1989). However, as drinking patterns have changed, so has price responsiveness. In the UK, for example, there has been a major increase in the amount of wine drunk over the past thirty years and price responsiveness has more than halved (Godfrey 1994). Other factors may influence changing beverage price responsiveness in individual countries over time. For example, beer prices in the UK rose very rapidly in the 1980s, mainly due to producer increases which resulted in beer price elasticities changing from -0.5 to -1.0 (Godfrey 1994). Österberg (1995) also details changes in price elasticities for different beverages in Finland as incomes rose.

It may be expected that as relative prices change, consumers may switch and substitute between beverages. Although these cross-price effects have been included in most studies, the estimates of the effects are small. This may be because drinkers have established drinking patterns and switch within beverage types rather than with the mix of the beverages consumed.

Governments also have an interest in the price responsiveness of different beverages if they are concerned with revenue yield. If a beverage is too price responsive, an increase in tax, although meaning more tax per item sold, may actually result in a loss in overall revenue. This would occur if the price rise resulted in a large drop in the amount of the drink sold. In many countries alcohol consumption is responsive to price, but usually the overall impact is at or less than unity, that is, a 1 per cent increase in price leading to a 1 per cent or less decrease in consumption. This implies in economic terms that, overall, alcohol may be price inelastic. This does not imply that there is no price effect; indeed, the majority of studies have found significant price effects on overall consumption. Few other policies have such clear evidence for effectiveness on overall consumption.

Do Heavy Drinkers Respond to Price?

While it is clear that a consistent 'price/tax' policy could have an important impact on the overall level of drinking, aggregate studies do not allow an examination of the differential response to price changes across different groups of the population. Given the skewed distribution of alcohol consumption, an overall effect of price is unlikely to be found unless some of the heavy drinkers also were responsive. Part of the difficulty in discovering whether heavy drinkers respond to price or not lies in obtaining a consistent definition of a 'heavy drinker'.

It also may be useful to distinguish between 'binge' drinkers and other heavy drinkers. With some data this is possible. Chaloupka and Wechsler (1995), for example, found an estimated price elasticity of binge drinking at -0.145 compared to an average estimated price elasticity of drinking participation of -0.066. These elasticity estimates are somewhat different to earlier examples and relate to the likelihood of an individual college student taking up binge, or any, drinking as prices change.

Other recent studies have reached differing conclusions. Manning et al. (1995) concluded that moderate drinkers are more sensitive to price changes than light or heavy drinkers, using US evidence. This study had only one year's data – 1983 – available and the price, while varying across the USA, would not show much variation in a year. Sutton and Godfrey (1995), using UK information on males aged eighteen to twenty-four pooled over the years 1978–90, found that the heaviest drinking group were the most sensitive to price.

Differences in the results of studies using different models and evidence from different time-periods and countries are not surprising. There is likely to be no one answer to the question, are heavy drinkers responsive to price? Age and other factors have been found to interact with price responsiveness.

Prices and Problem Rates

Cook (1981), using a quasi-experimental approach, estimated the effect of price changes on road traffic accident deaths and liver cirrhosis deaths. The calculated price elasticities were –0.7 and –0.9 respectively. Cook and Tauchen (1982) examined the relationship between spirits consumption and cirrhosis mortality and found significant effects of tax changes on this problem rate.

More recently, a number of studies in the USA have examined the comparative effects of tax and alcohol control measures and drinking and driving policies. Saffer and Grossman (1987) and Chaloupka et al. (1991) have suggested that an increase in beer tax in the USA would reduce drink-driving fatalities. Chaloupka et al. (1991) concluded that maintaining beer tax at its real 1951 value would have reduced fatalities by 11.5 per cent annually from 1982 to 1988. Also, Cook and Moore (1993a) and Moore and Cook (1995) have indicated the importance and long-term effects of drinking for the young. As the young tend to be more sensitive to price, tax may be an effective policy in reducing the lifetime incidence of problems.

Grossman et al. (1993), using a number of studies and an economic framework, concluded that for the USA, a substantial increase in alcohol taxes was required, given external costs generated by alcohol, and that tax was more potent than a uniform drinking age of twenty-one (see Chapter 9, this volume). They suggest the welfare losses to individual drinkers are lower with a tax increase (that is, from the lost benefits of consumption to those drinkers not causing third-party effects but who reduce drinking because of tax increases) than similar welfare losses that occur from raised drinking ages.

There is considerable evidence for the positive effects of tax in reducing harms in the USA where tax is relatively low. There is a paucity of similar studies set in other countries and such policy comparisons would vary across time and countries. However, the available research does suggest that price rises are likely to result in fewer problems and that tax changes should be considered alongside more direct problem-orientated approaches.

Prices and Taxes

It is clear that increasing prices will reduce consumption, other things being equal. However, tax is only one component of price and in judging whether tax policy would be effective it is necessary to consider the relationship between changes in taxes and changes in prices. Tax systems also differ between countries. In some countries specific rates are set by volume of alcohol. These rates are usually established in monetary terms and hence with inflation their real value will fall over time unless regularly up-rated. In other countries tax is set on an *ad valorem* basis, with taxes being set as some proportion of final price. The amount taken in *ad valorem* taxes rises as the price rises.

Ad valorem taxes may seem advantageous as there is no need to undertake regular up-rating. However, the tax levels are based on price and are not related to the harms. It could be argued that for a harm minimisation policy, tax levels should vary with the strength of the beverage, not the costs of producing and retailing the beverage. In the UK there is a combination of both systems, with beverages being subject to specific taxes and then to a general sales tax.

In Figure 3.1, trends in the real specific duty rates in the UK are shown, expressed as rates per litre of pure alcohol. The rate per litre of alcohol on spirits is far higher than any other beverage, with the rate on cider being remarkably low. The period covered by Figure 3.1 shows a decline in the real value of spirits duty and some stability in those of other beverages. This may indicate an approach which seeks to maintain the government revenue. There seems no logic in terms of harm for the continuing discrepancies in the tax rates between beverages.

An examination of real price changes of individual beverages during the same period illustrates the importance of other factors on price. Beer prices, for example, rose dramatically from 1982 to 1993. While the tax component per pint was almost constant over the period shown in Figure 3.1, the manufacturers' and retailers' cost and profit component rose by 60 per cent.

Prices, therefore, are not only influenced by tax changes. Manufac-

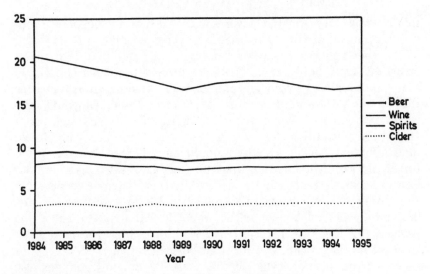

Figure 3.1: Real specific tax rates UK, 1990 prices
Source: Centre for Health Economics Database.

turers could also try to subvert tax policy by not passing on any tax changes and absorbing the increases in duty by reducing their profit per item. In fact, evidence suggests that manufacturers increase prices by more than the amount needed to cover the increased duty rates (Cook and Moore 1993b).

Implementing Tax Policies

The evidence would suggest that tax policy could form one part of a harm minimisation policy package. It could prove effective in reducing problems, but at the cost of affecting those not experiencing problems. This may suggest that a tax policy could be unpopular and this may be one of the barriers which prevent policy implementation despite the evidence of effectiveness.

In reality a number of influences will affect the implementation of a tax policy. Governments have other concerns, in particular the revenue generated by alcohol. The strength of such concern is difficult to judge. The importance of revenue from alcohol has tended to fall as governments or states have imposed more general sales taxes. However, governments like to preserve diverse sources of revenue and may therefore be reluctant to use tax more proactively for health or public welfare ends. However, the use of alcohol tax in this way suggests that governments are not too anxious about the disapproval of voters, at least in between election periods.

Another concern has been that high tax rates may lead to increases in cross-border trade. This has been of particular concern in high tax countries which are part of wider trading groups such as the European Union. In reality, legal cross-border shopping only becomes significant where there are low travel costs and high population concentrations; for example, on the Canadian and United States borders. Incentives to engage in cross-border shopping when prices are compared rather than tax are generally small (see for example, Buck et al. 1994). In the UK there is no evidence that the ability to shop freely in Europe has led to a decrease in the amount of alcohol bought within the UK. Attempts to 'solve' the problem by lowering tax can also lead to a higher revenue loss than would have resulted from cross-border shopping.

Effects on overall levels of inflation and employment are also frequently cited as being impediments to implementing a tax policy, although evidence about these effects is not robust. Political lobbying from trade groups remains an influence. The strongest lobby groups tend to be in countries with major producer interests. In studying UK tax decisions, Leedham and Godfrey (1990) concluded that concern over revenue yield had the most influence on budget decisions. This concern and the effects of political cycles and inflation were found to act as the major impediments to the application of a consistent health-based tax policy.

Conclusions

Economic approaches to the evaluation of different policy options favour one sort of harm minimisation approach. The decision rules are determined by the cost needed to reduce problems. If the cost of reducing the harm is greater than the benefits which would arise from lower rates of problems, then it would not be efficient in terms of society's welfare to pursue that policy.

Tax policy could be applied within this framework although there are a number of different costs and benefits associated with tax changes. In particular, tax can be seen as a blunt policy instrument affecting all drinkers. However, the amount of tax paid will increase with the amount consumed and potentially with the problems caused.

There is considerable evidence that prices affect both levels of consumption and problem rates. There is less consistent evidence on the effect of prices on the heaviest drinkers. The number of studies is small and this is an area which deserves further research, especially to identify the specific groups of the population where price may have a low or even no effect. It is clear that tax cannot be the only strategy for achieving alcohol policy objectives.

Tax is only one component of price but, in general, prices rise if tax rises. More problematic is overcoming the political impediments to adopting a consistent tax policy. Within an overall policy strategy for minimising harm, however, appropriate levels of tax could play an important role in increasing welfare for society by minimising the harms associated with inappropriate drinking.

References

Becker, G. and Murphy, K. (1988) 'A theory of rational addiction', *Journal of Political Economy*, 96: 675–700.

Buck, D., Godfrey, C. and Richardson, G. (1994) *Should Cross-Border Shopping Affect Tax Policy?* York, YARTC Occasional Paper 6, Centre for Health Economics, University of York.

Buck, D., Godfrey, C. and Sutton, M. (1996) 'Economic and other views of addiction: implications for the evaluation of policy options', *Drug and Alcohol Review*, 15: 357–68.

Chaloupka, F.J., Saffer, H. and Grossman, M. (1991) *Alcohol Control Policies and Motor Vehicle Fatalities*, Cambridge, MA, National Bureau of Economic Research, Working Paper 3831.

Chaloupka, F.J. and Wechsler, H. (1995) *The Impact of Price, Availability, and Alcohol Control Policies on Binge Drinking in College*, Cambridge, MA, National Bureau of Economic Research, Working Paper 5319.

Cook, P.J. (1981) 'The effect of liqour taxes on drinking cirrhosis and auto fatalities', in Moore, M. and Gerstein, D. (eds) *Alcohol and Public Policy: Beyond the Shadow of Prohibition*, Washington, D.C., National Academy of Sciences, pp. 255–85.

Cook, P.J. and Moore, M. (1993a) 'Drinking and schooling', *Journal of Health Economics*, 12: 411–29.

Cook, P.J. and Moore, M. (1993b) 'Taxation of alcoholic beverages', in Hilton, M.E. and Bloss, G. (eds) *Economics and the Prevention of Alcohol-Related Problems*, Rockville, MD, National Institute on Alcohol Abuse and Alcoholism Research Monograph No. 25, US Department of Health and Human Services, pp. 33–58.

Cook, P.J. and Tauchen, G. (1982) 'The effect of taxes on heavy drinking', *Bell Journal of Economics*, 13: 379–90.

Crain, M., Deaton, T., Holcombe, R. and Tollison, R. (1977) 'Rational choice and the taxation of sin', *Journal of Public Economics*, 8: 239–45.

Godfrey, C. (1989) 'Factors influencing the consumption of alcohol and tobacco: the use and abuse of economic models', *British Journal of Addiction*, 84: 1123–8.

Godfrey, C. (1994) 'Economic influences on change in population and personal substance behaviour', in Edwards, G. and Lader, M. (eds) *Addiction: Processes of Change*, Oxford, Oxford Medical Publications, Oxford University Press, pp. 163–87.

Grossman, M., Chaloupka, F.J., Saffer, H. and Laixuthai, A. (1993) *Effects of Alcohol Price Policy on Youth*, Cambridge, MA, National Bureau of Economic Research, Working Paper 4385.

Leedham, W. and Godfrey, C. (1990) 'Tax policy and budget decisions', in Tether, P. and Maynard, A. (eds) *Preventing Alcohol and Tobacco Problems*, Aldershot, Avebury, pp. 96–116.

Leung, S.F. and Phelps, C.E. (1993) ' "My kingdom for a drink. . . ?" A review of estimates of the price sensitivity of demand for alcoholic beverages', in Hilton, M.E. and Bloss, G. (eds) *Economics and the Prevention of Alcohol-Related Problems*, Rockville, MD, National Institute on Alcohol Abuse and Alcoholism Research, Monograph No. 25, US Department of Health and Human Services, pp. 1–31.

Manning, W.G., Blumberg, L. and Moulton, L.H. (1995) 'The demand for alcohol: the differential response to price', *Journal of Health Economics*, 14: 123–48.

Moore, M. and Cook, P.J. (1995) *Habit and Heterogeneity in the Youthful Demand for Alcohol*, Cambridge, MA, National Bureau of Economic Research, Working Paper 5152.

Österberg, E. (1995) 'Do alcohol prices affect consumption and related problems?' in Holder, H. and Edwards, G. (eds) *Alcohol and Public Policy: Evidence and Issues*, Oxford, Oxford University Press, pp. 145–63.

Pogue, T.F. and Sgnotz, L.G. (1989) 'Taxing to control social costs: the case of alcohol', *American Economic Review*, 79: 235–43.

Richardson, J. and Crawley, S. (1994) 'Optimum alcohol taxation: balancing consumption and external costs', *Health Economics*, 3: 73–87.

Saffer, H. and Grossman, M. (1987) 'Beer taxes, the legal drinking age, and youth motor vehicle fatalities', *Journal of Legal Studies*, 16: 351–74.

Single, E., Collins, D., Easton, B., Harwood, H., Lapsley, H. and Maynard, A. (1996) *International Guidelines for Estimating the Costs of Substance Abuse*, Ottawa, Canadian Centre on Substance Abuse.

Sutton, M. and Godfrey, C. (1995) 'A grouped data regression approach to estimating economic and social influences on individual drinking behaviour', *Health Economics*, 4: 237–47.

4 Local Control to Prevent Problems of Alcohol Availability: Experience in California Communities

Friedner D. Wittman

Drinking around the world occurs in varied contexts of local alcohol availability. In California, drinking occurs daily in all kinds of settings throughout the community – in residences, public buildings, hospitals, parks, schools, workplaces, theatres. Drinking also accompanies a wide variety of social events ranging from christenings to funerals, sports events to dinner with friends. Alcohol also is sold through a corresponding variety of retail outlets – bars, restaurants, hotel rooms, cruise-boats, liquor stores, convenience stores, mortuaries, gun shops, sports stadiums, discount stores, pharmacies, grocery stores, private clubs, park kiosks, flower boutiques, gas stations, and street fairs.

Alcohol researchers, local officials and community groups have begun looking at the contributions made by alcohol availability to the community's alcohol-related problems. Attention is being directed to retail alcohol outlets (Wittman and Shane 1988, Wittman 1994), to policies for drinking in public places and at events open to the public (Gliksman et al. 1995), and to 'high-risk' environments that are especially prone to alcohol-related problems (Hawkins et al. 1992).

Scientific evidence and practical experience are mounting to show that a community's alcohol-related problems can be reduced by modifying problematic environments of alcohol availability. US localities that have authority to control land use, especially cities and counties, have considerable legislative power and related community resources to accomplish these modifications. These capabilities, dormant since the Prohibition era, are of increasing interest for their potential to reduce health, safety, and well-being problems associated with alcohol availability (Wittman 1982, 1994).

This chapter reviews the emergence of 'local control', a community's exercise of its own local powers and resources to prevent availability-related problems. Attention is focused on experiences in the state of California, where cities and counties have substantially increased their local control efforts in the last decade. Five areas are reviewed: (1) overview of local control in the state; (2) environments of alcohol availability that are subject to local control; (3) documentation of relationships between alcohol outlets and alcohol problems; (4) strategies for community action to modify problem environments; and (5) examples of practical applications.

Local Control in California

Local control is taken here to mean the use of local laws, policies, and related programmes to protect a community's people and institutions from harm and loss due to the sale and public use of alcoholic beverages. Authority to establish local control comes from powers conferred on the states by the Constitutional repeal of Prohibition in 1933. In practice, states share their powers in varying degrees with cities and counties to regulate retail alcohol outlets.

The State of California permits cities and counties to control the conditions under which alcohol is sold, but not the sale of alcoholic beverages per se (Alcoholic Beverage Control Act 1993). Local control over the conditions of sale is accomplished through (1) planning and zoning ordinances that regulate the number, location and operation of retail alcohol outlets; (2) through standards for service of alcoholic beverages in public places and at public events; and (3) through nuisance abatement laws that require property owners to eliminate conditions detrimental to public health and safety. Each city and county has broad latitude to establish these controls as it sees fit, and it is up to each jurisdiction to enact and administer the Alcoholic Beverage Control Department's (ABC) own local control policy.

For forty years following the repeal of Prohibition, California communities mostly left control of alcohol outlets to the state's alcoholic beverage control agency. A scandal in the early 1950s led to the agency's re-establishment in 1955 in its current form as the Alcoholic Beverage Control Department. Things went smoothly during the Department's first decade as a new, well-supported reform agency. The agency's budget did not keep pace as demands for service increased, and the alcoholic beverage industry lobbied to keep the ABC's powers from expanding. From the mid-1960s to the mid-1980s the ABC's operating strength declined to less than one-half of its original design.

From the mid-1970s on, California communities began looking for alternatives to ABC management of retail alcohol outlets. Inner-city communities especially sought relief from disruption to community life and expensive use of local police resources to offset the ABC's glacial delays in acting on complaints about retail outlets. Community groups used mass public demonstrations to communicate frustration over problems emanating from high concentrations of poorly operated alcohol outlets (Wittman and Shane 1988: 119–26). Local developers and community leaders were upset that problems with alcohol outlets foreclosed other desirable land uses (Wittman and Shane 1988: 127–35).

As inadequacies of the ABC and local police enforcement policies became apparent, cities began to restrict alcohol outlets in selected inner-city areas through conditional-use permits (CUPs) written into their local planning and zoning ordinances. The ABC Act provided that 'no license shall be granted contrary to a valid zoning ordinances of any city or county' (Alcoholic Beverage Control Act 1993, S.23790). Cities found they could tailor their zoning ordinances to manage problem outlets, drawing on a broad palette of possible restrictions on location, distance between alcohol outlets and other sensitive uses, outlet density, types of establishments, opening hours and conditions of operation (Wittman 1982, 1986, 1994).

Cities quickly gained confidence in their planning and zoning ordinances as useful tools to prevent availability-related problems. Zoning had become particularly useful for local control following a US Supreme Court decision that recognised localities' powers to use local zoning to protect the community's 'public health, safety, welfare and morals' (City of Euclid v. Ambler Realty, 1926). Following Euclid, zoning could be used for these protective purposes to restrict uses of private property, including alcohol outlets, provided: (1) state law did not pre-empt the field; (2) the best information available at the time was used to verify the presence of problems warranting restrictions; and (3) rights of private property owners were protected regarding due process and reasonable return on the value of their property.

Although modern zoning was available at the time of repeal, fifty years passed before its potential for policy to prevent availability-related problems was looked at systematically (Wittman 1980, 1982, 1983, 1986, 1994). Interest in availability appeared among alcohol researchers during the 1960s in studies on alcohol problems in the general population (Cahalan et al. 1969, Cahalan 1970). These studies sparked curiosity in the contributions of historical, political, and social contexts to drinking problems (Moore and Gerstein 1981), and led to interest in the use of public policy to prevent these problems (Beauchamp 1980, Mecca 1982). Meanwhile, cities and counties learned the uses and limits of planning and zoning ordinances for the prevention of social and health problems related to land use (Babcock 1966, Christoffel and Teret 1993, Florence Dolan v. City of Tigard, 1994).

By the mid-1980s, many California cities required CUPs for alcohol outlets generally and started to place other restrictions on the sale/use of alcohol at public events and public places (Wittman and Hilton 1987). Three trends had converged: The decline of strength in the state ABC left cities increasingly on their own to solve problems with alcohol outlets; the alcohol research field and alcohol policy advocates became increasingly interested in availability-related issues; and city planning and zoning advanced from purely physical planning to encompass socio-physical, health and economic issues. This convergence made it possible for interested planning researchers and policy activists to prick the interest of local officials, alcohol researchers and community organisers, to explore the potentials of local planning and zoning to prevent availability-related problems.

As the potential usefulness of local control became clear (Watts and Rabow 1983, Wittman 1983), activity increased rapidly among California cities to impose preventive restrictions on retail alcohol outlets. For example, growing concern about alcohol sales in gasoline stations, a prime example of mushrooming alcohol availability at the time, led to a grass-roots movement to ban the practice. In about two years, city agencies and local prevention activists roughly doubled the percentage of cities restricting the practice. This movement triggered a state-level legislative backlash by the alcoholic beverage industry that eliminated localities' powers to impose such bans (ABC Act 1993, S.23790.5).

Despite sometimes chilling industry counter-attacks, California cities and counties continued to adopt CUP ordinances for retail alcohol outlets. Estimates by the League of California Cities in late 1993 suggested that about one-half of California's 475 cities had CUP requirements for on-sale and off-sale alcohol outlets (League of California Cities 1994). Cities began to require special training for service of alcoholic beverages (responsible beverage service, or RBS), following a state-wide symposium (Responsible Hospitality Institute 1991), and the establishment of a state-wide organisation to certify RBS training programmes (Peters 1996). (This is also discussed in Chapter 5, this volume.) Cities and counties also adopted policies to control drinking in public settings during national and state holidays, and at street fairs, county fairs, agricultural product fairs and ethnic celebrations (Wittman 1991, Wittman et al. 1991). Absorbing the lessons of the alcohol/gasoline defeat in 1986, activists and local governments successfully obtained state-level legislation to support local control.

The cities were stimulated by several sources. The state ABC provided technical back-up and liaison. The state Office of Traffic Safety approved grants to use National Highway Traffic Safety Agency for environmental prevention projects related to drink-driving. A model zoning ordinance for retail alcohol outlets provided useful guidance for a number of cities (Model Conditional Use Permit for Retail Alcohol Outlets 1988). A manual on municipal planning to prevent availability-related problems (Wittman and Shane 1988) led to a state-wide demonstration project to create a city-wide planning process that could manage all aspects of local alcohol availability (Wittman and Biderman 1992). Cities took advantage of no-cost and low-cost informational presentations and technical assistance supported by the California Department of Alcohol and Drug Programs, with considerable logistical support from the League of California Cities. Additional support came from federal grants to conduct 'community trials' studies and community planning demonstration programmes, and from in-state and national foundations to support demonstration projects that included advocacy for local control.

By the mid-1990s, concepts and strategies for local control had gained broad acceptance among California communities as a useful means for reducing alcohol-related problems. A bridgehead had been made, but difficult work lay ahead to refine concepts, improve practice and disseminate local control experience.

Community Environments of Alcohol Availability

California cities and counties find it useful to consider the local alcohol environment in three separate domains for purposes of local control (Wittman and Shane 1988): (1) Commercial availability; (2) Public availability; and (3) Social (normative) availability. A given community-level alcohol problem most likely will be expressed in all three domains; but different control strategies apply to each domain, and all of these strategies can be combined to focus on specific problems.

Commercial Availability

Commercial availability refers to places where alcoholic beverages are sold under licence by the state. The California ABC classifies commercial retail alcohol outlets into seven basic types for on-sales and off-sales (Alcoholic Beverage Control Act 1993). On-sales outlets are bars, restaurants, taverns and other places where alcoholic beverages are sold for consumption on the premises where the beverages are purchased. Off-sales outlets are liquor stores, grocery stores, and other places where alcoholic beverages are sold for consumption away from the premises where the beverages are purchased.

Typically about 20–25 per cent of all the retail outlets in California cities sell alcoholic beverages, and an estimated 10–15 per cent of the city's taxable retail sales come from alcohol, although precise figures are not available (Benham 1983). Planning and zoning laws are the primary vehicles for local control of retail alcohol outlets. Local participation in the ABC licensing and enforcement processes also is important, particularly when approached through local zoning review and the police department.

Public Availability

Public availability of alcohol refers to the presence of alcoholic beverages at public places of all types. These settings include parks, sidewalks, civic facilities, and all other places owned or operated by public agencies. Public availability also includes events open to the public, such as street fairs and rock concerts.

Public availability is controlled by local ordinances and by the regulations of local public agencies, rather than by the state ABC. Local communities vary considerably in the extent to which they impose controls on drinking in public, depending on the site or the circumstances: alcohol sales and consumption are permitted; consumption is permitted, but not sales; or no drinking is permitted. Communities also vary greatly in the diligence with which drinking-in-public ordinances are enforced. Control policies must contend with the fact that public health and safety issues compete with economic interests and the community's history, culture and beliefs about government intrusion into everyday life. Local policies on public drinking are politically volatile since they mirror the community's many orientations towards availability. Conflicts over public availability often are managed by tolerating slippage between what the law says and what local officials actually enforce.

Social availability

Social availability refers to customary beliefs and practices (norms) that guide the use of alcoholic beverages in the community, (Smart 1980, Wittman 1980, Rabow et al. 1982, Rush et al. 1986). Alcohol is a widely accepted part of family life for most Californians, and beyond the family lies a complex network of community norms on drinking. Community norms in California's diverse society are a complex product of local history, culture, external and internal economic influences, and the community's physical features and natural ecology.

Most local drinking norms, such as the use of wine in weekly religious ceremonies, are relatively trouble free. Some of the norms are in conflict with each other, particularly those pertaining to young people and regarding risks for the drinker during and after drinking (Morgan 1979, Room 1980).

Strategies to control problems with social availability include traditional passive public information and education programmes, and increasingly involve active participation by local organisations and the public. Organisations are encouraged to adopt prevention policies, and community leaders are asked to provide endorsements and to actively support prevention initiatives. Public participation in policy making is encouraged through social advocacy (Douglas 1986), community organising (Prevention Plus II 1989, Wittman 1995c), and media advocacy (Wallack et al. 1993). These approaches engage the public in shaping opinion and framing concerns about drinking and the management of its sequelae from a public health perspective.

California communities' ethnic diversity greatly complicates prevention issues related to drinking norms. Different community groups vary widely in their drinking styles and customs, and attach very different meanings, some not compatible with those of other groups, to the use of alcohol. Combating racism and respecting ethnic differences are critical parts of community planning in California to prevent problems associated with social availability. Several leading prevention strategists find it preferable to focus on common problems in shared environments that people from different backgrounds can tackle together, rather than focus on problems or practices that single out particular groups (Institute for the Study of Social Change 1991a).

Alcohol Problems and Alcohol Outlets

Alcohol problems that concern local communities include trauma, chronic illness, existential problems, decorum, violence, and economic and property loss (Room 1980). Application of local controls to these problems depends upon defining the problems as risks associated with their environmental contexts (Room 1984). In the technical parlance of the ABC and local zoning officials, a 'nexus', or connection, must be established to link a specific alcohol-related problem (or pattern of problems) to a specific alcohol outlet (or group of outlets) (Wittman 1986, 1994). Three mutually reinforcing sources of information are useful for describing the community's alcohol problem nexus: formal research findings, official reports from local public agencies and organisations, and personal experience (Wittman and Shane 1988).

The more clearly the connections can be shown between alcohol availability and alcohol problems, the more robust and effective will be local control initiatives. In the mid-1990s, these three sources of information were still far from full development and rationalisation for local application to high-risk environments (Wittman 1993a).

Public Health and Safety Research

Public health and public policy researchers are finding increasingly strong evidence of relationships between alcohol availability and alcohol-related problems. Researchers look across communities to compare availability variables, consumption variables, and problem variables. Ecological studies are particularly promising for guiding the development of local control (Gruenewald 1993, Gruenewald et al. 1993, Edwards et al. 1994: 129–42, Harding and Wittman 1995). Local availability is proving to be a significant factor in several problem areas, summarised below. The ecological basis for problem relationships suggests that alcohol outlets in a given community make simultaneous contributions to all of these problems:

Driving under the influence. The minimum purchase age, the density of bars and restaurants, and the quality of alcohol service in drinking establishments influence drink-driving rates and traffic-crash rates

(Douglass et al. 1979, Russ and Geller 1986, Saltz 1987, McKnight 1991, O'Malley and Wagerman 1991, Scribner et al. 1993, Van Oers and Garretson 1993, Holder and Wagenaar 1994, Gruenewald et al. (forthcoming)). This topic is discussed further in Chapter 8.

Youth access to alcohol. Ready access to alcohol both through retail alcohol outlets and in social settings generally, such as parties in private homes, is routinely reported by young people below legal drinking age (Preusser and Williams 1992, Wittman 1993b, Wagenaar and Wolfson 1994). (See also Chapter 9, this volume, for a further review of this subject.)

Alcohol and violence. The density of alcohol outlets (number of alcohol outlets per unit of population) is associated with homicide and assault (Gerson and Preston 1979, Scribner et al. 1993, Cook and Moore 1993, Parker and Rebhun 1995).

Problems of public decorum. Litter, loitering, and other neighbourhood quality of life issues are closely associated with retail alcohol outlets, and are frequently the main reason for local regulation of alcohol outlets (Wittman and Hilton 1987). Establishments that routinely permit drinking to intoxication are a significant source of these problems (Saltz and Hennessy 1990).

Alcoholism and alcohol-related diseases. Rates of alcoholism and alcohol-related diseases are associated with the density of alcohol outlets and with the price of alcoholic beverages (Parker et al. 1978, Hooper 1983, Edwards et al. 1994).

This research helps persuade local officials and community groups in California of the need for local control, and guides local policy makers in the selection of control measures appropriate to the local community's availability-related problems. Additionally, the scientific demonstration of a nexus is critical to sustaining local zoning ordinances against court challenges. It is important that findings be communicated in ways that are useful and intelligible to local policy makers, many of whom lack familiarity with the prevention field and know little about public health and safety research.

Local Agency Reports

Local agency reports from city and county agencies are vital sources of 'nexus' information for local availability-related problems. Field staff from several agencies are in positions to report daily contact with alcohol-related incidents in settings and events throughout the community. These agencies include sheriff/police departments, planning departments, recreation and parks departments, schools, hospitals and emergency medical services.

In California, these local agency sources presently are under-developed as sources of nexus information (Wittman 1991, Wittman et al. 1991). Agency reports provide little information about alcohol and other drug involvement in the event, and usually lack important information about the event's context. Since agency incident reports are made primarily for individual case purposes, the reports are not easily aggregated, lack specification of alcohol or drug involvement unless alcohol and other-drug (AOD) problems are primary, and may be inaccessible due to confidentiality restrictions.

Police department call-for-service records and incident reports are one example of particular interest. Most departments report alcohol problems only as alcohol-specific offences, if at all. The context information is usually restricted to address and police beat. The reports are rarely used by agencies outside the department other than for handling the particular case.

Yet these routine police reports are a potential goldmine for 'nexus' information. One strategy for capturing this information is to use an alcohol-sensitive information planning system programme (ASIPS programme) that 'piggy-backs' on routinely collected police data to report the basic data needed to provide reliable alcohol-nexus information. The ASIPS programme tags the police department's computer information system to identify AOD involvement in all police calls-for-service and in all follow-up incident reports (Wittman et al. 1994).

AOD status is reported for each call for service incident, along with context variables describing time, location and type of setting. Also included from the incident report is basic demographic information about suspects/victims participating in the event. Aggregated ASIPS data can be reported outside of the police department without breaching confidentiality. Prevention planners (including the police department's staff) can work with ASIPS data in many ways, depending upon their interest in the problems, their contexts, and their participants. The data are much easier to understand and to analyse when they are displayed on a geographic information system (GIS) (Harding and Wittman 1995).

The ASIPS concept can be used to capture alcohol-related information in its environmental context in any agency that makes daily contacts with the public. Pilot research in five cities has demonstrated the ASIPS programme's usefulness both for documenting and managing high-risk availability. ASIPS data have been used both for problem solving at the case-level (individual addresses) and for policy planning at the aggregate level (geographical areas and/or types of settings).

Personal Experiences of Availability-related Problems

The local availability-related problems that receive the most attention are those that are of most concern to local officials, community groups and the public. California's local public agencies have stepped up efforts in recent years to encourage concerned citizens and local groups to report problems as they are observed. Several cities provide hot-lines and standard reporting formats to encourage citizens and neighbourhood defence organisations to file complaints. The reporting formats are designed to help the caller describe the environmental correlates of the health or safety problem. These reports can be used to co-ordinate interagency responses from police, code inspections (building, health, safety), health and social services, and other agencies.

Systematic reports on community perceptions of availability-related problems strengthen the credibility of personal experience as a source of planning and enforcement information. These reports provide opportunities for everyone in the community – residents, workers, officials, visitors and leaders – to contribute useful information about availability-related problems. The data collection process can also recruit participants into the local control planning process (Wittman 1995a, Tool Kit 1995).

For example, key informant interviews and local surveys provide useful information about problems in local contexts that identifies problem-environments and encourages action on them. One key-informant survey found close agreement between local perceptions of availability-related problems in four widely separated California cities. The same four problem areas vied for attention in each of the four communities – drinking/driving, youth access, public decorum/drinking in public, and crime/violence. Concern about these four problems, far greater than concern about alcoholism, health-related problems and workplace alcohol problems, strongly influenced the local planning groups' choice of environmental prevention initiatives.

Additional survey work assisted in the detailed specification of problem environments and precise targeting of problem-solving efforts. Brief follow-up surveys were given to occupants of the targeted problem settings to select the most critical settings and most appropriate intervention strategies. Surveys of DUI (driving under the influence) offenders helped identify preferred settings and environmental patterns associated with drinking and driving; focus groups with teenagers clarified the sites and circumstances of youth access to alcohol and drugs.

Engaging the Public in Environmental Approaches to Prevention

Reporting the environmental contexts of alcohol problems is easier when people living and working in the community understand prevention and realise the significance of high-risk availability. Media advocacy (Wallack et al. 1993) and social marketing (Gliksman et al. 1990, Gliksman et al. 1995) inform people of the value of local control and persuade them to support it. Engaging the public in support for local control is particularly important to offset resistance by the alcoholic beverage industry and others opposed to it (Casswell and Gilmore 1989).

Much needs to be done to improve the quality and the utility of information for planning local control policies. The work of researchers and local officials could improve steadily, as suggested above, provided state and federal agencies support robust and rigorous local planning information systems, including complete data about the extent of local retail alcohol sales.

Taking Action on Community Environments of High-risk Availability

Even with perfect knowledge of alcohol problems and their contexts, local prevention planners still face the hard work of establishing local environmental change initiatives to reduce availability-related problems. Several community-based projects have been developed over the last decade that focus on reducing or eliminating high-risk environments of alcohol and drug availability through public policy and environmental approaches (Prevention Plus II 1989, Gibbs and Bennett 1990, Wittman 1990, Aguirre-Molina and Van Ness 1991, Join Together 1995, Wittman 1996b, Join Together (no date)).

Underlying these projects is a generic participatory problem-solving model.

- What community AOD-related problems would the people living and working here like to reduce or prevent?

- What can the community's agencies, groups, and concerned individuals do about these problems using local resources?

- Who (what agencies, which individuals) will take action on the problems?

- Are people happy with the results of these actions?

A Model for Action: Problem-solving Through Participatory Environmental Planning and Design

The Community Alcohol Problem Prevention Program (CAPP Program) applies this basic problem solving approach specifically to local control. The CAPP Program uses *participatory environmental design methods* for its problem-solving approach. Drawing on the fields of architecture and community planning, this approach brings together stakeholders in the community who have a specific interest in preventing problems in a particular environment (Alexander 1979, Wittman and Shane 1988, Schoen 1983).

The CAPP Program conducted a five-year demonstration project, the Community Prevention Planning Demonstration Project (CPPD Project, 1990–95), to test this approach. Community Alcohol Problem Prevention Planning Projects (CAPP Projects) were established in four mid-sized California municipalities. Working through the mayor's office, CAPPP planning groups were formed consisting of twelve to twenty members drawn from local government, residential, commercial, human service, professional, faith, educational and voluntary service sectors of the community. Each CAPPP planning group set out to answer three questions: (1) in what ways are local uses of alcohol environments harming people and damaging property? (2) What local and external resources are available to modify the high-risk environments? (3) How shall these resources be deployed to reduce or eliminate the risk? (Wittman and Biderman 1992).

'Environment' here means any of the settings and circumstances in the community in which alcoholic beverages are sold or consumed in retail, public and social environments. High-risk environments of concern might appear at a variety of scales, or sizes: problem settings could range from single facilities, to neighbourhoods and districts, to certain classes of facility or setting types throughout the city; problem circumstances could range from one-time events, to regularly scheduled activities, to mass events on special occasions.

'Uses of the environment' refers to activities of stakeholders with interests in the setting or circumstance in question. The stakeholders consist of three groups of individuals: *occupants and neighbours* (including drinking/drug-using individuals); *owners and managers* of the premises in which the setting is located; and *public officials and other interested parties* (such as insurance companies and human service provider agencies) responsible for the premises or the occupants of the setting (Wittman 1995b).

The CAPP model holds that for alcohol problems in any given setting or event, each stakeholder group contributes to the problems in certain ways, and each group can do something to reduce or eliminate the problems. The CAPPP projects brought the three groups together to review the problems and to identify ways that community resources could be used to reduce or prevent them. This work, called *environmental accountability analysis*, challenges all three groups to respond to the problems: occupants/neighbours to change problematic drinking behaviours; owner/managers to change practices regarding the presence and use of alcohol; and officials and other interested parties to apply or improve oversight policies and services (Wittman 1995b).

'Resources' refers to all of the community's capacities to deal with problem environments: prevention ideas (concepts and strategies), funds, organisational powers and individual concerns.

Each CAPPP demonstration project pursued four basic tasks to carry out this environmental management process (ISSC 1991a):

(1) *Get started* by building a core community planning group dedicated to the CAPPP process. This entailed major commitments from local leadership and adequate staffing by a trained community organiser.

(2) *Assess problem environments* by documenting the problems systematically and analysing them in a format useful for planning and monitoring environmental prevention initiatives. Key-informant interviews and other problem-elicitation methods proved sufficient for identifying problems and planning prevention initiatives. However, the absence of usable alcohol problem data in local agencies stimulated development of the ASIPS Program and underscored the need for a local system to monitor and evaluate the initiatives.

(3) *Commit resources* to prevention initiatives selected by the planning group to modify targeted high-risk environments. Choices were based on environmental accountability exercises to agree upon problem-selection and to choose risk-reduction activities.

(4) *Implement* selected strategies to carry out the initiatives and monitor and adjust their application to achieve actual problem-reductions. The CPPD Project identified nine strategies in use by California cities to prevent availability-related problems. CAPP planning groups used combinations of these strategies to zero in on specific problems. For example, regulatory activity, negotiation with owners, environmental design, media exposure, and work with the ABC were all applied to reduce alcohol sales at public events in Antioch, one of the demonstration cities (see case example below).

- *Planning and zoning ordinances* to manage retail alcohol outlets according to spacing and number of outlets (density), locations, types and conditions of operation, including requirements for sale/service of alcoholic beverages.

- *Other local ordinances and public agency regulations* that govern drinking and the availability of alcohol in public places and at events to which the public has access.

- *Organisational policies* for drinking at the organisation's social events, and for drinking by the organisation's officers and employees.

- *Negotiated agreements* between parties to resolve immediate concerns about availability-related problems, such as neighbours concerned about a nearby merchant's sale of alcoholic beverages.

- *Public information and education campaigns* to alert people to environmental risks associated with events and conditions of availability that merit special attention, such as drink-driving during holidays.

- *Environmental design* to use architecture, space planning, and decor to maintain security, provide surveillance and communicate expectations for people's use of a setting.

- *Active support for alcohol-free and alcohol-safe social events* by community leaders as the community's norm for the use of alcohol; and active discouragement of high-risk and highly objectionable drinking.

• *Economic measures* to set economic development policies and to collect service fees to offset local agency costs to manage alcohol availability.

• *Work with state agencies and other outside resources*, such as state ABCs, state and county alcohol and drug programme agencies, foundations and other local communities, to develop the community's own environmental prevention policies and programmes.

The participatory environmental planning process is demanding and recursive, sometimes requiring two steps back to move one step forward (Rittel and Webber 1973, Alexander 1979, Schoen 1983). The process requires skill in the arts of both adversarial and co-operative planning (Zander 1990). However, the process also can produce prompt, effective results (see Antioch example below).

Each of the four demonstration grant communities completed the general planning process to target problem environments and identified policies and environmental modifications to prevent or reduce problems (Hitao 1994). Three of the four communities undertook changes in public policy specifically to reduce high-risk environments identified through the local control planning process (Wittman 1995a). Within two years of making these changes, two communities observed reductions in the targeted alcohol-related problems (Wittman and Hudson 1995). Three of the four communities continued their CAPPP projects as prevention programmes assigned to designated city or county agencies.

Local Control in Action

Among the approximately 200 California municipalities estimated to have adopted some form of local control (League of California Cities 1994), the examples below show local control's flexibility to meet the needs and special characteristics of particular communities.

The City of Antioch (population 62,000) agreed in 1991 to participate in the four-city demonstration CPPD Project (see above). The century-old riverfront city had a colourful drinking history associated with public events during summer holidays, a large county fairground located in the city limits, and a number of troublesome bars. The Antioch Community Alcohol Problem Prevention Project (ACAPPP) began a key-informant assessment of the community's availability-related problems. The ACAPPP Planning Group chair, also the head of the community organisation that sponsored an annual Fourth of July riverfront celebration, quickly saw the value of responsible beverage service (RBS) policies for the annual celebration. Before the assessment was completed, on his own initiative, he implemented RBS requirements and restricted alcohol sales hours at the celebration. The new alcohol policies reduced police time, reduced clean-up expenses, and increased family participation in the event. Some non-profit community organisations complained about losses at their traditional fund-raiser beer-booths, leading to changes in fund-raising procedures that were welcomed by some observers (Hitao 1994).

Over the next two years, the assistant city manager redefined ACAPPP as an interagency oversight committee within city government, implemented RBS policies at the city's other riverfront holiday celebrations, regulated drinking in a major public park and added preventive environmental design features, and helped strengthen alcohol policies at the county fairgrounds. The city also passed a conditional use permit zoning ordinance for alcohol outlets and stepped up enforcement to regulate troublesome bars. By fall of 1995, problems with on-sale outlets and public uses of alcohol in Antioch had diminished to barely noticeable levels. Issues of social availability in the city's rapidly growing residential areas were left to the county alcohol and drug prevention programme, which took on CAPPP functions for Antioch and other cities in its region (Wittman and Hudson 1995).

The City of Woodland (population 45,000) is the county seat of a rural agricultural area under increasing pressure from a rapidly growing metropolitan area. In the late 1980s, Woodland's planners were faced with a growing and changing population, static funding for police and other public services, and an economically depressed downtown with a long history of public inebriation and rowdy 'country and western' bars. In 1990, a study by the Woodland Police Department concluded that better-managed alcohol outlets offered the most efficient means to reduce alcohol-related police calls for service. Woodland city council adopted a conditional use permit ordinance in 1991 setting requirements for future retail alcohol outlets and for existing outlets making major changes in operation. The new ordinance, based on the state's Model Conditional Use-permit Ordinance for Retail Alcohol Outlets (1988), is administered by a senior officer in the Woodland Police Department. The officer uses pre-application contacts with prospective operators to review their business plans, explain the intent of the ordinance and introduce the operator to the neighbours.

Woodland's CUP ordinance has not been difficult to administer, and appears to have reduced alcohol-specific problems considerably. By 1995, Woodland's arrest rates for DUI and drinking-in-public had dropped to about one-third of rates prior to the CUP's passage. These drops were greater than secular declines occurring simultaneously in other Yolo County cities due to changes in county arrest-booking procedures. Woodland residents and merchants reported fewer disruptions due to drinking. Fewer alcohol outlets were cited for selling alcoholic beverages to underaged purchasers caught in ABC 'stings' than was typical for the state (12 per cent in Woodland compared to a state-wide rate of about 50 per cent). Results were mixed for other alcohol-involved offences: disturbing-the-peace offences dropped to about one-half of former rates, but assault rates increased (Wittman and Hudson 1995).

South Central and South East Los Angeles (population 650,000, located in two of fifteen city council districts) gained prominence in April 1992 due to a civil disturbance following a police-brutality trial. The disturbance, involving a complex network of civil rights issues, economic grievances, and urban neglect (Sonenshein 1993), brought with it the destruction of about 250 of more than 700 alcohol outlets in the two council districts. Many of the destroyed alcohol outlets had been magnets for crime, vice, loitering, harassment and assault. A local community coalition for prevention of AOD problems prevailed on the city council to follow existing city planning department regulations, rather than grant waivers to rebuild as quickly as possible. These regulations called for case-by-case 'plot-plan reviews' for any project involving new construction or significant remodelling (Mosher and Works 1994).

Plot-plan review applications from alcohol outlets with problem histories were jointly protested by neighbours and police, with organising assistance from the community coalition. The reviews slowed down the approval process and required that the store operators respond to neighbour complaints and police problems. The city planning department placed special operating requirements on outlets with problem histories. By spring of 1996, about fifty-five alcohol outlets had reopened, and about thirty former alcohol outlets converted to merchandise other than alcohol. It appeared highly unlikely that more of the shut-down outlets would apply to reopen. The community coalition began using the city's ordinances to abate nuisances at other problem environments (prostitution hotels and crackhouses), and started training young people interested in community service how to use the city's planning and zoning process to address neighbourhood social and health problems. Formal studies are under way to test local perceptions that alcohol-related problems are fewer than before the 1992 disturbances (Bass 1996).

Discussion

These examples suggest that local control initiatives are capable of limiting or reducing certain availability-related problems. These problems include highly visible community problems (loitering, harassment, public inebriation) and other alcohol-related problems that are major concerns for local agencies and community groups: drink-driving, youth access and youth drinking, and crime/violence.

California experience with local control suggests the following considerations to make successful use of local control initiatives to reduce or prevent availability-related problems:

Build a supportive local constituency. A policy coalition is necessary to pursue local control. Political processes are involved in any local environmental change that is sufficiently potent to significantly reduce alcohol-related problems. Environmental change at this level is likely to threaten economic interests and to challenge social conventions. Successful local control initiatives in California communities seem to thrive on *combined* support from responsive public agencies, concerned local groups, and trained organisers. Sympathetic participation by well-informed officials and community leaders also is vital, particularly from the police and planning departments.

Use local control planning processes to change both norms and regulations. Simultaneous pursuit of 'normative' and 'regulatory' approaches appears to be more fruitful than pursuit of the one without the other, in keeping with observations by Watts and Rabow (1983) and Wittman (1982, 1983) of interactions between socionormative and regulatory forms of 'control'. Movement in both areas appears necessary to secure significant and lasting changes; the regulation of availability without consent is easily subverted, and good intentions quickly become meaningless without proper support. Active participation by each of the three stakeholder groups can help meld social, economic and management perspectives on alcohol availability into policy that is fully implemented and honoured. At its worst, the local control planning process becomes destructively divisive. At its best, it contributes to community building and to the solution of other health and social problems.

Obtain external support to assist the planning process. California cities and counties make great use of outside technical assistance, training, and information to develop useful local control policies. In addition to technical expertise, external supports are an important source of fresh ideas and stimulation to tackle the community's alcohol problem environments. Those county alcohol and drug programmes that have encouraged development of strong local control policies are agencies most likely to seek external support on a continuing basis. Demand has increased from year to year for help from the California Department of Alcohol and Drug Program's prevention technical assistance programme.

Seek continuing improvements in local management of alcohol availability. After twenty years, proficiency in local control in California is still in its early stages of development in most cities and counties. Early experience points to the need for more robust and better-rationalised information systems to support community-based planning and evaluation for local control, well-trained and well-supported community organisers, continuing formal research studies on the relationship between alcohol outlets and alcohol-related problems, and a common planning framework through which cities and counties can share experiences on a consistent basis. It is encouraging to note considerable movement to meet these needs. It is discouraging to observe the impending evaporation of support from state and federal agencies and from private foundations which have done much to nurture development of local control to this point. It remains to be seen whether local control in California will survive on slimmer rations, find fresh sources of support, and become more self-sufficient.

Can Local Control Contribute Significantly to Harm Reduction in California Communities?

Experience to date suggests that self-directed local control can play an important part in significant reductions in morbidity and mortality rates, but cannot alone achieve wholesale reductions. It is very difficult to imagine local communities creating and sustaining massive changes within themselves without some outside assistance. In California, major influences on the community's drinking norms and control policies originate outside the community in the alcoholic beverage industry and from state alcohol control policy. Under these circumstances it is difficult (but not impossible) to imagine a city or county becoming the 'mouse that roared', replacing these influences with its own prevention-friendly environment for alcohol availability.

Local environmental initiatives to reduce problems at the community level can be considered from short-term problem solving and long-term planning perspectives. Short-term prevention takes prompt action to reduce 'hot spots' of high-risk availability, such as bad bars or dangerous stretches of road, where the risks already are locally acknowledged to be unacceptably high (Wittman et al. 1996). High-risk availability that involves trauma – drink-driving crashes, fights, domestic violence – can be significantly reduced by well-planned local control measures aimed at the hot spots.

Long-term prevention involves sustained efforts to lower the acceptable threshold of risk for the local alcohol environment. This effort requires painstaking co-operative efforts from local officials, local organisations and concerned individuals living and working in the community. Education and advocacy, buttressed by credible 'nexus' documentation, must first associate the given alcohol environment with unacceptable problems, and then must take appropriate initiative to reduce or eliminate the problems. *With sustained support from the larger prevention community at institutional and state-wide levels,* change-agents in local communities currently are undertaking these efforts. Many California cities are ready to move past the demonstration phase to the next levels of development: adequate problem documentation, improved efficacy and staff deployment, and better monitoring and policy feedback.

California's experience supports Edwards et al. (1994: 125–45), to affirm that local initiatives directed at specific problem environments can achieve significant reductions in certain availability-related problems. This observation should be viewed not as an opportunity to unload state and federal prevention responsibilities onto localities, but as a prospect for building powerful working partnerships between state and federal agencies and local prevention initiatives. Local control measures 'should not be viewed in isolation, but as elements in a coherent alcohol control policy which structures the alcohol market so as to limit consumption ... *the effectiveness of environmentally-directed measures should be viewed as a means to a policy end, rather than as restrictiveness for restriction's sake'* (Edwards et al. 1994: 207, italics in original).

In California: (1) close co-operation between local control agencies and state ABC administration of licensing and enforcement; (2) state legislation that encourages local control initiatives through both normative (social and economic) and regulatory approaches; (3) state support for research on relationships between alcohol problems and alcohol outlets, including complete data about retail sales activities; (4) mutually supporting and combined state and local public information campaigns to address availability-related problems; (5) continuing technical assistance, training and clearing-house activity from state and federal sources to transfer knowledge, skills, and resources to support local initiatives. These are the supports that can translate local control's promising beginnings into permanent community infrastructures that prevent or minimise harm from alcohol and other drugs.

References

Aguirre-Molina, M. and Van Ness, E. (1991) *Communities Take Charge! A Manual for the Prevention of Alcohol and Other Drug Problems Among Youth*, Piscataway, N.J., University of Medicine and Dentistry of New Jersey – Robert Wood Johnson Medical School, Dept. of Environmental and Community Medicine, Division of Consumer Health Education.

Alcoholic Beverage Control Act (1993) Business and Professions Code, Division 9. State of California Department of Alcoholic Beverage Control.

Alexander, C. (1979) *The Timeless Way of Building*, New York, Oxford University Press.

Babcock, R.F. (1966) *The Zoning Game*, Madison, WI, University of Wisconsin Press.

Bass, K. (1996) (Program Director, Community Coalition for Substance Abuse Prevention and Treatment, Los Angeles, Calif.), 'Community organizing/mobilization as a method of addressing alcohol problems', Presentation at the Alcohol Policy Ten Conference, 4–8 May, Toronto: Addiction Research Foundation.

Beachamp, D.E. (1980) *Beyond Alcoholism: Alcohol and Public Health Policy*, Philadelphia, PA, Temple University Press.

Benham, K. (1983) *San Francisco Alcohol Fact Book*, San Francisco, CA, Trauma Center Foundation, San Francisco Prevention Project, November.

Cahalan, D. (1970) *Problem Drinkers: A National Survey*, San Francisco, CA, Jossey-Bass, Inc.

Cahalan, D., Cisin, I.H. and Crossley, H.M. (1969) *American Drinking Practices: A National Study of Drinking Behavior and Attitudes*, New Brunswick, N.J., Rutgers Center of Alcohol Studies.

Casswell, S. and Gilmore, L. (1989) 'An evaluated community action project on alcohol', *Journal of Studies on Alcohol*, 50.

Christoffel, T. and Teret, S.P. (1993) *Protecting the Public: Legal Issues in Injury Prevention*, New York, Oxford University Press.

City of Euclid v. *Ambler Realty Company* (1926) 272 US 365 467 S.Ct. 114.

Cook, P.J. and Moore, M.F. (1993) 'Violence reduction through restrictions on alcohol availability', *Alcohol Health and Research World*, 117, 151–6.

Douglas, R.R. (1986) 'Alcohol management policies for recreation departments: Development and implementation of the Thunder Bay model', in Giesbrecht, N. and Cox, R. (eds) *Prevention and the environment*, Toronto, Addiction Research Foundation.

Douglass, R., Wagenaar, A. and Barkey, P. (1979) *Alcohol Availability, Consumption, and the Incidence of Alcohol-Related Social and Health Problems in Michigan*, Highway Safety Research Institute, University of Michigan, Ann Arbor, MI, US Dept. of Commerce, National Technical Information Service, May.

Edwards, G., Anderson, P., Babor, T.F., Casswell, S., Ferrence, R., Giesbrecht, N., Godfrey, C., Holder, H., Lemmens, P., Mäkelä, K., Midanik, L., Norström, T., Österberg, E., Romelsjö, A., Room, R., Simpura, J. and Skog, Ø-J. (1994) *Alcohol Policy and the Public Good*, New York, Oxford University Press.

Florence Dolan v. *City of Tigard* (1994) 93-518, US Supreme Court, Writ of Certiorari to Supreme Court of Oregon, June.

Gerson, L.W. and Preston, D.A. (1979) 'Alcohol consumption and the incidence of violent crime', *Journal of Studies on Alcohol*, 41: 307–12.

Gibbs, J. and Bennett, S. (1990) *Together We Can Reduce the Risks*, Seattle, WA, Seattle Health Education Foundation.

Gliksman, L., Douglas, R.R., Rylett, M. and Narbonne-Fortin, C. (1995) 'Reducing problems through municipal alcohol policies: the Canadian experiment in Ontario', *Drugs: Education, Prevention and Policy*, 2: 105–18.

Gliksman, L., Douglas, R.R., Thomson, M., Moffat, K., Smythe, C. and Caverson, R. (1990) 'Promoting municipal alcohol policies: An evaluation of a campaign', *Contemporary Drug Problems*, 17: 391–420.

Gruenewald, P.J. (1993) 'Alcohol problems and the control of availability: Theoretical and empirical issues', in Hilton, H.E. and Bliss, G. (eds) *Economics and the Prevention of Alcohol-Related Problems*. NIAAA Research Monograph No. 25, DHHS Pub. No. (NIH) 93-3513. Washington, D.C., Supt. of Documents, US Government Print Office.

Gruenewald, P.J., Millar, A.B., Treno, A.J., Yang, Z., Ponicki, W.R. and Roeper, P. (1996) 'The geography of availability and drinking and driving', *Addiction* (forthcoming).

Gruenewald, P.J., Ponicki, W.R. and Holder, H.D. (1993) 'The relationship of outlet densities to alcohol consumption: A time-series cross-sectional analysis', *Alcoholism: Clinical and Experimental Research*, Jan/Feb, 17: 38–47.

Harding, J.R. and Wittman, F.D. (1995) 'ASIPS and community-level prevention planning using police incident data with a GIS', Paper presented at the Annual Conference of the Urban and Regional Information Systems

Association, 16–20 July, San Antonio, Texas, Berkeley, CA, CLEW Associates, July.

Hawkins, J.D., Catalano, R.F. and Miller, J.Y. (1992) 'Risk and protective factors for alcohol and other drug problems in adolescence and early adulthood: Implications for substance abuse prevention', *Psychological Bulletin*, 112: 1.

Hitao, G. (1994) *How to Prevent Alcohol Problems in Cities: An Evaluation of the Community Prevention Planning Demonstration Project, June 1990–September 1993*, Berkeley, CA, Institute for the Study of Social Change, University of California, Berkeley, January.

Holder, H. and Wagenaar, A. (1994) 'Mandated server training and reduced alcohol-involved traffic crashes: A time-series analysis of the Oregon experience', *Accident Analysis and Prevention*, 26: 89–97.

Hooper, F. (1983) 'The relationship between alcohol policies, control policies and cirrhosis mortality in United States counties', Paper presented at the Annual Meeting of the American Public Health Association, Dallas, Texas, 16 November.

Institute for the Study of Social Change (1991a) *The Diversity Project. Final Report*, Berkeley, CA, University of California, Berkeley, November.

Institute for the Study of Social Change (1991b) *Handbook: Community Planning Project*, Berkely, CA, University of California, Berkeley.

Join Together (No date) *Alcohol and Drug Abuse in America: Policies for Prevention*, Boston, Join Together, Boston University School of Public Health, and Institute for Health Policy, Heller School, Brandeis University.

Join Together (1995) *A community substance abuse indicators handbook*, Boston, Join Together, Boston University School of Public Health, and Institute for Health Policy, Heller School, Brandeis University.

League of California Cities Conditional Use Permit Ordinances and Alcohol-Related Problems Survey (1994) Unpublished, Spring.

McKnight, A.J. (1991) 'Factors influencing the effectiveness of server-intervention education', *Journal of Studies on Alcohol*, 52: 389–97.

Mecca, A. (ed.) (1982) 'Future of alcoholism services in California', *Proceedings of Think Tank II*, San Rafael, CA, California Health Research Foundation.

Model Conditional Use Permit Ordinance for Retail Alcohol Outlets (1996) Prepared by Assemblyman Gary Condit's office, Sacramento, CA, 1988. Modifications made by James F. Mosher (Marin Institute for the Prevention of Alcohol and Other Drug Problems, San Rafael, CA) and Friedner D. Wittman (Institute for the Study of Social Change, University of California, Berkeley).

Morgan, P. (1979) 'The evaluation of California alcohol policy', Paper presented at second Plenary Meeting of the International Study of Alcohol Control Experiences, Pacific Grove, California, April.

Morgan, P. (1980) 'The state as mediator: Alcohol problem management in the post-war period', *Contemporary Drug Problems*, Spring, 9: 107–40.

Moore, M.H. and Gerstein, D.H. (eds) (1981) *Alcohol and Public Policy:*

Beyond the Shadow of Prohibition, Washington, D.C., National Academy Press.

Mosher, J. (1979) *The Alcoholic Beverage Control System in California*, Prepared for the Second Plenary Meeting of the International Study of Alcohol Control Experiences, Pacific Grove, CA, February, Berkeley, CA, Alcohol Research Group.

Mosher, J.F. and Colman, V. (1989) *Alcoholic Beverage Control in a Public Health Perspective: A Handbook for Action*, San Rafael, CA, Center for Injury Prevention, Trauma Foundation, San Francisco, General Hospital, and Marin Institute for the Prevention of Alcohol and Other Drug Problems.

Mosher, J.F. and Works, R. (1994) *Confronting Sacramento: State Preemption, Community Control and Alcohol-Outlet Blight in Two Inner-City Communities*, San Rafael, CA, The Marin Institute.

O'Malley, P.M. and Wagenaar, A.C. (1991) 'Effects of minimum drinking age laws on alcohol use, related behaviors and traffic crash involvement among American youth, 1976–1987', *Journal of Studies on Alcohol*, 52: 478–91.

Parker, D., Wolz, M. and Harford, T. (1978) 'The prevention of alcoholism: An empirical report on the effects of outlet availability', *Alcoholism: Clinical and Experimental Research*, 2: 339–43.

Parker, R.N. (1993) 'The effects of context on alcohol and violence', *Alcohol Health and Research World*, 17: 117–22.

Parker R.N. and Rebhun, L.A. (1995) *Alcohol and Homicide: A Deadly Combination of Two American Traditions*, New York, State University of New York Press.

Pernanen, K. (1991) *Alcohol in Human Violence*, New York, Guilford Press.

Peters, J. (1996) 'Training: An investment in managing your future', *Beverage Industry News*, 61, 8.

Preusser, D.F. and Williams, A.F. (1992) 'Sale of alcohol to underage purchasers in three New York counties and Washington, D.C.', *Journal of Public Health Policy*, 13: 306–17.

Prevention Plus II (1989) *Tools for Creating and Sustaining Drug Free Communities*, US DHHS Publication No. (ADM) 89-1649: Rockville, MD, Office of Substance Abuse Prevention.

Rabow, J., Schwartz, C., Stevens, S. and Watts, R. (1982) 'Social psychological dimensions of alcohol availability: The relationship of perceived social obligations, price considerations, and energy expended to the frequency, amount, and type of alcoholic beverages consumed', *International Journal of the Addictions*, 17: 1259–71.

Rabow, J. and Watts, R.K. (1982) 'Alcohol availability, alcoholic beverage sales, and alcohol-related problems', *Journal of Studies on Alcohol*, 43: 767–801.

Responsible Hospitality Institute (RHI) Proceedings and Recommendations, California Symposium on Responsible Beverage Service (1991) March, Santa Clara, CA, Scotts Valley, CA: RHI.

Rittel, H. and Webber, M.M. (1973) 'Dilemmas in general theory of planning', *Policy Sciences*, Vol. A: 155–69.

Room, R. (1980) 'Concepts and strategies in the prevention of alcohol-related problems', *Contemporary Drug Problems*, 9: 85–106.

Room, R. (1984) 'Alcohol control and public health', *American Review of Public Health*, 5: 293–317.

Rush, B.R., Gliksman, L. and Brook, R. (1986) 'Alcohol availability, alcohol consumption and alcohol-related damage. II. The role of socio-demographic factors', *Journal of Studies on Alcohol*, 47: 11–18.

Russ, N.W. and Geller, E.S. (1986) *Evaluation of a Server Intervention Program for Preventing Drunk Driving*, Final report no. DD-3. Blacksbury, VA, Virginia Polytechnic Institute and State University, Department of Psychology.

Saltz, R.F. (1987) 'The roles of bars and restaurants in preventing alcohol-impaired driving: An evaluation of server education', *Evaluation of Health Professionals*, 7: 5–27.

Saltz, R.F. and Hennessy, M. (1990) *The Efficacy of 'Responsible Beverage Service' Programs in Reducing Intoxication*, Berkeley, CA, Prevention Research Center.

Schoen, D.A. (1983) *The Reflective Practitioner: How Professionals Think in Action*, New York, Basic Books.

Scribner, R., Dwyer, J. and Mackinnon, D. (1993) *The Risk of Assaultive Violence Associated With Alcohol Outlets in Los Angeles County*, Alhambra, CA, University of Southern California School of Medicine, Dept. of Preventive Medicine.

Scribner, R., Mackinnon, D. and Dwyer, J.H. (1993) *Alcohol Outlet Density and Motor Vehicle Crashes in Los Angeles County Cities*, Alhambra, CA, University of Southern California School of Medicine, Dept. of Preventive Medicine.

Single, E. and Storm, T. (eds) (1985) *Public Drinking and Public Policy*, Toronto, Addiction Research Foundation.

Smart, R. (1980) 'Availability and the prevention of alcohol-related problems', in Hartford, T.C., Parker, D.A. and Light, L. (eds) *Normative Approaches to the Prevention of Alcohol Abuse and Alcoholism*, NIAAA Research Monograph No. 3, Rockville, MD: US Department of Health, Education and Welfare.

Sonenshein, R.J. (1993) *The Battle Over Liquor Stores in an Inner City: The Los Angeles Community Case Study*, Report prepared for DHHS Substance Abuse and Mental Health Services, July.

Tool Kit for Prevention of Alcohol-Related Problems (1995) Berkeley, CA, Community Prevention Planning Demonstration Project, Institute for the Study of Social Change, University of California, Berkeley.

Van Oers, J.A.M. and Garretson, H.F.L. (1993) 'The geographic relationship between alcohol use, bars, liquor shops and traffic injuries in Rotterdam', *Journal of Studies on Alcohol*, 54: 739–44.

Wagenaar, A.C. and Wolfson, M. (1994) 'Enforcement of the legal minimum drinking age in the United States', *Journal of Public Health Policy*, 15: 317–53.

Wallack, L., Dorfman, L., Jernigan, D. and Themba, M. (1993) *Media Advocacy and Public Health: Power for Prevention*, Newbury Park, CA, Sage Publications.

Watts, R. and Rabow, J. (1983) 'Alcohol availability and alcohol-related problems in 213 California cities', *Alcoholism: Clinical and Experimental Research*, 17: 47–58.

Wittman, F.D. (1980) *Tale of Two Cities: Policies and Practices in the Local Control of Alcohol Availability*, Preparation supported by a National Institute on Alcohol Abuse and Alcoholism National Research Center Grant AA-03524. Berkeley, CA, Social Research Group, October.

Wittman, F.D. (1982) *Zoning Ordinances, Alcohol Outlets, and Planning: Prospects of Local Control of Alcohol Problems*, Prepared under funding provided by the National Institute on Alcohol Abuse and Alcoholism, Grant Nos. AA-04868-01/AA-05622-02. Berkeley, CA, Alcohol Research Group, December, 1981, revised April 1982.

Wittman, F.D. (1983) *Local Regulation of Alcohol Availability in Selected California Communities: Introduction and Summary of Findings*, Prepared for the California State Health and Welfare Agency, Department of Alcohol and Drug Programs, under Contract A-0138-2. Berkeley, CA, Prevention Research Group, Institute of Epidemiology and Behavioral Medicine, Medical Research Institute of San Francisco, October.

Wittman, F.D. (1986) 'Issues in controlling alcohol availability', in *Western City: League of California Cities*, Sacramento, CA: November.

Wittman, F.D. (1990) 'Environmental design to prevent problems of alcohol availability: Concepts and prospects', in *Research, Action, and the Community: Experiences in the Prevention of Alcohol and Other Drug Problems*, OSAP Prevention Monograph-4, DHHS (ADM) 89-1651.

Wittman, F.D. (1991) *Information Based Community Planning for Prevention of Alcohol Problems*, Prepared for the Bureau of Alcohol Services, Santa Clara County Health Department in San Jose, California. Berkeley, CA, CLEW Associates, May.

Wittman, F.D. (1993a) *Local Information Sources for Planning Alcohol/Drug Prevention Programs*, Berkeley, CA, Institute for the Study of Social Change, University of California, Berkeley, February.

Wittman, F.D. (1993b) *Survey of Alcohol and Other Drug Experiences Among Castro Valley High School Students in 1987, 1990, and 1993*, Prepared for CommPré, Horizon Services, Inc., Hayward, CA. Berkeley, CA, CLEW Associates.

Wittman, F.D. (1994) *Development and Use of Conditional Use Permits to Prevent Problems Related to Retail Alcohol Outlets: An Overview*, Community Prevention Planning Demonstration Project. Institute for the Study of Social Change, University of California at Berkeley, September.

Wittman, F.D. (1995a) *The Community Prevention Planning Demonstration Project: Changing Community Alcohol Environments to Reduce AOD-Related Problems in Four California Cities*, Presented at the 37th International Conference on Alcohol and Drug Dependence, San Diego, CA, 23 August 1995. Berkeley, CA, Institute for the Study of Social Change, University of California, Berkeley.

Wittman, F.D. (1995b) *Environmental Accountability Analysis*, Presented to the Annual Conference of the League of California Cities, San Francisco, California, 24 October 1995, Berkeley, CA, Community Prevention Planning Demonstration Project, Institute for the Study of Social Change, University of California, Berkeley, October.

Wittman, F.D. (1995c) *Overview on Community Organizers for Community Alcohol Problem Prevention Projects*, Berkeley, CA, Community Prevention Planning Demonstration Project, Institute for the Study of Social Change, University of California, Berkeley.

Wittman, F.D. (1996a) 'Case study: Escondido country alcohol planning project', Prepared for Wittman, F.D. *The Environmental Approach to Community AOD Prevention. An Action Manual*, EMT Group, Inc. Sacramento, CA: California Department of Alcohol and Drug Programs.

Wittman, F.D. (1996b) *The Environmental Approach to Community AOD Prevention. An Action Manual*, EMT Group, Inc. Sacramento, CA: California Department of Alcohol and Drug Programs.

Wittman, F.D. (1996c) 'Local zoning to prevent problems related to retail alcohol outlets: Progress report on fifteen years of experience in California', Prepared for Alcohol Policy Ten Conference, 4–8 May 1996. Toronto, Addiction Research Foundation.

Wittman, F.D., Harding, J.R. and Kessler, K.H. (1994) *Recommendations to the City of Berkeley for an Information Planning System to Prevent Problems Related to the Availability and Use of Alcohol and Other Drugs (Long Form)*, Berkeley, CA, CLEW Associates, December.

Wittman, F.D. and Biderman, F. (1992) 'The California community planning demonstration project: Experiences in planning for prevention of alcohol problems in four municipalities', in *Experiences With Community Action Projects: New Research in the Prevention of Alcohol and Other Drug Problems*, CSAP Prevention Monograph 14. Center for Substance Abuse Prevention, US Department of Health and Human Services.

Wittman, F.D. and Burhenne, R. (1985) *Planning, Zoning, and Alcohol Outlets in San Diego: Community Planning for the Prevention of Alcohol Problems*, Prepared for California Department of Alcohol and Drug Programs contract no. AA-0032-4. Berkeley/San Diego, CA, September.

Wittman, F.D. and Harding, J. (1994) *The Hayward ASIPS project: Design and Use of a Community-Based Information Planning System to Prevent Alcohol and Other Drug Problems*, Berkeley, CA, CLEW Associates, June.

Wittman, F.D., Harding, J.R. and Biderman, F. (1994) *ASIPS Summary*

(Alcohol-Sensitive Information Planning System), Berkeley, CA, CLEW Associates and the Institute for the Study of Social Change, University of California, Berkeley, January 1993, updated May 1993.

Wittman, F.D., Harding, J.R. and Kessler, K.H. (1994) *Recommendations to the City of Berkeley for an Information Planning System to Prevent Problems Related to the Availability and Use of Alcohol and Other Drugs (Long Form)*, Berkeley, CA, CLEW Associates, December.

Wittman, F.D., Harding, J.R. and Sparks, M. (1996) *Pilot Project to Use ASIPS/GIS to Assist Vallejo Fighting Back Partnership in Planning to Prevent Alcohol and Drug-Related Problems*, Prepared for Robert Wood Johnson Foundation, Princeton, NJ, Berkeley, CA, CLEW Associates, 15 March.

Wittman, F.D., Helmke, C., Biderman, F., Graudenz, D. and Footer, K. (1991) *Alameda County Community Readiness Project, Final Report for North County Cities*, Prepared for Alameda County Department of Alcohol and Drug Programs. Berkeley, CA, CLEW Associates, June.

Wittman, F.D. and Hilton, M.E. (1987) 'Uses of planning and zoning ordinances to regulate alcohol outlets in California cities', in H. Holder (ed.) *Control Issues in Alcohol Abuse Prevention: Strategies for States and Communities*, Greenwich, CT, JAI Press.

Wittman, F.D. and Hudson, M. (1995) *Local Initiatives to Prevent Problems Related to alcohol availability: Notes From Three Communities*, Berkeley, CA: Community Prevention Planning Demonstration Project, Institute for the Study of Social Change, University of California, Berkeley.

Wittman, F.D. and Shane, P. (1988) *Manual for Community Planning to Prevent Problems of Alcohol Availability*, Prepared under the support from the California Department of Alcohol and Drug programs contract nos. A-0154-5, A-0143-6, A-0024-7; additional support provided by National Institute on Alcohol Abuse and Alcoholism Research Center grant AA06282 to the Prevention Research Center, Pacific Institute for Research and Evaluation. Berkeley, CA, Prevention Research Center, September.

Zander, A. (1990) *Effective Social Action by Community Groups*, San Francisco, CA, Jossey-Bass.

5 Prevention Where Alcohol is Sold and Consumed: Server Intervention and Responsible Beverage Service

Robert F. Saltz

A hallmark of strategies to minimise harm related to the consumption of alcohol is that they are targeted at times and places proximal to where and when drinking and the risk of subsequent harm are present. Because these are also the times and places where the drinker's judgement is likely to be most impaired, it seems best that interventions to reduce harm do not depend on the drinker's initiative. The use of air bags in motor vehicles is often cited as a prototypical strategy for harm reduction in that its employment occurs just at the point where harm is likely (that is, during a collision), and its operation is automatic and independent of the driver's intentions or behaviour.

Server intervention's potential as a prevention strategy stems from its sharing these basic features. At a minimum, server intervention refers to servers of alcoholic beverages making sure that no intoxicated or impaired customer is left to drive away in that condition. More generally, under the rubric of Responsible Beverage Service (RBS), it refers to the steps that servers of alcoholic beverages can take to reduce the chances that their patrons (or guests) become intoxicated in the first place. The intervention thus occurs in close proximity to when the risk arises (that is, while the patron is drinking or has become impaired), and its invocation does not depend on the drinker's judgement (though, of course, the drinker may respond in various ways to the server's attentions).

The idea that those who serve alcohol might be in a position to prevent subsequent harm to drinkers and others stems from several observations primarily in North American settings. First, as summarised by O'Donnell (1985), a significant proportion (about half) of legally impaired drivers had been drinking at licensed outlets. This implies that someone presumably not impaired by alcohol (the commercial server) is in a position to intervene when the drinker's own judgement may well be impaired. Second, as summarised by Mosher (1984), there had been a legal precedent (in the USA) for holding alcohol servers and establishments liable for monetary costs in the case where a customer known to be intoxicated was served more alcohol which then contributed to damages or injury to innocent third parties. This in turn implies not only that there is a legal and cultural support for servers to take responsibility for their serving practices, but that a mechanism is already in place to encourage them to do so.

As Mosher points out, however, these supports and mechanisms have not been directed toward prevention per se, and thus far have not been adequate to constitute a major inducement for bar owners and managers to implement effective RBS programmes. A key question for server intervention today is in finding the best incentives for its adoption (with disincentives for irresponsible service). Before this question could be pursued, however, research had to show that there is, indeed, a potential for server intervention or RBS programmes to reduce alcohol-related deaths and injuries.

Early Research into the Efficacy of Server Intervention

While responsible beverage service evaluations have been already reviewed in the published literature (see Saltz 1989, McKnight 1993), we will summarise them here for convenience and include newer studies as well. One of the early evaluations of server intervention, the Navy Server Study (Saltz 1985, 1987, Hennessy and Saltz 1989, Saltz and Hennessy 1990a), sought simply to answer the question of whether the concept of server intervention had potential merit as a prevention strategy. Two similar Navy clubs for enlisted personnel were selected, with one serving as a programme site and the other as a comparison. The programme involved extensive consultation with the club manager, producing several changes in club policies and practices, and an eighteen-hour training course for all staff. The outcome measure was the proportion of patrons whose drinking (either by self-report or direct observation) was estimated to put them over the legal limit of intoxication (at the time, 0.10% BAC (blood alcohol content). The programme resulted in a fairly dramatic reduction in that proportion (from 33% to 15%), at least over the short run (that is, two months after implementation).

The policy changes included promoting non-alcoholic beverages and food, overtly delaying service of an alcoholic beverage if it would put the patron at or above the legal limit for intoxication, and the discontinuance of beer sold in pitchers. Where food service had been previously segregated from the bar area, a food service station was installed in the bar-room, and money incentives were provided for servers and cooks to promote food sales. In addition, where servers had been free to roam anywhere in the building to serve customers, the new programme required their being assigned to specific sections of optimal size, so that customers' consumption could be monitored. The food and beverage menus were expanded, and drink prices raised marginally to cover the programme costs.

The training course, broken into five modules and spread out over as many weeks, included giving reasons for change, alcohol's effects on the body, monitoring a customer's consumption to know when he or she has reached the limit, and techniques to pace service and refuse it when necessary. Group discussions and visual presentations were used throughout the eighteen-hour programme, with role-play exercises dominating the last two sessions.

In this case study, care was taken to find a programme site in which there was (1) heavy drinking, but also (2) a high level of interest and co-operation on the part of the manager. As with other efficacy studies, it sought optimum conditions, delivered a comprehensive programme with high intensity, and limited the scope of application to one or two establishments to maintain that level of intensity. In the early evaluations of any programme, issues of generalisability are postponed while investigating the inherent merit of the prevention strategy. Thus, optimum conditions are more appropriate to the task than seeking out, say, a 'typical' setting.

Other early evaluations have been similarly modest in scope. Russ and Geller (1987; see also Geller et al. 1987) evaluated one of the commercially available server training programmes, TIPS (Training for Intervention Procedures by Servers of Alcohol) (Chafetz 1984). This programme comprised a six-hour course that included video vignettes, group discussion and role-playing, with an emphasis on identifying signs of impairment, pacing service, checking patrons' age, and promoting alternatives to alcoholic beverages. The trainees then had to score at least 70% correct on a forty-question written test to become certified servers. The authors recruited seventeen trainees from two commercial establishments, ending up with about half of the employees having been trained.

Research assistants, posing as customers, attempted to order and consume a drink every twenty minutes over a two-hour period. The authors found that while the untrained staff intervened no more than was the case at baseline (about 0.75 interventions), the trained staff intervened more frequently (3.24 interventions). A second measure of the programme's impact was the pseudo-patron's BAC taken after the two-hour drinking period was over. Whereas those served by the untrained staff had BACs as high as baseline (mean of 0.103%, with four of nine pseudo-patrons above the legal limit), none of those served by the trained staff was over the legal limit (mean of 0.059% BAC).

Another evaluation was conducted by researchers of the Addiction Research Foundation in Toronto, Canada (Gliksman et al. 1993). Here, manager and complementary server training courses were given to four different establishments in Thunder Bay, Ontario, with four other sites used for comparison. The study adapted and expanded on the 'pseudo-patron' approach used by Geller et al. (1987) and the outcome variable was the server's response scores (with highest score for the 'best' responses to the pseudo-patron's behaviour). Where the mean scores of the comparison sites increased slightly from about 16.3 to 16.9, the experimental sites' mean score rose from about 15 to over 21 (that is, the trained servers had moved towards more appropriate responses to the problematic scenes acted out by the pseudo-patrons).

A study reported by Howard-Pitney and others (1991) was conducted in Park City, Utah, where a newly expanded state law required servers and managers to be trained every three years. Twenty-six different establishments participated in a one-day training, and again pseudo-patrons (and observers) were used to evaluate the training's impact on server behaviour. Here, no differences in interventions were observed between the treatment and control servers. Observers did note, however, that the trained establishments were more likely to have some responsible alcohol service policies (for example, advertising low- or non-alcoholic drinks, offering information on transportation). The number of places was too small for differences to be statistically significant, however.

Each of these studies was small in scale with outcomes measured over a short period following implementation. The mixed results suggest that responsible beverage service programmes have potential to reduce the risks of intoxication, but other factors may act to facilitate or impede implementation. One cannot help but notice, however, that the shorter training (or awareness) interventions seemed to produce the smallest impacts.

Two other evaluations have started to move away from a focus on efficacy and towards implementation issues (sometimes referred to as 'effectiveness' studies, cf. Flay 1986). Saltz and Hennessy (1990b) reported on an evaluation of a responsible beverage service programme implemented in the cities of Santa Cruz and Monterey, California. Within each city, two bars or restaurants were given different training programmes while a third served as a no-treatment comparison. Here, positive effects on lowering the risk of intoxication were found for the programme sites in Santa Cruz, but not in Monterey. No differences were found for type of programme. The report suggests that the two communities differed in ways that affected the managers' commitment to the server programme. The study design thus included an explicit comparison across two dimensions of implementation (programme type and community), as well as serving as a replication study of the efficacy of responsible beverage service programmes more generally.

Another evaluation, by McKnight (1988), involved the development and delivery of a responsible beverage service programme to 100 establishments in eight different cities across the USA. In this study, a three-hour training was given to servers and managers, with three additional hours for the managers alone. In all, 1079 people were trained. A group of 135 matched establishments was used for comparison. Research assistants were used in this study, too, to pose as customers, and were to feign intoxication when entering the establishment to see if they would be served a drink despite their condition. While the frequency of *some* form of intervention rose from 14 to 27% at the trained businesses (no change at comparisons), outright refusal of service to the pseudo-patrons remained unchanged, with a rate of about 5%.

If only because of the scale of programme delivery, McKnight's study represents something much closer to a 'real world' intervention and would probably be seen as a more meaningful demonstration to a policy maker than the smaller 'test cases' described earlier. Of course, the small studies, taken as a whole, can tell us more about the *potential* for RBS than might one or two full-scale implementations.

Research on Implementation Issues

The early efficacy studies seem to show that under some conditions, and to differing degrees of success, RBS programmes *can* reduce levels of intoxication and raise levels of server intervention.

That these results are 'mixed' should not be surprising since each study's programme was developed and implemented without benefit of systematic research into what approach works best in a given setting. We really do not know, for example, whether current serving practices (which typically do not entail preventing intoxication or intervention to prevent impaired driving) reflect ignorance of laws (where they apply), lack of training in how to intervene, lack of motivation to change, resistance to change due to licensees' fear of lost revenue or servers' fear of adverse customer response, or, more likely, some combination of these and other factors.

The question for RBS is, then, to find the most effective mechanism by which servers and their managers will intervene to prevent alcohol-related harm. There are several approaches and some research that can help us evaluate their relative merits. The leading strategies include:

- Manager and/or server training
  (a) using persuasion with licensees to adopt RBS principles and attend voluntary training programmes
  (b) make server training mandatory

- Enact server liability laws that hold servers responsible for injury or damage caused by a customer who was given too much alcohol

- Enforce laws that require servers to refuse service to intoxicated patrons

The 'persuasive' approach is the one most used by the early research, of course, and usually over a small number of businesses (excepting McKnight 1988). This has led some to argue that RBS is doomed to failure as persuasion is unlikely to work in the face of economic incentives to sell as much alcohol as customers will drink. Apart from the fact this is an empirical question that should be argued from evidence, we have described several other mechanisms that are not dependent on a licensee's 'good will'.

A more recent community-wide demonstration programme relying on voluntary compliance was reported by Stockwell et al. (1993). The 'Freo Respects You' programme was aimed at over fifty licensed establishments in Freemantle, Western Australia. The programme planners started with the premise that server training alone would not be sufficient to change serving practices unless accompanied by management support and co-operation from law enforcement agencies. Having organised support from both the state Hotels and Hospitality Association and local public authorities, the programme was launched with a media campaign and comprised two key components: conducting formal (and confidential) 'risk assessments' for each licensee or manager; and organising workshops for licensees, managers and bar staff. The training covered 'liquor licensing laws, signs of approaching and actual drunkenness, strategies for dealing with customers, general facts about alcohol and the development of house policies' (Stockwell et al. 1993: x). The training sessions were staffed by members of both the hospitality industry and the Police Liquor Squad.

The experience seems to provide some support for those sceptical of voluntary approaches, in that only ten businesses took part in the programme (within a seven-month period), manager attendance at training was lower than desired, and there were difficulties in maintaining fidelity to the training curriculum. Seven of the ten establishments were considered 'medium to high risk' for producing drink-driving offenders, and these were used in an evaluation along with seven similar businesses from another community. The programme increased staff knowledge of the serving laws and encouraged more positive attitudes toward responsible service. The individual risk assessments did seem to encourage change in management policies in some cases.

The evaluation included sending youthful-looking eighteen-year-olds into the participating outlets to see if identification would be asked for, and while there was an increase in such checks, staff were just as likely to accept non-photo IDs as before the training. Pseudo-patrons were also used to simulate drunkenness, but refusals were made only eight times out of seventy-eight attempts, with no difference between communities. Surprisingly, then, exit breath tests with actual patrons showed a statistically significant drop in the proportion of them with breath alcohol levels in excess of 0.08 (in comparison with the control community). This difference seemed due to large decreases in three of the participating businesses, with the researchers suggesting that this could reflect different levels of implementation of the programme and policies at the outlets.

There is no a priori imperative for manager and server training to be offered on a voluntary basis. While future evaluation may show that voluntary attendance at training sessions produces greater change for these who attend, mandatory training may reach more servers and convey to them a greater significance of RBS (by virtue of the training being required).

In the United States, Oregon, and more recently New Mexico, mandate training for all commercial servers. Holder and Wagenaar (1994) evaluated the state of Oregon's mandatory server training programme by looking at single-vehicle night-time crashes for the period 1976–89. The training programme began in December of 1986 with half of the servers having been trained by the end of 1989. Time series analysis estimated a reduction in crashes of 23% net of other potential effects (including 0.08% BAC laws and others aimed at reducing impaired driving). This is quite a sizeable effect, especially given the modest results from the studies summarised above, which should be an additional incentive to look more closely at the implementation process to see what might account for the apparent disparity. It may be, for instance, that in the case of Oregon, a 'critical mass' of trained servers produced a change in serving practices that one would not find when training is limited to only a few businesses at a time.

The use of training, whether voluntary or mandatory, is predicated on the premise that the greatest barrier to adopting RBS practices is either lack of awareness on servers' part, or lack of specific skills and techniques to intervene with those whose alcohol consumption puts them at risk of injuring themselves or others. It may be, however, that licensees need more motivation than training per se, though most training curricula include a motivational element. That extra motivation might be provided via any combination of incentives (for example, liability insurance premium discounts, favourable notation in files kept by regulatory agencies) or disincentives such as fear of liability lawsuits or other legal action.

The effects of liquor liability laws are difficult to estimate as they are not subject to experimental manipulation. We do have the opportunity of 'natural experiments' whenever such laws have changed. Wagenaar and Holder (1991) have analysed single-vehicle night-time traffic crash data from the State of Texas over a ten-year period that included two well-publicised successful dram shop liability lawsuits. After controlling for national trends and other historical interventions (for example, minimum drinking age changes and mandatory seat belt laws), it appears as though the lawsuits themselves accounted for drops of 6.5% and 5.3% in the crash rates. The analysis, of course, cannot directly link the dram shop suits to changes in serving practices, but future research may be able to prospectively investigate these practices during changes in liability laws as they happen. A report by Holder et al. (1990) provides some limited information about how liability laws affect bars and restaurants. Using liability risk scores derived from a panel of legal experts, questionnaires were mailed to a sample of licensees in five states (USA) with the lowest risk and four states with high-risk scores. The response rate was low (12%), so the results should be viewed with caution, but the sample size itself was fairly large (839) and there were no overt differences in the types of businesses represented in the two sets of states (high and low liability).

Results showed a definite relationship between liability and awareness, with people in high liability states much more likely to know of liquor liability lawsuits, more likely to report that such suits are possible in their state, and much more likely to characterise the business climate as 'hostile' toward their organisation. Interestingly, if there were any differences between the two groups with regard to training, it would appear that the businesses in the low liability states were more likely to have formal training for their staff on matters of service to minors or intoxicated patrons than were the high liability bars and restaurants, though the differences were small. Similarly, there was little difference in checking age identification or offering drinks in oversize servings (pitchers or bottles). On the other hand, it did appear that business in the high liability states were much less likely to use price promotions (happy hours or two-for-one sales), and were more likely to refuse service to intoxicated patrons.

In sum, these findings suggest that owners and managers are aware of the liability climates in which they operate, and perceive their need and ability to obtain liability insurance to likewise be affected by that climate. Training per se does not seem to be encouraged by working in a high liability environment, or at least the encouragement is not sufficient to overcome the costs of providing that training. Nevertheless, higher risk of liability does seem to influence certain management and serving practices that may, in the end, prove to be as important if not more important than training per se in reducing the risk of driving while impaired. The Texas evidence in particular implies that changes in legal environments for licensees can directly result in lowered alcohol-related crashes.

Finally, there is limited, but persuasive evidence that visible enforcement of laws against service to intoxicated patrons may have a large effect on serving practices even in the absence of any training at all. A study by McKnight and Streff (1993) evaluated the impact of increased enforcement of laws prohibiting service to obviously intoxicated patrons. Notices were sent to licensed establishments in Washtenaw County, Michigan, and plainclothes police officers visited bars and restaurants monitoring beverage service over the course of one year. Service to pseudo-patrons feigning intoxication declined from 84% to 47% (later rising to 58%) while service in a comparison site showed declines of a much smaller magnitude. The proportion of DUI (driving under the influence) arrestees coming from licensed establishments declined from 32% to 23% (with no changes in DUI enforcement practices) where the proportion increased slightly in the comparison site.

Though most server intervention and RBS programmes emphasize the risk of drink-driving, one should keep in mind that intoxication is associated with a number of other problems and harm as well, not the least of which is violent behaviour. It is noteworthy, then, that in at least one instance, RBS was a central part of an effort to reduce assault. The Surfers Paradise Safety Action Project was a demonstration project focusing on the use of responsible beverage service practices to lower alcohol-related violence and disorder in the central business district of that tourist area on Australia's Gold Coast. An evaluation covered programme activities between April and December of 1993. The programme comprised three major strategies: the development of community-based task forces; conducting risk assessments similar to those done in Freemantle, with subsequent implementation of a community 'code of practice'; and increased enforcement of licence laws, particularly those tied to the prevention of assaults. Training was offered, primarily to security staff, in ways to deal with patron intoxication, and the code of practice emphasized refusal of service to intoxicated patrons, along with responsible advertising and, most importantly perhaps, the elimination of free drinks and extreme price promotions. At the same time as these efforts were directed at behaviour inside licensed businesses, police officers were stepping up response to unlawful behaviour on the streets of the same commercial zone.

Though the evaluation limits our drawing strong conclusions by virtue of its not including any control community, observed physical assaults in a sample of outlets declined from 9.8 per 100 hours of observation to 4.7 (Homel and Clark 1994: 40). Observations also found a significant reduction in binge drinking among men and in rates of intoxication. Business during this time did not appear to suffer any patronage. Police data also showed a decline in violence and other offences for the central business district while rates for the larger jurisdiction were increasing, though it would be difficult to segregate the effects of the RBS activities with increased general law enforcement.

Conclusions

For those whose interest lies in preventive action, there seems sufficient evidence that server intervention or responsible beverage service programmes can measurably, and sometimes dramatically, reduce alcohol impairment and intoxication. It would also seem that server training on its own may have limited impact (though the Oregon experience should not be overlooked). The enactment and enforcement of laws requiring refusal of alcoholic beverages to intoxicated patrons holds promise to the degree that those laws can be effectively enforced. Likewise, liquor liability laws can be effective, if drafted with a strong prevention orientation and subsequently publicised. In all cases, there must be an emphasis on house policies and serving practices, backed up with management support and community commitment to the programme.

Practical experience with RBS programmes in the field leads one to sound a note of caution. There often, if not always, is tremendous pressure to focus on the design and delivery of training programmes. Perhaps this is because the technology of training is familiar and well developed, whereas achieving changes in local regulation is more challenging and unfamiliar. Whatever the reason, lopsided attention to server training at the expense of working on changing house policies and community law enforcement would seem to ensure failure.

For the research community, this cursory review of results points out how much more we should like to know about implementing an effective responsible beverage service programme. The demonstrated potential of server intervention provides the necessary motivation to continue the pursuit of this particular strategy, while the research we do have is sufficient to focus our efforts on which programme components are most likely to achieve the desired effect. There is every reason to believe that further refinement of responsible beverage service programmes will show them to be one of the most cost-effective weapons we have to battle alcohol-related injuries and deaths.

References

Chafetz, M.E. (1984) 'Training in Intervention Procedures: A Prevention Program', *Alcohol, Drugs, and Driving: Abstracts and Reviews*, 5: 17–19.

Flay, B. (1986) 'Efficacy and effectiveness trials (and other phases of research) in the development of health promotion programs', *Preventive Medicine*, 15: 451–74.

Geller, E., Russ, N. and Delphos, W. (1987) 'Does server intervention make a difference?' Alcohol Health and Research World, 11: 64–9.

Gliksman, L., McKenzie, D., Single, E., Douglas, R., Brunet, S. and Moffatt, K. (1993) 'The role of alcohol providers in prevention: An evaluation of a server intervention program', Addiction, 88: 1189–97.

Hennessy, M. and Saltz, R.F. (1989) 'Adjusting for Multi-Method Bias Through Selection Modeling', Evaluation Review, 13: 380–99.

Holder, H. and Wagenaar, A. (1994) 'Mandated server training and reduced alcohol-involved traffic crashes: A time series analysis of the Oregon experience', Accident Analysis and Prevention, 26: 89–97.

Holder, H., Wagenaar, A., Saltz, R., Mosher, J. and Janes, K. (1990) 'Alcohol beverage server liability and the reduction of alcohol-related problems: Evaluation of dram shop laws', Non-Technical Final Report (7–88/6–90) DOT HAS 807 628 to the National Highway Traffic Safety Administration (Contract DTNH–22–88–C–07068). Available through the National Technical Information Service, Springfield, VA 22161.

Homel, R. and Clark, J. (1994) 'The prediction and prevention of violence in pubs and clubs', in Clarke, R.V. (ed.) Crime Prevention Studies, Vol. 3, Monsey, N.Y., Criminal Justice Press.

Homel, R., Hauritz, M., Wortley, R., Clark, J. and Carvolth, R. (1994). The impact of the Surfers Paradise Safety Action Project, Centre for Crime Policy and Public Safety, School of Justice Administration, Griffith University.

Howard-Pitney, B., Johnson, M.D., Altman, D., Hopkins, R. and Hammond, N. (1991) 'Responsible alcohol service: A study of server, manager, and environmental impact', American Journal of Public Health, 81: 197–9.

McKnight, A.J. (1988) Development and Field Test of a Responsible Alcohol Service Program, Final Report, National Highway Traffic Safety Administration, US Department of Transportation, Contract No. DTNH22-84-C-07170.

McKnight, A.J. (1993) 'Server Intervention: Accomplishments and Needs', Alcohol Health and Research World, 17: 76–83.

McKnight, A.J. and Streff, F.M. (1993) 'The effect of enforcement upon service of alcohol to intoxicated patrons of bars and restaurants', in Alcohol, Drugs and Traffic Safety–T92, Proceedings of the 12th International Conference on Alcohol, Drugs, and Traffic Safety. Cologne, Germany, Verlag TÜV Rheinland, 1296–1302.

Mosher, J.M. (1984) 'The Impact of Legal Provisions on Barroom Behavior: Toward an Alcohol-Problems Prevention Policy', Alcohol, 1: 205–11.

O'Donnell, M. (1985) 'Research on drinking locations of alcohol-impaired drivers: implication for prevention policies', Journal of Public Health Policy, 6: 510–25.

Russ, N.W. and Geller, E.S. (1987) 'Training bar personnel to prevent drunken driving: A field evaluation', American Journal of Public Health, 77: 952–54.

Saltz, R.F. (1985) 'Server intervention: Conceptual overview and current developments', *Alcohol, Drugs, and Driving: Abstracts and Reviews*, 1: 1–14.

Saltz, R.F. (1987) 'The roles of bars and restaurants in preventing alcohol-impaired driving: An evaluation of server intervention', *Evaluation and the Health Professions*, 10: 5–27.

Saltz, R.F. (1989) 'Research Needs and Opportunities for Health Educators in Server Intervention Programs', *Health Education Quarterly*, 16: 429–38.

Saltz, R.F. and Hennessy, M. (1990a) *The Efficacy of 'Responsible Beverage Service' Programs in Reducing Intoxication*, Berkeley, CA, Prevention Research Center.

Saltz, R.F. and Hennessy, M. (1990b) *Reducing Intoxication in Commercial Establishments: An Evaluation of Responsible Beverage Service Practices*, Berkeley, CA, Prevention Research Center.

Stockwell, T., Rydon, P., Lang, E. and Beel, A. (1993) *An Evaluation of the 'Freo Respects You' responsible alcohol service project*, National Centre for Research into the Prevention of Drug Abuse, Curtin University, Perth, Western Australia.

Wagenaar, A.C. and Holder, H.D. (1991) 'Effects of Alcoholic Beverage Server Liability on Traffic Crash Injuries', *Alcoholism: Clinical and Experimental Research*, 15: 942–7.

6 Standard Unit Labelling of Alcohol Containers

Tim Stockwell and Eric Single

Introduction

A 'unit' or 'standard drink' of alcohol has become a central concept in alcohol education campaigns over the past two decades in the English-speaking world. Whenever advice is given to the public regarding low-risk levels of use, whether for general health or safety reasons, almost invariably levels of daily and/or weekly alcohol consumption are provided in 'units' of alcohol or 'standard drinks'. Such advice is usually accompanied by an illustration of typical servings of beer, wine, spirits and sherry or port which contain approximately the same amounts of alcohol and comprise one 'unit' or 'standard drink'. In different countries, health educators tend to employ different definitions of a standard unit supposedly reflecting typical serving sizes in that country. For example, a unit or standard drink in Canada is 13.6 grams, in the UK it is 8 grams, in the USA 14 grams and in both New Zealand and Australia it is 10 grams of alcohol.

The notion of labelling alcohol containers with their alcohol content expressed in units or standard drinks has gained rapid acceptance since it was first proposed by the British Royal Medical Colleges in 1987. From 22 December 1995 it became law in Australia for all alcohol imported or manufactured to include a statement on the packaging expressing the number of 10 g 'standard drinks' to one decimal place. Such labelling has also been recommended by the Alcohol Advisory Council of New Zealand (Courtney 1989), Alcohol Concern in the UK (Appleby 1992) and the Policy and Research Director of the Canadian Centre on Substance Abuse (Single 1994). On 9 July 1992 Representative Patricia

Figure 6.1: Standard drink illustrations
Sources: Alcohol Advisory Council (ALAC), New Zealand, Health Department, Western Australia and the Medical Council on Alcoholism, UK.

Schroeder introduced a bill into the US Congress to require basic consumer information on beverage containers including alcohol content expressed in standard units (*Booze News*, Center for Science in the Public Interest, July 1992).

Standard unit labelling falls into the category of those strategies which assist people to reduce hazardous use of alcohol by sticking to relatively safe limits. It is not a strategy which can be expected to work in isolation since it requires that drinkers are already motivated to observe a particular drinking limit.

A chain of supermarkets in the UK (Tesco) introduced a form of standard unit labelling in Britain in 1989. It is too early to evaluate the impact of standard unit labelling on the community at large as no evaluation of this initiative has been made publicly available. A number of experiments, focus group studies and community surveys have, however, examined drinkers' reactions and their abilities to utilise the information from such labelling. Collectively, these studies provide a strong rationale for the adoption of standard unit labelling and were, indeed, influential in the decision by the Australian government to adopt standard unit labelling in 1995. This chapter will summarise these studies and discuss their implications for the ways in which the beneficial impact of such labelling can be maximised.

Standard Units and Low Risk Consumption Levels

The issue of standard units is closely related to that of recommended upper limits for alcohol consumption. There now exists a large scientific literature documenting both the adverse and the beneficial consequences of different levels and patterns of alcohol use (English and Holman 1995). In the main, these studies have examined the risk of different long-term health consequences as a function of a measure of average daily intake of alcohol of individuals assessed at usually one earlier point in time. A recent review of such long-term studies which also met a set of basic criteria for scientific adequacy concluded that risk of death from all causes increased significantly above an average of 40g alcohol per day for men and above 20g for women (English and Holman 1995). For people drinking below these levels, there was evidence of a reduced risk of death in comparison with total abstainers, presumed to be the result of a protective effect of moderate alcohol consumption against coronary heart disease.

Different authorities around the world have exercised varying

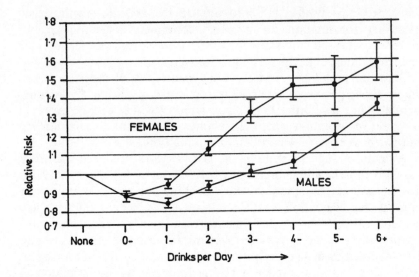

Figure 6.2: Relationship of all-cause mortality to alcohol intake based on pooled results of sixteen cohort studies.
Reproduced by permission of the Commonwealth of Australia from 'The quantification of drug-caused morbidity and mortality in Australia 1995. Part 1' Australian Government Publishing Service: Canberra.

degrees of caution when interpreting the scientific data in order to devise recommended upper limits of consumption. At one extreme, Swedish authorities have adopted the level of no more than one 'drink' per day (Rydberg 1992). At the other, the British Royal College of Psychiatrists (1979) advocated that men should restrict their drinking to less than 56 drinks per week (that is, 8 drinks or 64g per day) and women to less than 35 drinks (40g per day). As epidemiological evidence regarding the long-term adverse effects of drinking has mounted this level has crept downwards so that until very recently the advice in Britain was to drink less than 21 drinks per week for men (24g per day) and 14 for women (16g per day). Under controversial circumstances, the British government announced in December 1995 that these limits were to be revised upwards to 4 per day for men (32g) and 3 for women (24g). Both this revision and the additional advice that abstainers should consider using alcohol in moderation to gain the protection from heart disease were resisted strongly by the medical establishment (Edwards 1996, Marmot 1996). In both Canada and Australia the recommended levels are expressed as daily limits but at different levels – 4 and 2 in Australia (40g and 20g), 2 and 1 in Canada (27g and 14g).

New Zealand (Alcohol Advisory Council of New Zealand 1996) alone provides specific advice both for weekly (21 and 14) and daily upper limits of consumption (6 and 4, or 60g and 40g). This advice is consistent with growing evidence that (i) the risk of acute health problems from episodes of intoxication is most pronounced at levels slightly higher than the average daily levels recommended to reduce the risk of chronic health problems (Stockwell et al. 1996), and (ii) a pattern of 'binge' drinking increases the risk of chronic health problems at any level of average daily consumption (Hansagi 1995).

Upper levels of alcohol consumption are also advised for road safety reasons and the concept of standard units is utilised for this purpose almost universally. There appears to be less international variation in the basis of this advice since it is based on pharmacological studies of rates of alcohol metabolisation (Blaze-Temple et al. 1988). While it is usually advised by road safety authorities that drivers should avoid all prior alcohol consumption, it is evident that the enforcement of drink-driving laws results in a healthy interest from drinkers in how much they can drink and still remain below legal blood alcohol limits (Davey and McLean 1988).

In Australia, advice on how to remain below a blood alcohol level of 50mg per 100ml focuses on drinking rate rather than on total sessional intake: drivers are only advised to drink less than one standard drink per hour (men can also drink two in the first hour).

In the UK at least, the first stirrings of interest regarding drinking limits expressed as 'units' of alcohol occurred in relation to yet another domain of alcohol-related harm: 'problem drinking'. In the early 1980s there was even a network of self-help groups in major cities which went under the name of Drink Watchers (Ruzek 1987). Members kept weekly diaries of their alcohol use and endeavoured to remain below 40 units per week if they were men and 30 for women. A number of self-help guides for problem drinkers who wished to control their drinking also appeared, all of which contained detailed information regarding the number of units of alcohol contained in different drinks. In one of the more comprehensive guides (Robertson and Heather 1986), the contents of twelve varieties of alcoholic beverages were listed, along with three detailed footnotes outlining exceptions.

It was in the context of working with problem drinkers on controlled drinking programmes that the potential value of unit labelling occurred to the first author of this chapter. In his experience, clients, health professionals and even alcohol experts were frequently unable to estimate the number of units of alcohol in commonly available drinks – particularly when these were either unusually strong or weak. He subsequently had the opportunity to recommend this strategy to the meeting of the British Royal Medical Colleges referred to above.

From the preceding discussion, it should be clear that there are many types of educational message regarding alcohol consumption that employ the concept of a unit of alcohol. These include: (i) weekly drinking limits to avoid long-term health risks, gain health benefits and/or gain control over a drinking problem; (ii) daily limits to avoid both acute and chronic health problems; and (iii) hourly limits to remain below the legal blood alcohol level for driving.

The particular recommended limits vary across place and time and are sometimes only partially related to scientific evidence. Standard unit labelling is intended to assist consumers who wish to restrict their drinking within such limits for the above or other purposes. A national survey of public opinion in Australia regarding standard unit labelling found that many respondents claimed they would also use the information in order to monitor their own or someone else's drinking and to calculate the amount of alcohol to purchase for a party. This last point also suggests that standard unit labelling may also be a strategy which promotes and facilitates the emerging concept of 'host responsibility' in the service of alcohol whether to paying customers or private guests.

Impediments to Observing Drinking Limits in the Absence of Standard Unit Labelling

In the absence of unit labels on containers, several major difficulties have been identified for drinkers who attempt to follow advice to drink within limits expressed in standard drinks or units.

(i) Drinks are often not served in standard units
Containers for alcoholic beverages vary considerably in size. For example, beer containers in Canada may contain 7oz, 12oz, one quart, one half-litre, one litre or two litres, not to mention different size kegs. Wine and spirits similarly come in a variety of different size containers.

Furthermore, drinking often occurs at home or at private parties. Over 60% of drinking occasions in Australia take place in unlicensed settings (Lang et al. 1992) where it has been shown that typical serve sizes are significantly larger than the 'standards' employed in alcohol education campaigns. In a survey of the size of wine servings on licensed premises in an Australian city (Stockwell 1992), it was found that the average serve contained 1.7 10g units – theoretically enough to put the average women over the legal drinking limit after one drink. Two studies, one Scandinavian (Lemmens 1994) and one Australian (Carruthers and Binns 1987), have shown that serve sizes used at home can be widely discrepant from the supposed standard.

(ii) Standard serve sizes will have varying alcohol content
The serve sizes specified by alcohol educators for standard units only apply to beverages of 'average' strength. In Australia, beers are available in strengths between 0.9% and 11%, wines between 6% and 15%, and spirits from 37% to 59%. Drinkers' knowledge of the percentage alcohol content of commonly available drinks is poor (Stockwell and Honig 1990) and they usually fail to compensate for this when estimating the number of units in standard serves of beer and wine (Stockwell and Stirling 1989). In order to make such a compensation with any accuracy requires a somewhat complex calculation and precise knowledge of serve size and the conversion formulae from millilitres to grams to standard units.

(iii) Drinkers do not always count in standard units
Beer drinkers – and especially those with a high intake – typically recall their consumption in terms of bottles and/or cans of beer, rather than beer glasses (Stockwell et al. 1990). They therefore need information about the alcohol content of each individual bottle and can, not of a hypothetical standard glass size. In Australia, the UK and New Zealand, units of beer are defined in terms of glasses (usually 'middies' or half pints). In Canada, a unit of beer refers to a 340ml bottle. In practice, with the increasing internationalisation of the alcohol market it is likely that beer (and other beverages) are consumed in similar varieties of glasses and containers the world over. Standard units are frequently defined in terms of volumes of a given beverage (for example, 100ml of wine in Australia or 5oz of wine in Canada). Unfortunately, one study has shown that few drinkers have an accurate idea of what an amount of a liquid defined in terms of millilitres actually looks like (Stockwell et al. 1990).

(iv) Drinkers have poor knowledge of the number of units in alcohol containers
A survey of 1003 adults in four Australian states (Stockwell and Beel 1994) found that only 30% of beer drinkers could correctly state the number of units in a regular sized can or bottle of beer (to the nearest half unit) and 3% of wine drinkers correctly guessed the number of units in a regular strength bottle of wine (to the nearest whole unit). In short, alcohol often is not available, is not consumed and is not thought of in defined standard units containing equal amounts of alcohol. Standard unit labelling is intended to rectify this for those situations where drinkers know how many alcohol containers (for example, cans of beer) or what proportion of one container (for example, half a bottle of wine) they have personally consumed over a particular period of time – be it an hour, a day or a week.

Does Standard Unit Labelling Assist Drinkers to Keep Track of Their Drinking?

A series of studies conducted in Perth examined whether the addition of unit labels was of assistance to drinkers when they attempted to follow advice on low-risk drinking (Stockwell et al. 1990). These were performed on beer and wine drinkers recruited from a busy shopping mall who were taught and tested on their knowledge of units. Subjects served as their own controls in a variety of alcohol estimation tasks in which alcohol containers were given large and easy-to-read labels that were systematically rotated between a percentage alcohol by volume message and one on standard units. The main findings were:

- When offered containers with labels which presented only the percentage alcohol content by volume, both beer and wine drinkers significantly underestimated the number of standard units in their preferred drink (Stockwell et al. 1991a). The task for beer drinkers was to estimate the total number of units in an array of three 375ml beer cans, while wine drinkers attempted the estimation task with one half-full bottle of wine.

- With percentage alcohol content by volume labels, beer drinkers had significant difficulty in pouring amounts of beer corresponding to a standard unit if either glass size or beverage strength differed from the supposed standard of a 285ml glass of 5% beer (Stockwell et al. 1991b).

- The addition of standard unit labels substantially and significantly reduced these errors in both the above tasks (Stockwell et al. 1991a, b). To illustrate the difference, with unit labels 96% of beer drinkers and 88% of wine drinkers estimated the presented drinks contained four or more units of alcohol – an amount that would put the average male over the then legal limit for driving of 80mg per 100ml if consumed in one hour (Blaze-Temple et al. 1988). With percentage alcohol by volume labels only 25% of beer drinkers and 28% of wine drinkers estimated, correctly, that the drinks contained this amount of alcohol.

Consumer Reactions and Support for Unit Labelling

A variety of studies, both published and unpublished, have touched on the acceptability of unit labelling to drinkers. Quantitative studies employing an individual interview format have tended to find strong support and expressed need for such labelling. Focus group studies have provided more qualified support and underline the need for drinkers to be motivated to monitor their drinking. These studies are summarised in Table 6.1.

(i) Alcohol estimation experiments and survey data
Stockwell and Stirling (1989) surveyed a convenience sample of 217 adults attending a road safety display at a popular public show in Devon, England. As a consequence of the existence of a number of local and national alcohol education campaigns which employed the concept of a 'unit' of alcohol, as many as 69% of the sample claimed to have heard of the term 'unit' before. All subjects were then taught and tested on their understanding of the unit system and asked to apply it to a range of alcoholic drinks which varied in alcoholic strength: wines between 0.05% and 13%; beers between 0.9% and 8.6%. The drink containers only had percentage alcohol by volume labels. The study revealed that few subjects were able to make the estimates with any accuracy. After performing the alcohol estimation tasks and receiving feedback on their performance, 91% of subjects agreed with the statement 'it would be a good idea for bottles and cans of alcoholic drinks to display their alcohol content in units'.

Table 6.1: Studies on public support for unit labelling

Authors, date, country	n	Sample	Question	Agree
Stockwell & Stirling, 1989, UK	217	Convenience sample at a public show	'would it be a good idea for bottles and cans of alcoholic drinks to display their alcohol content in units?'	95%
Stockwell, Blaze-Temple & Walker, 1990, AUS	257	Convenience sample, shopping mall	'if safe drinking advice used the same terms, which of the following labelling methods would you find easiest to use?'	77% prefer units* vs gms
Lang, Stockwell Rydon & Gamble, 1992, AUS	1160	Random household survey, Perth	'Which of the following labels would best help you to keep track of how much alcohol you drink?'	55% prefer units* vs % or gms
REARK Research, 1991, AUS	501	Random household survey, 5 cities	'information on labels about standard drinks would help people to know how many drinks they were consuming?'	86% agree
Stockwell & Beel, 1994, AUS	1003	Random telephone survey, 4 cities	'Do you think cans and bottles of alcoholic drinks should be labelled with the number of standard drinks they contain?'	88% 'yes'

* The actual term used was 'standard drinks' in these studies.

In the Australian studies described above, data were collected on the proportion of subjects who approve of unit labelling in a convenience sample of 257 shoppers in a city mall who took part in alcohol estimation tasks (Stockwell et al. 1990). In these studies subjects were questioned only in relation to labelling on their preferred beverages – either beer or wine. After completing the estimation tasks, mostly performing poorly, and then receiving feedback on their performance, they were asked which form of labelling they preferred on alcohol containers: percentage alcohol by volume or 'standard drinks'. Two-thirds preferred the standard drink labels, 23% the percentage labels and the rest were undecided. Subjects were also asked which form of labelling they would find 'easiest to follow' if it was to be used both on labels and in advice on safe drinking. With this more focused question, 77% chose 'standard drinks' over grams, decigrams and units. Although used interchangeably in this chapter, the term 'standard drink' is used in Australia in preference to units in alcohol education. In this study, 67% of subjects claimed to have heard of the term before. It could be argued that this high level of support for unit labelling is simply due to the 'demand characteristics' of such experiments and also that the samples obtained were not representative of the wider community. Lang et al. (1992) assessed the level of support for standard unit (that is, 'standard drink') labelling as part of a household survey concerned with patterns of alcohol use and problems. A representative sample of 1160 adults from Perth, Western Australia, were asked to view pictures of alcohol containers carrying percentage alcohol by volume, grams or unit labels. Male preferences were equally divided between percentage and unit labels, while females greatly preferred unit labels. Overall, 55% preferred units and less than 4% preferred grams. Subsequent analyses confirm that the preference for unit over percentage labels was statistically significant for each of the wine, beer and spirit examples used. It is possible that the substantial minority of respondents who preferred percentage labels included many (for example, young males) who used the information to select strong drinks to get the most 'bang for their buck'. No analyses were conducted, however, which would have tested this hypothesis.

Prompted by a submission based on some of the above evidence, the Commonwealth Department of Health in Australia commissioned a market research company to assess community attitudes and knowledge of units (REARK Research 1991). A sample of 501 adults was drawn from five of the most populous states. After being shown examples of unit labelling, 86% of subjects stated that such labelling would help people to know how many units of alcohol they were drinking and 67% claimed they were likely to use this information themselves.

A larger multi-state survey was conducted in Australia in 1994 by the National Centre for Research into the Prevention of Drug Abuse (Stockwell and Beel 1994). A telephone survey of 1003 subjects from four states in which results were weighted for age and sex to offset sampling bias demonstrated a high level of awareness of the term 'standard drink'. Furthermore, 88.1% of the sample were supportive of standard drink labels being introduced on all alcohol containers and 89% of the sample claimed they would make use of such labelling to help themselves (or someone who was driving them) remain below the legal limit for driving. In addition, 74% reported that they would use standard drink labels to stay below recommended daily limits for health reasons. A smaller but still significant proportion (38%) said they would use the information to get the best value for money when buying alcohol! Arguably, the percentage alcohol by volume labelling is just as useful in this regard in most situations.

In the context of a continuing evaluation of the introduction of warning labels on alcohol containers in the USA, Greenfield et al. (1993) have found levels of support for standard drink labelling almost as high as in Australia.

(ii) Focus group research
Focus group studies have been conducted in Canada and Australia to examine whether drinkers want to monitor their drinking and whether they think they need more information to assist with this. The advantage of focus groups over more structured surveys is that they permit a more in-depth exploration of what people have to say about these issues. The format is generally for small groups of about eight to twenty persons to be asked to talk openly and freely in response to open-ended questions from a facilitator. The facilitator must not show any personal views or reveal any agenda for the discussion but attempt to clarify the views of the group members. The group members are normally strangers to each other prior to the discussion. A possible disadvantage of such groups is that biases may arise as a consequence of participants 'faking good' to impress the others.

In both the Canadian and Australian studies the subjects were unlikely to state that they themselves had any need to monitor their own drinking more carefully. They were far more likely to state that other people (younger if old, older if young, problem drinkers) would benefit from using units to monitor their drinking. In the Canadian study, participants were likely to state that they already had enough information to enable them to keep track of their drinking (Millward Brown 1994). Although objectively the Canadian subjects performed poorly in alcohol estimation tasks, subjectively they did not express a strong need or desire for better information on alcohol content. However, when they were shown examples of unit labelling they tended to respond positively to these. The Australian study (Lenahan et al. 1994) concluded that most drinkers lack any real motivation to want to cut down on their consumption and hence have limited interest in different types of labelling to achieve this.

The Canadian focus group study found evidence that there was considerable confusion among drinkers regarding the concept of a 'standard serve' and an objective need for better information. Some of the confusion centred around whether subjects conceptualised the standard serve as an amount of liquid as opposed to an amount of alcohol.

These focus group studies are not necessarily inconsistent with the more positive findings from the other studies reported above. It would appear that when starting 'cold' (that is, in the absence of seeing unit labels or having their purpose explained) and in a group of strangers, drinkers do not express a strong desire for better consumer information to help them monitor the amount of alcohol they drink. However, when drinkers are familiar with the unit system, are interviewed on a one-to-one basis and have attempted to apply this both with and without unit labels then they are highly receptive and supportive of the concept.

As a community-wide harm reduction strategy, it must be concluded that standard unit labelling will benefit those drinkers who are motivated to count their drinks whether for health, road safety, personal safety or economic reasons. It is worth also noting a further finding common to the Canadian focus group study (Millward Brown 1994) and an earlier Australian study (REARK Research 1991) that there is a marked preference for unit labels which are accompanied by graphics or symbols of some kind. This would be especially important for the various groups in society who are not sufficiently literate, numerate or keen-sighted to read small unit labels. If experience with other products is any guide, the standard unit information should also be large and prominent (Rootman et al. 1995).

Impediments to the Introduction of Standard Unit Labelling

Thus far, a reasonably convincing case can be made that standard unit labelling would assist most people who drink alcohol to monitor their consumption if they so choose. It would also appear that there is considerable latent popular support for such labelling. However, the concept is relatively new and has only (at the time of writing) recently been introduced as a compulsory measure into one country. What impediments lie in the way of this seemingly innocuous harm reduction strategy being introduced?

There are several impediments to the introduction of standard unit labelling. First, the introduction of new information on labels represents a cost to the industry which would be passed on to consumers. Estimates of the size of the cost are not available, but it may be assumed that it would not be significant. Second, in many countries there is public apathy concerning the issue of standard unit labelling. Although research subjects have generally reacted favourably when shown standard unit information, they generally have not expressed a spontaneous desire for such information. This apathy appears to derive from a lack of understanding of the concept of standard 'units' or 'drinks'. For unit labelling to have its maximum positive impact, it may be necessary to combine the introduction of such labelling with a public education campaign explaining the concept and its utility.

Third, some public health advocates are lukewarm in their support for unit labelling due to concerns that it will used by some drinkers to 'get the biggest bang for the buck', that is, to maximise their alcohol intake for the least amount of money. This appears to be particularly the case in the United States where even percentage alcohol by volume labels are not provided on beer bottles for fear of this outcome. From an Australian and a consumer perspective, this argument seems extraordinary. There are about seventeen varieties of beer available in Australia with a strength of less than 3.5%. There are also beers on sale (usually imported) with strengths of up to 11%. Given the potential hazards of drinking the latter before driving out of ignorance and the famous US concern for civil liberties it is surprising that this situation should persist. In countries where percentage alcohol by volume information is already provided it can be argued that this already provides an efficient means of enabling drinkers to discern the relative strengths of different beverages, that is, the addition of unit labelling is unlikely to contribute to more efficient binge drinking.

The lack of an international standard may also represent a barrier to effective communications about the alcohol content of drinks. Imported products would presumably have to indicate the number of units in terms of the size of these in the country of sale rather than the country of origin. This means that exported alcohol will have to either be exempt from unit labelling requirements or have different standard unit information depending on the country of sale. In Australia, importers are required to add an additional unit label to imported products.

Finally, sectors of the alcohol industry have opposed the introduction of unit labelling in many countries. In Australia, it took almost five years for standard unit labelling to become compulsory following a meeting of the state and federal health ministers at which there was unanimous support for the concept (Stockwell 1993). There was tremendous political pressure applied from brewing and distilling interests in Australia to prevent this initiative. This is well exemplified by a glossy leaflet produced early in 1994 by the Australian Associated Brewers entitled 'Standard drinks: facts, myths and some surprises'. This was distributed to all members of parliament and numerous media outlets. It stated that:

Brewers support:

- Giving consumers the information they need to make informed decisions about drinking for health and safety.

- Reducing alcohol misuse through education. Brewers do not support:

- Standard drinks labelling – it gives consumers dangerously misleading information.

As revealed in an Australian Broadcasting Corporation television news report in mid-1994, a lobbyist representing the distillers, Mr Gordon Broderick, travelled the country to pay personal visits to each minister for health to present a similar viewpoint. He also had several letters published in major daily newspapers on the subject. A representation was made from the offices of the General Agreement on Tariffs and Trade (GATT) in Brussels to the Australian government protesting that standard unit labelling would create a unilateral barrier to trade. Throughout this period it is interesting that the Australian wine industry was consistently supportive of unit labelling and some wineries even introduced their own labels well in advance of the regulation coming into effect.

In addition to the support from the wine industry, there was also a well-orchestrated nation-wide campaign by alcohol advocacy groups, the medical establishment, consumer associations and various professional societies to put the pro-labelling point of view. The issue was covered extensively in the media and almost invariably in a manner supportive of unit labelling. The evidence cited above that there was almost universal public support for the concept across Australia (Stockwell and Beel 1994) was quoted by the Federal Minister for Health, the Rt. Hon. Carmen Lawrence, when the decision to introduce the measure was first announced. It is possible that similar opposition might be mounted by the alcohol industry to oppose unit labelling were serious attempts made to introduce it in other countries. While a national regulation on this matter might be the preferred strategy, it is also possible to work with individual sectors of the manufacturing and retailing arms of the alcohol industry to improve information regarding alcohol content of drinks in a piecemeal fashion. The British supermarket chain Tesco and the Australian wine makers voluntarily introduced unit labelling. Clearly, alcohol manufacturers and distributors can play a leading role in providing better information on the alcohol content of their products if they choose.

Conclusions

There is a strong case for the introduction of unit labelling both on consumer and on health grounds. With increasing medical knowledge regarding the adverse and beneficial effects of different patterns of alcohol use it is increasingly important that consumers are given the information they need to drink within limits of their choosing. These limits may make reference to levels of hourly, daily or weekly consumption. As a population-wide harm reduction strategy, unit labelling cannot work in isolation. It requires that a significant number of drinkers are both aware of drinking guidelines and are motivated to apply these, at least in some situations and for some purposes. Media information campaigns are a necessary adjunct to the labels (or, we would argue, vice versa) if there is a realistic chance of the strategy contributing to measurable reductions in consumption and harm. We would suggest that the evidence from focus groups is that there may be difficulties in motivating drinkers to monitor their drinking (or at least to admit to needing to do this publicly), but that the most effective motivators might be: the need to remain below the legal blood alcohol level for driving, gaining the health benefits of moderate alcohol use, greater ease for planning amounts of alcohol to purchase for parties and the desire of many heavier drinkers to be knowledgeable about alcohol.

An additional argument in favour of using container labelling to relay health information to consumers comes from research concerning the US experience with warning labels. A series of national surveys have been conducted there to examine the impact of the 1989 warning label legislation (Greenfield et al. 1993). These surveys have shown that, while many drinkers do not notice the labels, it tends to be the heavier drinkers who are more likely to have seen and to remember them. It is rare indeed to find a health promotion strategy in which the main target group are most likely to be exposed to the intervention. Product labelling is obviously most likely to be seen by those people who most frequently use the product – in this case those who drink excessively.

While there will be much to learn from the Australian experiment with standard unit labelling, efforts to promote the practice of monitoring personal alcohol intake should not stop at product labelling. Other strategies will need to be devised to enable drinkers on licensed premises to also have accurate information since, very often, they do not see the container from which their drink is poured. Likely strategies would include efforts to standardise the serve size of particular beverages across different premises and to provide highly visible information about alcohol content of all drinks for sale expressed in terms of units.

There will always be resistance to the idea of monitoring personal alcohol consumption. Alcohol is usually consumed to help unwind and enjoy oneself. Keeping a close watch on intake and counting drinks might be thought to be inconsistent with these objectives. For this simple reason we do not believe that unit labelling is any kind of panacea for alcohol problems. It has the potential, however, to provide an essential platform upon which to advance a variety of other prevention strategies which assume that people already know how much alcohol they drink. At present and without reference to unit labelling, drinkers have a very poor appreciation of the alcohol content of drinks and hence of their own intake. It is our hope that unit labelling will ensure that ultimately 'units' or 'standard drinks' will become part of the conceptual landscape of most drinkers. This will greatly ease the important tasks of providing consumers with meaningful information regarding the possible implications for life and death of different drinking patterns.

References

Appleby, E. (1992) (Editorial) *Alcohol Concern*, vol. 7, Sept./Oct., London, UK.

Blaze-Temple, D., Binns, C.W. and Somerford, P. (1988) 'The utilisation of blood alcohol concentration formulae to establishing a responsible drinking level for females', *Australian Drug and Alcohol Review*, 7: 369–73.

Carruthers, S.J. and Binns, C.W. (1987) 'The standard drink and alcohol consumption', *Drug and Alcohol Review*, 11: 363–70.

Courtney, H. (1989) 'Fact or fable? The ineffective warning label', *Newsletter of the Alcoholic Liquor Advisory Council*, no. 45, Wellington, New Zealand.

Davey, J. and McLean, S. (1988) 'Drunken Driving and knowledge of blood alcohol levels', *Medical Journal of Australia*, 149: 226–7.

Edwards, G. (1996) 'Doctors should stick with the independent medical advice', *British Medical Journal*, 312:1.

English, D. and Holman, D. (1995) *The Quantification of Drug-Caused Morbidity and Mortality in Australia 1995*, Canberra, Commonwealth Department of Human Services and Health, Australian Government Publishing Service.

Greenfield, T. (1994) 'Mandated container warnings as an alcohol-related harm-reduction policy: first evidence from long-term US/Ontario surveys', Paper presented at 5th International Conference on the Reduction of Drug Related Harm, Toronto, 6–10 March.

Greenfield, T., Graves, K. and Kaskutas, L. (1993) 'Alcohol warning labels for prevention: national survey findings', *Alcohol Health and Research World*, 17(1): 67–75.

Hansagi, H. (1995) 'Alcohol consumption and stroke mortality: 20 year follow-up of 15,077 men and women', Paper presented at the International Conference on the Social and Health Effects of Different Drinking Patterns, Kettil Bruun Society, Toronto, Canada, 13–17 November.

Health Department of Western Australia (1988) 'Here's to your Health!' Perth, Western Australia, Health Promotion Services Branch.

Lang, E., Stockwell, T., Rydon, P. and Gamble, C. (1992) *Drinking Settings, Alcohol-Related Harm and Support for Prevention Policies. Results of a Survey of Persons Residing in the Perth Metropolitan Area.* Technical Report, National Centre for Research into the Prevention of Drug Abuse, Division of Health Sciences, Curtin University of Technology.

Lemmens, P. (1994) 'The alcohol content of self-report "standard drinks" ', *Addiction*, 89: 593–602.

Lenahan Lynton Blom Blaxterland Pty (1994) *Developmental Research: Adult Alcohol Consumption, Education and Awareness Campaign*, Report prepared for Public Affairs Branch, Department of Human Services and Health, Canberra.

McEwan, I. (1995) *Upper Limits for Responsible Drinking*, New Zealand, Alcohol Advisory Council.

Marmot, M. (1996) 'A not-so-sensible drinks policy', *Lancet*, 346: 1643–4.

Millward Brown (1994) *Consumer Awareness of Alcohol Content*, Ottawa, Canadian Centre on Substance Abuse.

REARK Research (1991) *A Study of Attitudes Towards Alcohol Consumption, Labelling and Advertising*, Canberra, Commonwealth Department of Community Services and Health.

Robertson, I. and Heather, N. (1986) *Let's Drink to Your Health! A Self-Help Guide to Healthier Drinking*, Leicester, British Psychological Society.

Rootman, B., Flay, D., Northrup, M., Foster, D., Burton, R., Ferrence, R., Raphael, D. and Single, E. (1995) *Plain Packaging of Cigarettes and Event Marketing to Advertise Smoking: A Study of Youth*, University of Toronto Centre for Health Promotion.

Royal College of Psychiatrists (1979) *Alcohol and Alcoholism*, London, Tavistock.

Ruzek, J. (1987) 'The Drinkwatchers experiment: A description and evaluation', in Clement, S. and Stockwell, T. (eds) *Helping the Problem Drinker: New Initiatives in Community Care*, London, Croom Helm.

Rydberg, U. (1992) 'Responsible drinking – is it responsible? A discussion on recommendations of "safe" limits of drinking', Paper presented to International Congress on Alcohol and Alcoholism Annual Conference, Glasgow.

Single, E. (1994) 'Standard Serving Information: Results of a Focus Group Study in Canada', Paper presented at the Perspectives for Change Conference (Alcohol Advisory Council of New Zealand), Rotorura, New Zealand.

Stockwell, T. (1992) 'Information provided in Australia about the size of "standard" drinks', (Letter to the Editor), *Medical Journal of Australia*, 156: 295.

Stockwell, T. (1993) 'Influencing the labelling of alcoholic beverage containers: informing the public', *Addiction*, 88 (Supplement): 53S–60S.

Stockwell, T. and Beel, A. (1994) *Public Support for the Introduction of Standard Drink Labels on Alcohol Containers*, Curtin University, Perth, Western Australia, National Centre for Research into the Prevention of Drug Abuse.

Stockwell, T., Blaze-Temple, D. and Walker, C. (1990) *An Experimental Test of the Proposal to Label Containers of Alcoholic Drink with Alcohol Content in 'Standard Drinks'*, Technical Report, Curtin University of Technology, Perth, Western Australia, National Centre for Research into the Prevention of Drug Abuse.

Stockwell, T., Blaze-Temple, D. and Walker, C. (1991a) 'A test of the proposal to label containers of alcohohic drink with alcohol content in standard drinks' *Health Promotion International*, 6: 207–15.

Stockwell, T., Blaze-Temple, D. and Walker, C. (1991b) 'The effect of "standard drink" labelling on the ability of drinkers to pour a "standard drink" ', *Australian Journal of Public Health*, 15: 56–63.

Stockwell, T., Hawks, D., Lang, E. and Rydon, P. (1996) 'Unravelling the preventative paradox for acute alcohol problems', *Drug and Alcohol Review*, 15(1): 7–16.

Stockwell, T. and Honig, F. (1990) 'Labelling alcoholic drinks: percentage proof, original gravity, percentage alcohol or "standard drinks"?' *Drug and Alcohol Review*, 9: 81–90.

Stockwell, T. and Stirling, L. (1989) 'Estimating alcohol content of drinks: common errors in applying the unit system', *British Medical Journal*, 298: 571–2.

7 Warning Labels: Evidence on Harm Reduction from Long-term American Surveys

Thomas K. Greenfield

Alcohol container warning labels have been mandated in a number of countries such as Mexico, India and, most notably, the United States. In the latter instance, an extensive impact evaluation has been done and results to date will be summarised. Health warnings on containers are an attractive harm reduction intervention for governments for several reasons. First, the 'mechanism of action' – how people are exposed to the label's message – makes it likely that appropriate 'target groups', such as those who purchase, handle and drink large quantities of alcoholic beverages, will be more exposed to them than are others (Greenfield et al. 1993). Second, warning label messages can, in principle, be chosen to focus on practical, plausible actions consumers may take to mitigate risks associated with certain consumption patterns or circumstances, such as avoiding drinking when going to drive a vehicle or operate machinery, or during pregnancy (among the several messages involved in the US label; see Greenfield 1994b). Third, labelling legislation can be enacted to assure extremely low governmental cost (limited to administrative, regulatory and enforcement functions) and even industry cost (limited to initial design and printing costs when rules permit the warning label to be combined with existing labelling, as in the US instance). Finally, palatable as the strategy is on a cost basis, the approach is also non-invasive and in principle non-manipulative. Mandatory warning labels may be justified to officials and the public on a right-to-know basis: consumers of the product are offered accurate information on which to base their choices about its use.

Thus, as a policy-based prevention strategy, a priori, this approach has the potential to avoid the 'preaching to the converted' problem of so many 'educational' programmes by reaching heavier drinkers; it can specify precautions individuals may take to avert unwanted harms associated with inappropriate or high-risk use, and can be supported as a low-cost, non-restrictive policy by major stakeholders – officials, industry, the public health community and the public itself. But in practice, how has it been accepted by the public? What is its credibility with heavy drinkers themselves, and have any impacts been observed?

This chapter describes the US policy and reviews evidence about the extent to which the federally mandated warning label on alcoholic beverage containers, in place now for more than five years, has lived up to its potential. It also considers whether there have been unwanted 'side effects' of the policy, or areas of failure, and whether alterations in the label's content or format could improve its functioning. More speculatively, the question is raised about the generalisability of this country's experience: could other countries with differing cultural traditions from those in the US also benefit by alcohol health warning labels?

The US Experience

Since November 1989, health warning labels have been mandated on all alcoholic beverage containers for sale in the United States (Public Law No. 100-690 1988). The act made clear that the intent of Congress was that the warning label serve to 'remind' the public of a number of the risks involved in drinking. The required label reads:

> **GOVERNMENT WARNING:** (1) According to the Surgeon General, women should not drink alcoholic beverages during pregnancy because of the risk of birth defects. (2) Consumption of alcoholic beverages impairs your ability to drive a car or operate machinery, and may cause health problems.

According to the law as implemented by rule-making in the US Bureau of Alcohol, Tobacco, and Firearms (ATF), the body that is responsible for regulating beverage alcohol product labelling, there are three essential requirements for the labels: (1) a minimum size for the height of the type (for most containers 2mm, although slightly larger type is used for bottles of larger than 3 litres);

(2) text size implying no more than 10 characters per centimetre; (3) the tag phrase 'GOVERNMENT WARNING' must appear in bold type and capital letters. There are no limitations on the typeface or the style of type that may be used (despite public health advocates' prior arguments for a ban on script or italic type) or on the colour of type or background; the label may appear anywhere except the bottom of the container, may even be vertical (by the side of the face label, for example), and requires no particular border. Thus, no requirements demand that the label be of a noticeable or attention-getting format. While some producers appear ingenious in disguising the label (one label parallels in density and size the bar code on the back label, for example), many and perhaps most are straightforward and reasonably legible, though generally not particularly prominent. Paradoxically, it is possible that the very lack of uniformity of *format* keeps the label fresher than it would be if it were more standardised, given the non-rotating, standardised *content* of the message. For more details about the labelling legislation and its history consult Greenfield and Hilton (1994) and Kaskutas (1995).

A comprehensive literature review (US National Institute on Alcohol Abuse and Alcoholism 1987) preceding the legislation was commissioned by the US National Institute of Alcohol Abuse and Alcoholism (NIAAA) finding, based on studies of other health warnings of various kinds, that labels could be effective if well implemented. The review's conclusion, based on other product labelling experience, that alcohol warning labels did have the potential to be effective *did* play a role in the hearings leading up to enactment. The report also urged Congress to mandate before – after study designs as part of such policy enactment. An evaluation of the national policy was subsequently required in the legislation and implemented by funding from NIAAA. In response, to serve as a baseline for later impact assessments, the Alcohol Research Group (ARG) of Berkeley, California, was commissioned to conduct a US national telephone survey in the Summer of 1989 ($n=2000$) prior to the introduction of the labels. ARG then conducted two subsequent cross-sectional surveys with equivalent samples in the US in 1990 and 1991, and smaller parallel surveys ($n=1000$) in Ontario, Canada, chosen as a no-treatment reference site. The 1989 Canadian National Alcohol and Drugs Survey (Eliany et al. 1990) conducted by telephone was available to serve as a partial pre-intervention reference point (see Giesbrecht and Greenfield 1991).

The National Impact Study

In attempting to evaluate possible impacts of the warning labels policy, researchers were challenged to design and conduct an adequately sensitive and comprehensive study. Greenfield (1994a) enumerated the major difficulties that confronted this policy evaluation research project as originally designed. The evaluation had to be mounted rapidly, making impossible the development of specific, *extended* baseline data (Cook and Campbell 1979). Since warning labels were mandated nationally, a randomised experiment was ruled out, as were in-country comparisons; instead, the quasi-experiment had to rely on a neighbouring province. Ontario has population demographics and cultural characteristics including a rural/urban balance making it not very unlike the US overall, but any non-equivalent quasi-experiment has inherent limitations (see Greenfield 1994a). Implementation was effectively gradual as new, labelled products gradually replaced old (Scammon et al. 1991), making effects harder to detect than if the programme was introduced in full force. (The prior literature review (US NIAAA 1987) recommended supportive media and programming to amplify and call attention to the label messages, but no such efforts were funded.) The expected sizes of intervention effects were small (plausible changes 1–10%) reducing power to detect change, especially in subgroups. Many necessary questions, for example 'have you seen the warning label?' could not be posed unobtrusively, initially ruling out a longitudinal design. It was difficult to control for confounding messages of similar content to the warning label messages such as radio and TV 'spots' on drink-driving. In addition, self-report survey questions on sensitive issues such as drinking and driving were indispensable but are prone to social desirability bias (Bradburn et al. 1979). Lastly, based on diffusion research (Ferrence 1989) and theory of mass media health campaigns (Greenfield 1994a), a slow rise in exposure to the warning label was expected, making it likely that any direct impacts would emerge only over a long time. The design and measures chosen attempted to reduce, but could not eliminate, these various threats to validity.

In the first three annual survey waves, 1989–91, extensive survey data were collected to examine possible changes in specific kinds of knowledge, attitudes and behaviour that might plausibly be attributed to seeing warning label messages, and study factors affecting label awareness. The initial research phase extended from six months before to only eighteen months after label introduction. Findings from this early period have been reported elsewhere (Kaskutas and Greenfield 1991, Kaskutas and Greenfield 1992, Graves 1993, Greenfield et al. 1993, Greenfield and Kaskutas 1993) and will be summarised presently. One discovery was that after eighteen months, the exposure levels were still climbing. For this reason, and to remedy some of the limitations of the initial surveys, the project was continued, again with NIAAA support, gathering comparable data in 1993 and 1994. An important aim in extending the project for the longer-term evaluation, to four and a half years post-implementation, was carefully to follow awareness or 'penetration' of the label and its messages, especially in groups that have elevated risk of alcohol harms – younger men and women, particularly those who are heavier drinkers. Parallel to the adult cross-sectional samples, longitudinal panel samples of men and women 18–40 years old were followed from 1993 to 1994. The split panel design (Curtin and Feinleib 1992) was used to allow sources of bias such as sensitisation and attrition to be controlled or at least estimated. However, here the focus will be on the cross-sectional component of the survey series as longitudinal analyses are just beginning. The US national survey included five cross-sectional probability samples of adults (18 and over) conducted by telephone in the summer months of 1989, 1990, 1991, 1993 and 1994 with parallel surveys between 1990 and 1994 in Ontario, Canada. Computer-assisted telephone interviews using closely similar instruments were secured from 2006, 2000, 2017, 1026 and 1016 US respondents from 1989 to 1994, respectively (omitting 1992). The Ontario surveys included the same key variables and interviewed 1045, 1028, 1022 and 1028 adults from 1990 on.

A workable theory of action modelling how the phenomena occur strengthens susceptibility to evaluation (Lipsey 1990). The new surveys include measures with increased sensitivity, such as degree of exposure, allowing us to test theories of action developed in the first phase of the research (Greenfield and Kaskutas, 1993). Within the original 18 month time frame, the effects that could reasonably be anticipated were not in variables such as overall consumption (Scammon et al. 1991). Behavioural and even attitudinal change outcomes should lie further out on the causal chain than simply noticing and recalling messages (McGuire 1974, Greenfield and Kaskutas 1993). It is theoretically plausible to expect a sequencing of outcomes with the early direct effects (those detectable within the first 18 months) mostly being instrumental steps – such as seeing the labels and recalling their messages, or having conversations related to the health warnings. Initial results were consistent with impacts of this sort (Graves 1993, Greenfield et al. 1993, Kaskutas and Graves 1994).

Short-term Outcomes

One promising early finding suggested a *possible* behavioural effect: between 1990 and 1991 in the US, increasing numbers of people reported sometime in the prior twelve months not driving after having had too much to drink, while in Ontario levels dropped; of course, competing explanations of the trend differences could not be ruled out (Graves 1993).

As mentioned before, the policy of requiring warning labels has the attraction that because labels are placed on the container that may be handled in proximity with ingestion, the intervention's 'dose' is automatically titrated to consumption level: the more the person drinks, the more she or he is likely to receive 'impressions' of the government warning (Greenfield et al. 1993, MacKinnon and Fenaughty 1993) serving as cues (or reminders) to adopt precautions (Weinstein 1988) that might reduce harm. Not only has the prior data confirmed that exposure is related to drinking variables, with heavier drinkers seeing the label more (Greenfield et al. 1993), but attention to and recall of the specific messages has been found, as hypothesised, to be influenced by those messages' perceived personal relevance (Greenfield and Kaskutas 1993). Additionally, based on analyses looking at possible mechanisms of influence, Greenfield and Kaskutas (1993) reported that two behavioural strategies which could reduce harm from drinking and driving – limiting drinking before driving and limiting driving after drinking – were both associated with exposure to the drinking driving message, as well as to salience factors predicted by theories of precaution adoption (Weinstein 1988). Taken together with Graves' (1993) US–Ontario comparison just mentioned, Greenfield and Kaskutas (1993) interpreted these results as 'consistent' with a possible effect of the label.

Independent of the policy's objective impact, for a policy to be effective it must remain in place for some time. Political and popular support for a policy is an important predictor of whether or not a policy will be sustained (Room et al. 1995). From 1989 on, the surveys have been used to study public opinion about the warning label policy in Canada and the US in the context of other alcohol control measures (Giesbrecht and Greenfield 1991, Room et al. 1995). In the US, Kaskutas (1993a) found that in general between 1989 and 1991 support for a range of alcohol policies stayed the same or declined. Of the thirteen policies studied, only support for having the alcohol warning label increased significantly, from 87% to 91% in the two years spanning implementation. Those exposed to the label were about twice as likely to support it as those who had not seen it. In each year, about the same percentage (60–61%) of those sampled believed placing warning labels on alcoholic beverages would be an effective way to change people's behaviour.

In the concluding part of this chapter several new findings from the complete series of surveys are presented, several based on multivariate results from analyses of all four post-implementation US cross-sectional surveys. Publications of the group, particularly Greenfield et al. (1993), contain further details of the sampling methods and measures used. Multivariate analyses controlling for demographic and other variables are important because empirical results have supported the proposition from information theory that 'receiver characteristics' play a role (Laughery and Brelsford 1991) in the selectivity process (Greenfield 1994b) that determines who becomes aware of the label and 'receives' specific warning messages (Greenfield and Kaskutas 1993, Greenfield et al. 1993). Ontario remains a no-treatment control site, though earlier studies have shown some 'leakage' of the intervention: warnings seen by some control respondents most likely involved cross-border travel and a few labels left on imported US alcohol products (Graves 1993, Graves et al. 1993). Although various Canadian jurisdictions have been considering labelling legislation (for example, the Province of British Columbia in 1983), a private member's bill which went through a second reading in the federal parliament warning label legislation in Canada has not been achieved at the time of writing.

Longer-term Findings

Exposure to the Label and its Messages in the US

A number of earlier reports have considered 'penetration' of the label among the adult population as a whole. Here the focus is on the percentage of *drinkers* seeing the label and the percentage recalling its specific messages. Consideration is limited to drinkers because abstaining groups do not interact much with the product (Greenfield and Kaskutas 1993) and tend not to see the label

(Mayer et al. 1991). For the most part, those not drinking in the last twelve months will have little *need* for the health warnings; for example, only a small minority of the 35% of US abstainers aged 18 and older are still deciding whether or not to begin drinking. Conversely, it is mostly drinkers that need to be reminded (as Congress put it) of harms that may be avoided or minimised by limiting drinking, or not drinking at all, in high risk situations, such as when about to drive or during pregnancy – the two main situations involving alcohol harm and warnings taken up here.

Figure 7.1 presents, for drinkers during the prior twelve months, percentages in each survey year who said they saw the label, and those levels when 'corrected' to remove possible 'false positives' using a minimal recall requirement requiring some knowledge of the label's contents (see Greenfield et al. 1993).

In each year, seven message recall items, three correct (drink-driving, pregnancy and operating machinery) and four incorrect (cancer, drug interaction, arthritis and addiction), were available for the criterion test. In order to be considered 'likely' to have seen the

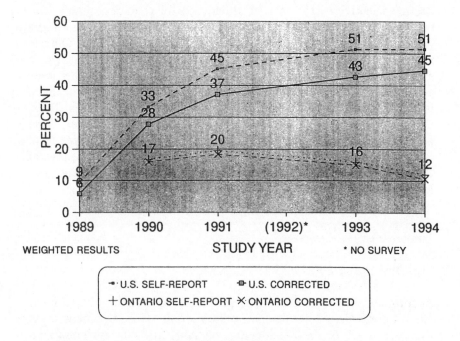

Figure 7.1: Percentages of drinkers seeing warning label by year and site. Note that correction for false positives involves message recall criterion (see text)

label, four answers out of seven could not be answered wrong, and at least one asking about messages really on the label had to be answered correctly (affirmed). As a check on the validity of this correction for false positives, in the summer 1989 baseline survey, from six to three months before the November implementation date, approximately 7% overall reported seeing the labels, a percentage similar to the correction. The criterion is probably conservative, since clearly some see the label with little specific recall of its contents. However, for the purpose of identifying the group that could be *influenced* by the labels, the 'corrected' measure seems apt.

In the US, exposure to the label and minimal awareness of its messages increased sharply in the early years and has been levelling off such that, after three to four and a half years, approximately half of all drinkers report label exposure in the prior year (in both 1993 and 1994, when an additional question was asked, 62% reported *ever* having seen the label). In Ontario, in 1990, after the US warning label introduction, exposure to labels was about half the US level, and it has fallen quite markedly to a 1994 level of only 12%. The pattern of results suggests levelling out, after several years, of numbers exposed to the label where it is mandated, and stagnation where it is only occasionally encountered (in a neighbouring province).

Other analyses not reported here have shown that the small number of Ontarians who see the labels, mostly when they travel or shop below the border (Graves et al. 1993), say they 'actually read the label' only slightly fewer times in the last year than their US counterparts (Greenfield 1994b). In both countries roughly one-tenth of drinkers claim to have read the label at least monthly, above one-third have read it three or more times, above half more than twice, and most at least once during the prior twelve months.

Because one may be vaguely aware of the label with little assimilation of its messages, it is important to consider recall of its contents. For each year and site, Figure 7.2 gives levels of recall of the 'pregnant women shouldn't drink' message (the first on the label), while Figure 7.3 gives the same for the 'driving impairment' message (label message number 2).

In the US the percentages of drinkers recalling the first message closely parallels the label awareness and 'corrected' exposure curves (Figure 7.1). This argues that almost all drinkers who see the label when it is on all containers are 'receiving the message' and being reminded that drinking during pregnancy is harmful. In Ontario, where exposure is less routine, equivalent recall levels in the early

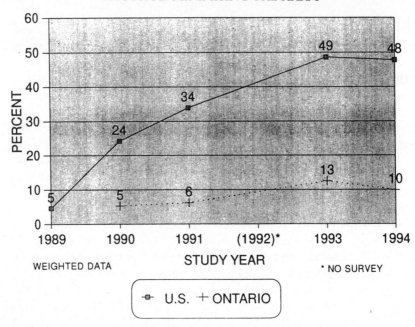

Figure 7.2: Percentages of drinkers recalling birth defects message by year in US and Ontario

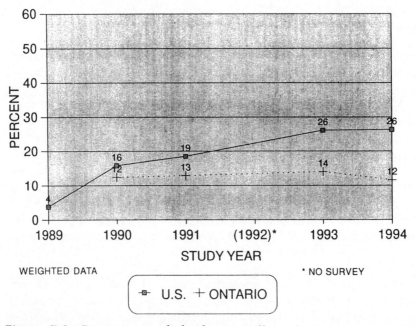

Figure 7.3: Percentages of drinkers recalling driving impairment message by year in US and Ontario

years were less than one-third of those exposed, but over time have climbed to much higher proportions (while exposure has faded). Thus it appears that a certain 'saturation' is necessary for good recall, emphasizing the importance of *mandating* that a label be on *all* containers. The driving impairment message, in contrast to the pregnancy message, is recalled by only about half those seeing the label (interestingly, a considerably higher proportion of Ontarians). Again, the time-trend appears to be reaching a plateau in the US. Why do fewer American drinkers recall this message? At least two explanations seem plausible. First, it is the second, in fact a middle, message, rather than one at the beginning or end (where psychologists find recall for material strongest). Second, there are more messages about drink-driving in the 'message environment' including TV spots, billboards and print advertising, making the discrimination task (did I really see it *there*?) harder than for the pregnancy message, which is rather more unique. Nonetheless, there is fair recall achieved after three or four years with 26% of drinkers recalling the message, nearly double the 1990 level. It remains a puzzle as to why proportionally more Ontarians seeing the label recall this message. 'Freshness' of the stimulus may suggest greater likelihood of attending to it (remember that Ontario drinkers, even though only exposed to the label occasionally, when they were, said they read it almost as frequently as did US counterparts). We believe these results argue for the merits of rotating, or introducing new messages periodically, in order to keep them 'fresh'. The levelling off of exposure and recall might be offset if the label's content was not increasingly becoming 'boring' through overexposure. Why bother to read something again when you think you already know what it says?

An important agenda is trying to understand how labels work by examining factors predicting greater exposure both to the label and specific messages. In the US 1993 sample, two segmentation analyses of seeing the label and recall of the driving impairment message as dependent measures were undertaken, using the CHAID programme (Statistical Programs for the Social Sciences Inc. 1993). This analysis searches for specific levels of selected variables which best account for the variance in the dependent variable. In this instance, subsamples defined by the predictors are yielded when they statistically distinguish increasing levels of exposure or recall. For more details see Greenfield (1994b).

Each analysis included gender, age (four levels), as well as number of times containers were purchased (five levels) and opened (six levels). In both cases, number of times containers were opened was the best predictor in the set for both exposure and message recall. Among those never opening containers, age was the best predictor. Of all subgroups identified by the analysis, respondents aged 30 or older who never opened containers were least exposed. Only 15% of them saw the label and only 10% knew it said something about drink-driving. Conversely, even for those not opening containers, those under 30 had about average exposure (39% seeing the label, 25% recalling its message). For those opening containers more often, analyses of label awareness and drink-driving message recall gave different results. For seeing the label, only the group opening containers five or more times were subdivided again, by gender: 75% of men (versus 54% women) saw the label. Men were further differentiated on purchase behaviour: men who opened five or more containers *and* who purchased three or more times in thirty days were the subgroup most likely to be exposed, with fully 83% seeing the label (almost two-thirds of those who purchased less often also saw the label). Clearly those buying and handling alcohol are very well reached by the label, especially the young.

For recalling the label's driving impairment message, lower subgroup percentages are to be expected. In this instance 36% of the group opening five or more containers recalled the message. The group opening containers one to four times in thirty days was subdivided by age, the greatest recall being by those under 30 (37%, versus 20% for those older). In summary, the drink-driving message was retained slightly more by younger individuals who open a moderate number, not many, containers.

Possible Effects on Behaviour

To examine the impact of seeing the warning label and recalling specific messages – either the driving impairment message or the drinking and pregnancy message – on related behaviours, multiple logistic regression models were fitted. The focus here is on the 1990–94 US samples which provide adequate groups of respondents exposed to the messages. These analyses controlled for year of study, gender, age (18–25, 26–30, 31–40, 41–60, 61 or more), ethnicity (black, white, Hispanic, and Other), education (less than high school, HS graduate, some college, college degree), as well as Conservative Protestant religion (which affects both drinking pattern and health behaviours) and the frequency of drinking five or more drinks a day (5+), which represents a risk for drinking and driving (Greenfield 1995). Analyses for drink-driving related outcomes included only respondents who reported driving during the past year and drank any alcohol in that period. Analyses were done separately for two drink-driving harm-reducing precautionary behaviours as dependent measures – limiting driving because of having drunk too much (reported by 37% overall) and having limited your drinking because you knew you had to drive (68% overall) as well as for conversations about drinking and driving. We examined whether or not seeing the warning label and recalling its driving impairment message contributed significantly to predicting each dependent behavioural variable.

In predicting the harm-reducing behaviour of deliberately not driving after drinking too much, the model correctly predicted 72.5% of the cases. Other factors being equal, those most likely to report using this precautionary strategy tended to be younger, male, white, and more often drank heavily; education and Conservative Protestantism were unrelated. Controlling for all these variables, those recalling the label's drink-driving message were significantly more likely to limit their driving after drinking (odds ratio (OR) = 1.86; confidence interval (CI) 1.67–2.30; $p < 0.0001$), than those unexposed. The harm-reducing behaviour was practised more in 1991 than in 1990, the rates in other years not differing from the 1990s.

The other precautionary behaviour, limiting drinking when going to drive gave a similar but less dramatic result for the association with recall of the label's message. Those adopting this harm-reduction strategy (which is practised by more drinkers but is inherently less safe than not driving after drinking) were also somewhat more likely to have recalled the drink-driving message (OR = 1.33; CI 1.07–1.64; $p < 0.01$). Younger men were again more likely than older to use the harm-reducing strategy (limiting drinking when they knew they would be driving), but in this instance the predictive relationships differed from those for the other precautionary behaviour: ethnicity played no role, while higher levels of education were positively related to limiting drinking, and Conservative Protestants were *less* likely to use the strategy, other predictors accounted for.

In a parallel logistic regression model, conversations about drink-driving were not found to be associated with recall of the drink-driving message, controlling for other variables. Conversely, in an equivalent logistic regression model (but substituting consumption volume for 5+ frequency), other factors accounted for, recall of the pregnancy warning *was* associated significantly with conversations about drinking and pregnancy (OR = 1.34; CI 1.13–1.59; $p < 0.001$). Such conversations were more likely with increasing education and in later years.

Evidence regarding effects of the pregnancy message have also indicated a possible role of warnings. Among those women who had been pregnant during the prior year in the combined post-implementation sample ($n=365$), Kaskutas and Greenfield (1995) reported all but 4% drank a maximum of two or less drinks per occasion (versus 44% who reported more than two drinks maximum in the prior twelve months, including some period when not pregnant). In all, 75%, when pregnant, reported no drinks, which represents perfectly following the label's injunction, in contrast to the same respondents reporting only a 25% abstinence rate in the prior twelve months. More importantly, among the 101 pregnant women who remembered seeing the label's message about not drinking during pregnancy, 66% (versus 43% for the 166 who did not recall seeing the label's message) indicated that their maximum when pregnant was lower than the maximum they reported for the whole prior twelve months, also including some period outside pregnancy. (In each case, only 1% indicated increased drinking and the rest reported the same maximum overall as when pregnant.)

Although not conclusive evidence of an effect due to the warning label's messages, these findings are at least consistent with the Congressional intent, by showing that the appropriate groups are being reminded of the harms, and that, other personal characteristics including drinking variables accounted for, those more exposed to the message appear more likely than others to be adopting harm-reduction strategies related to drinking and driving, and possibly drinking less per occasion when pregnant and having more conversations about drinking and pregnancy.

Public Opinion and Attitudes

Firstly, analyses of the opinions regarding thirteen alcohol policies in the US and Ontario indicate that warning labels on containers continue to be the most favoured policy measures in both jurisdictions. In the US, after implementation of the legislation, support for the warning label policy increased from pre-intervention levels of 87% (Kaskutas 1993a). It has continued to rise to a 1994 level of 92% favouring the policy ($p < 0.0001$). In the US, warning labels was the *only* alcohol policy opinion which showed positive change from an already very high level, support for four other policies significantly declining during the same five-year period. (An anonymous reviewer noted that in Australia there has been a similar experience with increased support for public health legislation following implementation in the case of the random breath-testing of drivers. A desirable mix of alcohol policies would include at least some showing this characteristic.) Clearly the public has strong acceptance of the warning label measure. In addition to supporting the policy, a majority of US adults believe that warning labels are an effective way to change people's behaviour, although the percentage in the US has fallen somewhat (55% in 1993; 53% in 1994) from the high of 61% in 1991. The public tends *not* to have much expectation that heavy drinkers will be affected by the label: soon after implementation, in 1990 and 1991, only 14% disagreed with the statement that heavy drinkers would *not* be affected and this rate has fallen to 10% by 1993 and 1994. Somewhat surprisingly, and speaking to the larger numbers of more 'moderate' drinkers, in 1991, eighteen months after implementation, a majority (55%) also agreed that 'Warning labels have affected my drinking' (20% with *strong* agreement), but in the longer term this rate too has fallen significantly (47% in 1993; 42% in 1994). Thus, there is some indication of increasing scepticism about effects as the label 'grows old' (although endorsement of the labelling *policy* has not abated and instead continues to increase). Finally, in 1993 and 1994 we added a question asking whether the label 'should include the number of standard drinks in the bottle or can', finding that 76% answered 'yes'.

Learning from the US Experience

The time-trends suggest that it has taken four to five years for exposure levels among drinkers (and the population) to flatten, and that by 1994 about half the drinkers were aware of the label and were being reached by at least some of its messages. This is encouraging. Additionally, the segmentation analyses confirm and strengthen the earlier findings (Greenfield et al. 1993) that target groups were being reached, as hoped by the policy's advocates. It is remarkable that over four-fifths of men who were the heaviest consumers were seeing the label three and a half years after its introduction and it is promising that over one-third of those under 30 who opened even moderate numbers of containers recalled seeing the message about drink-driving. Thus, in the longer term, the label is reaching its intended targets, those at elevated risk of harm.

Longer-term behavioural results not elaborated here but involving quasi-experimental comparisons with Ontario that parallel those conducted with the six- and eighteen-month post-implementation data (Graves 1993, Greenfield et al. 1993) suggest that changes in the US population levels of deliberately not driving after drinking, which earlier appeared to favour the US intervention site over the control site, have not been sustained. Nevertheless, the US results summarised here, pooling post-implementation surveys and showing associations between recall of the label's drink-driving message and harm-reducing behaviours related to drink-driving risks or risks to the foetus, are consistent with some influence. The two drink-driving results can be reconciled by noting that an overall decline in US concern about drink-driving (which may have peaked earlier when grass-roots organisations like Mothers Against Drunk Driving were vigorous) might be somewhat slowed among those paying attention to the label's message. Similar associations between recall of the drinking and pregnancy warning and lowered maxima are also promising. Thus, the label may indeed be reminding those at most risk to take precautions, as Congress intended. While these cross-sectional relationships cannot determine whether seeing the label *caused* the increase in precautionary behaviours, these relationships are suggestive. Our group has also found some evidence of a dose-response relationship when warning labels are considered along with other messages such as those in advertisements, on TV, billboards and point-of-sale signs (Kaskutas and Graves 1994). A clear recommendation for any country considering labels is to couple the introduction of warning labels with other messages using different modalities or community campaigns complementing the label, which have been recommended (US NIAAA 1987, MacKinnon et al. 1993) but not been implemented in the US. Synergy seems valuable. Several results also suggest altering order of messages, or better, rotating different messages could be helpful for reducing the tendency to 'tune out' unchanging stimuli.

Finally, the sustained public opinion in support of the warning label with more than 90 per cent in favour, and the continued belief by a majority of people that mandated labels can be effective, is striking. Even allowing for some social desirability bias, we find many people do believe the warning label has affected their own drinking. It has been argued by Hilton and Kaskutas (1991) that such non-invasive informational approaches are most supported 'precisely because they are expected to have the least impact on most drinkers' (p. 1332), a somewhat sceptical view to be sure. In the first years after the government warning appeared on containers, the public did not seem to be jaded by the 'insignificance' or 'redundancy' of the actual label which many believed, because of its widely known content, might occur. There does not seem to be widespread cynicism in America about its effectiveness, as some predicted, although scepticism is somewhat more evident in the longer term. On the contrary, the sustained public opinion findings suggest that politicians may well be advised to leave the warning label policy in place even in the absence of strong evidence of efficacy. It is not clear that strong evidence for such an intervention could ever be obtained unless the policy were to be introduced in a designed quasi-experiment (the label being withheld in selected places). But this may not be practical. In a mass programme like this, weak evidence of potentially modest effects may have to suffice. Advocates may reasonably argue that, in the absence of documented negative impacts, continuing the very inexpensive policy is warranted, based on the proposition in jurisprudence, now widely applied in the US, that the public has a 'right to know' about products that have the potential to harm, if improperly used. This is a viable harm-reduction strategy, one that relies on providing accurate consumer information about real risks, and how these may be reduced.

It would appear that other countries could improve upon the US policy were they to have the fortitude to adopt a labelling law that employed all we know now about informational health campaigns both in label design and in concurrent programming. Other countries would need to judge the public acceptance of such messages, undoubtedly varying in their cultural attitudes toward the appropriateness of government warnings regarding alcohol. In the US it does not appear likely that the labelling policy will be rescinded or retooled, at least for some time. The industry is not enamoured of the product warning, and fought it for years, but once implemented quite 'painlessly' it has not made major efforts to overturn the policy. Perhaps this is so because, in the end, the advent of the label has not had much impact on overall sales, which continued on a slight downward trend from the early 1980s (Midanik and Clark 1994), and it may have been perceived to offer producers a modicum of legal protection against suits arguing negligence in failing to inform about associated risks when marketing a potentially hazardous substance to an unwitting public. There are periodic 'probes' to test governmental will, as in the case of the Wine Institute, a lobbying group, which in May 1996 applied to the warning label regulatory agency for inclusion of an announcement as part of the warning label inviting consumers to call the Federal

Department of Agriculture regarding its new dietary guidelines. These guidelines, though not changing recommended safe limits of consumption, for the first time acknowledged the findings about cardiovascular health effects of moderate drinking. Advocacy groups remain vigilant and are mounting a response. The petition is unlikely to succeed. Nor is it clear that public health efforts to improve the labelling regulations would prosper, and the attempt to strengthen the policy, for example by requiring rotating, different, or more legible messages, might well upset the balance of forces that seems now to prevail. Given the difficulty of changing legislation, once enacted, it would seem that countries considering warning labels would be best advised to instate rotating messages from the outset, should these be deemed desirable. As recent experience has shown, alcohol and particularly wine producers are keen to amplify potential health benefits of moderate drinking. The warning label as it stands remains a counterbalance to such assertions, which are receiving plenty of publicity.

Acknowledgement

This chapter is based in part on a paper presented at the 5th International Conference on the Reduction of Alcohol-Related Harm, Toronto, Ontario, 6–10 March (Greenfield 1994b). The research was supported by a grant from the US National Institute on Alcohol Abuse and Alcoholism (NIAAA) to the Alcohol Research Group, Western Consortium for Public Health (Grant No. AA08557). The opinions expressed are those of the author and do not necessarily represent those of the supporting agencies. I thank Michael Hilton, Lee Kaskutas, Norman Giesbrecht, Karen Graves, Mija Lee and Robin Room for various important contributions to this study.

References

Bradburn, N.M., Sudman, S. and Associates (1979) *Improving Interview Method and Questionnaire Design: Response Effects to Threatening Questions in Survey Research*, San Francisco, CA, Jossey-Bass.

Cook, T.D. and Campbell, D.T. (1979) *Quasi-Experimentation: Design and Analysis Issues for Field Settings*, Boston, MA, Houghton Mifflin.

Curtin, L. and Feinleib, M. (1992) 'Considerations in the design of longitudinal surveys of health', in Dwyer, J.H., Feinleib, M., Lipert, P. and Hoffmeister, H. (eds) *Statistical Models for Longitudinal Studies of*

Health, Monographs in Epidemiology and Biostatistics No. 16, New York, Oxford University Press, pp. 49–67.

Dwyer, J.H., Feinleib, M., Lipert, P. and Hoffmeister, H. (1992) *Statistical Models for Longitudinal Studies of Health*, Monographs in Epidemiology and Biostatistics No. 16, New York, Oxford University Press.

Eliany, M., Giesbrecht, N., Nelson, M., Wellman, B. and Wortley, S. (eds) (1990) *National Alcohol and Other Drugs Survey: Highlight Report*, Ottawa, Health and Welfare Canada.

Ferrence, R.G. (1989) *Deadly Fashion: The Rise and Fall of Cigarette Smoking in North America*, New York, Garland.

Frey, J. (1989) *Survey Research by Telephone*, Newbury Park, CA, Sage Publications, Inc.

Giesbrecht, N. and Greenfield, T.K. (1991) 'Public opinions on alcohol policy issues: a comparison of American and Canadian surveys', Presented at Alcohol Policy Section, 36th International Institute on the Prevention and Treatment of Alcoholism, ICAA, Stockholm, Sweden.

Graves, K.L. (1993) 'An evaluation of the alcohol warning label: A comparison of the United States and Ontario, Canada between 1990 and 1991', *Journal of Public Policy and Marketing*, 12: 19–29.

Graves, K.L., Giesbrecht, N. and Ferris, J. (1993) *Leakage of the Alcohol Warning Label from the United States Across the Border to Ontario, Canada*, Berkeley, CA, Alcohol Research Group.

Greenfield, T.K. (1994a) 'Improving causal inference from naturalistic designs: Self-selection and other issues in evaluating alcohol control policies', *Applied Behavioral Science Review*, 2: 45–61.

Greenfield, T.K. (1994b) 'Mandated container warnings as an alcohol-related harm reduction policy: First evidence from long-term US/Ontario surveys', Presented at 5th International Conference on the Reduction of Drug Related Harm, Toronto, Ontario, 6–10 March.

Greenfield, T.K. (1995) 'Pattern of drinking, gender, age and risks for self-reported alcohol-related social and health harms: A strategy for applying nonparametric regression', Presented at Conference on Social and Health Effects of Different Drinking Patterns, Toronto, Canada, 13–17 November.

Greenfield, T.K., Graves, K.L. and Kaskutas, L.A. (1993) 'Alcohol warning labels for prevention: national survey findings', *Alcohol, Health and Research World*, 17: 67–75.

Greenfield, T.K. and Hilton, M. (1994) 'Warning labels on alcoholic beverage containers in the United States', Presented at 38th Annual International Institute on the Prevention and Treatment of Alcoholism, International Council on Alcohol and Addictions, Prague, 6–10 June.

Greenfield, T.K. and Kaskutas, L.A. (1993) 'Early impacts of alcoholic beverage warning labels: national study findings relevant to drinking and driving behavior', *Safety Science*, 16: 689–707.

Greenfield, T.K. and Kaskutas, L.A. (1994) 'Changes in public opinion about alcohol control and intervention policies in the US: A five-year trend study', Presented at American Public Health Association Annual Meeting, Washington, D.C., 30 Oct.–4 Nov.

Hilton, M.E. and Kaskutas, L.A. (1991) 'Public support for warning labels on alcoholic beverage containers', British Journal of Addiction, 86: 1323–33.

Kaskutas, L.A. (1993a) 'Changes in public attitudes toward alcohol control policies since the warning label mandate of 1988', Journal of Public Policy and Marketing, 12: 30–7.

Kaskutas, L.A. (1993b) 'Differential perceptions of alcohol policy effectiveness, Journal of Public Health Policy, 14: 415–36.

Kaskutas, L.A. (1995) 'Interpretations of risk: The use of scientific information in the development of the alcohol warning label policy', International Journal of the Addictions, 30: 1519–48.

Kaskutas, L.A. and Graves, K. (1994) 'Relationship between cumulative exposure to health messages and awareness and behavior-related drinking during pregnancy', American Journal of Health Promotion, 9: 115–24.

Kaskutas, L.A. and Greenfield, T.K. (1991) 'Knowledge of warning labels on alcoholic beverage containers', in Proceedings of the Human Factors Society 35th Annual Meeting – 1991, pp. 441–5.

Kaskutas, L.A. and Greenfield, T.K. (1992) 'First effects of warning labels on alcoholic beverage containers', Drug and Alcohol Dependence, 31: 1–14.

Kaskutas, L.A. and Greenfield, T.K. (1995) 'Reach and effects of health messages on drinking during pregnancy', Presented at American Public Health Association Annual Meeting, Washington, D.C., 30 Oct.–4 Nov.

Laughery, K.R. and Brelsford, J.W. (1991) 'Receiver characteristics in safety communications', Proceedings of the Human Factors Society 35th Annual Meeting – 1991, pp. 1068–72.

Lipsey, M.W. (1990) 'Theory as method: Small theory of treatments', in L. Sechrest, E. Perrin, and J. Bunker (eds) Research Methodology: Strengthening Interpretations of Nonexperimental Data (DHHS Publication No. (PHS)90-3454). Agency for Health Care Policy and Research, pp. 33–51.

MacKinnon, D.P. and Fenaughty, A.M. (1993) 'Substance use and memory for health warning labels', Health Psychology, 12(2): 147–50.

MacKinnon, D.P. Pentz, M.A. and Stacy, A.W. (1993) 'The alcohol warning label and adolescents: The first year', American Journal of Public Health, 83: 585–7.

Mayer, R.N., Smith, K.R. and Scammon, D.C. (1991) 'Evaluating the impact of alcohol warning labels', Advances in Consumer Research, 18: 706–14.

McGuire, W.J. (1974) 'Communication methods for drug education', in M. Goodstadt (ed.) Research on Methods and Programs of Drug Education, Toronto, Ontario, Addiction Research Foundation, pp. 1–26.

Midanik, L.T. and Clark, W.B. (1994) 'The demographic distribution of U.S. drinking patterns in 1990: Descriptions and trends from 1984', American Journal of Public Health, 84: 1218–22.

Public Law No. 100-690 (1988) *Alcoholic Beverage Labeling Act of 1988*, in Washington, D.C.: 100th Congress, 2nd session.

Room, R., Graves, K., Giesbrecht, N. and Greenfield, T.K. (1995) 'Trends in public opinion about alcohol policy initiatives in Ontario and the US: 1989–91', *Drug and Alcohol Review*, 14: 35–47.

Scammon, D.L., Mayer, R.N. and Smith, K.R. (1991) 'Alcohol warnings: How do you know when you have had one too many?' *Journal of Public Policy and Marketing*, 10: 214–28.

Statistical Programs for the Social Sciences Inc. (1993) *The CHAID manual for SPSS for Windows*, Chicago, IL: SPSS, Inc.

Survey Design and Analysis Inc. (1989) *Alcohol Warning Label Study: Technical Report*, Ann Arbor, MI, Survey Design and Analysis, Inc.

Survey Design and Analysis Inc. (1990) *Alcohol Warning Label Study: Technical Report*, Ann Arbor, MI, Survey Design and Analysis, Inc.

Survey Design and Analysis Inc. (1991) *Alcohol Warning Label Study: Technical Report*, Ann Arbor, MI, Survey Design and Analysis, Inc.

Survey Design and Analysis Inc. (1993) *Alcohol Warning Label Study: Technical Report*, Ann Arbor, MI, Survey Design and Analysis, Inc.

Survey Design and Analysis Inc. (1994) *Alcohol Warning Label Study: Technical Report*, Ann Arbor, MI, Survey Design and Analysis, Inc.

US National Institute on Alcohol Abuse and Alcoholism (1987) *Review of the Research Literature on the Effects of Health Warning Labels: a Report to the United States Congress* (No. ADM 281-86-0003). Washington, D.C.: US National Institute on Alcohol Abuse and Alcoholism.

Weinstein, N.D. (1988) 'The precaution adoption process', *Health Psychology*, 7(4): 355–86.

8 Driving Under the Influence of Alcohol

Kathryn Stewart and Barry M. Sweedler

Over the last decade, the number of deaths and injuries related to impaired driving has declined significantly in the United States as well as in other industrialised countries. For example, in 1982, 57 per cent of all highway fatalities in the US involved a driver or pedestrian with a measurable blood alcohol level. By 1995, this figure had decreased to 41 per cent of fatalities. The total number of traffic fatalities decreased from 43,945 in 1982 to 41,465 in 1995 (a decline of 6 per cent) while alcohol-related fatalities decreased from 25,170 to 17,130 in the same time period (a decline of 32 per cent) (National Highway Traffic Safety Administration 1995).

Similar reductions have occurred in other industrialised countries, including Great Britain, Germany, the Netherlands, Canada and Australia (Transportation Research Board 1994). Some countries have experienced slight increases in the last few years, causing some concern. (See, for example, Simpson et al. 1995 for a discussion of recent increases in Canada.) The general trend, however, has been very encouraging. The harm that has been avoided is truly monumental. For example, in the United States, if alcohol-involved crash rates had continued unchanged since 1982, almost 13,000 more people would have died in 1993. Many thousands of serious injuries were also avoided.

What accounts for these changes, which have occurred in different countries with different cultural, legal, economic and social environments? It is possible that some portion of the reductions observed is due to global economic or demographic shifts. There is sufficient research evidence, however, to indicate that a significant portion of the change has resulted from changes in social norms, laws, policies and practices aimed at reducing the harm that results from impaired driving (Stewart et al. 1995).

An evolution in social attitudes has occurred in recent years that appears to have had an effect on impaired driving and on the laws and policies that control it. For many years after the invention of the automobile, the public tended to perceive traffic injuries as unpredictable accidents – just bad luck. Then people began to recognise that crashes were not random occurrences; in particular, alcohol played a role in many crashes. The reaction was to blame the irresponsible, uncontrolled driver who had committed a criminal act and in so doing caused injury or death. The public – especially victims of drunken drivers – demanded severe punishment of offenders. This punishment satisfied a need for justice and was thought to deter others from drinking and driving.

More recently has come an era in which alcohol-related traffic crashes are recognised as the result of social and cultural patterns and environmental conditions as well as individual transgressions. The consumption of alcohol is a socially condoned behaviour. Driving is essential to the daily functioning of the citizens of many countries. It is not surprising that these two behaviours combine in destructive ways. Ross (1992a) has made the point that drink-driving 'is a predictable product of our social institutions, especially transportation and recreation'.

When an impaired individual gets into a car and causes injury or death, this incident is the result of many influences, including social norms; the availability, pricing and promotion of alcohol; the laws governing the licensing of drivers; the availability or lack of availability of other means of transportation; the driver's perception of the likelihood of arrest and punishment; the vigour of law enforcement; the presence of road hazards, and the safety of automobiles. Each of these elements has been the focus of strategies that have the potential to reduce the harm resulting from alcohol-impaired driving.

Many of the strategies that are designed to reduce alcohol-related harm in general also reduce alcohol-related crashes. These strategies include limits on the availability of alcohol, increases in price and public education about alcohol. These strategies are discussed in other chapters. This chapter will deal only with strategies that are specifically aimed at impaired driving. The strategies to be discussed include those related to establishing legal limits on alcohol while driving, enforcement practices, penalties for impaired driving and the transportation environment.

Legal Limits on Alcohol

Per se Laws

A landmark event in the development of policies regarding impaired driving was the establishment of the fact that consumption of alcohol does, in fact, increase the probability of traffic crashes. A study carried out by Borkenstein et al. (1964) compared the blood alcohol content (BAC) of drivers in fatal crashes to the BACs of randomly selected drivers at the same time of day and day of the week in the places where the fatal crashes occurred. The study indicated that drivers with BACs of 0.05 to 0.099 per cent were twice as likely to crash as drivers with a zero BAC. Drivers with BACs from 0.10 to 0.149 per cent were ten times as likely to have a fatal crash. A BAC between 0.15 and 0.19 per cent increased the probability of a fatal crash by almost thirty-two times and a BAC at or above 0.20 per cent increased the probability by over forty times. Up until 1967, in the United States as well as other countries outside of Scandinavia, in order for a driver to be convicted of drunken driving, evidence was required that his or her behaviour clearly indicated intoxication, including such evidence as slurred speech or inability to walk a straight line. Blood alcohol levels were measured and used as corroborative evidence of intoxication. In 1967, a per se law was adopted in Britain to establish levels of blood alcohol as per se evidence of intoxication, that is, it became illegal to drive with that level of blood alcohol regardless of other behavioural or performance impairment. Canada adopted a per se law in 1969 and states in the US began to do the same (Evans 1991). Currently, all but two states in the US have established per se laws. These laws make prosecution of impaired driving cases far easier and more effective.

Reductions in the Legal BAC Limit

The BAC level at which driving becomes illegal varies widely throughout the world. Research has not established a 'safe' level of blood alcohol (Moskowitz and Burns 1990). In most countries the BAC limit is based on what is politically and socially acceptable. Most states in the United States have established 0.10 per cent as the legal limit.[1]

Reductions in the legal BAC limit are beginning to be more widely applied in the United States. Currently, fifteen states have reduced the BAC limit to 0.08 per cent, which is also the limit in Canada, Great Britain and Germany. Other European countries, including France, Belgium, Finland, Norway, the Netherlands and Portugal, have established 0.05 per cent as the limit, as has Australia. Sweden's limit is 0.02 per cent.

Lowering the legal BAC limit has three purposes. First, a lower BAC is presumed to make conviction of drivers apprehended with marginal BACs more likely. For example, in states in the US with a limit of 0.10 per cent, prosecutors often do not pursue cases in which the arrest BAC was under 0.12 or even 0.15 per cent because of difficulties obtaining a conviction. Second, lowering the limit appears to have a general deterrence effect. That is, drivers perceive that they are more likely to be arrested and punished for driving after drinking, therefore they are less inclined to do so. This second effect has far more potential to improve traffic safety than the first. The third purpose of lowering the legal BAC limit is to send a more rational and consistent message about levels at which drivers are impaired.

Evaluations of the effects of decreasing the legal limit have been conducted in a number of countries. Kloeden and McLean (1995) reported a reduction of late-night drink-driving in Adelaide after the legal blood alcohol limit in South Australia was lowered from 0.08 to 0.05 per cent in 1991. Road surveys showed a small reduction in drink-driving, both legal and illegal, shortly after the BAC was lowered. Two years later, in 1993, the level of drink-driving had continued to decrease and was at the lowest level observed in the seven years of roadside surveys. In 1994, the US National Highway Traffic Safety Administration (NHTSA) conducted a preliminary assessment of changes in alcohol-related crashes in the states that had passed 0.08 BAC legislation. The five states studied had the law in effect for at least two years. The comparisons of six different measures of driver involvement in alcohol-related fatal crashes for the five states suggest that significant decreases occurred following implementation of the 0.08 legislation (Johnson 1995).

Not surprisingly, lowering the BAC level has met with vigorous opposition from the alcoholic beverage industry (see, for example, Moore 1992).

Lower BAC Levels for Underage Drivers

As described in Chapter 9 (this volume), in the United States, raising the legal age for purchase of alcohol to twenty-one has been highly successful in reducing alcohol-related crashes among young drivers. As part of this effort, it has been increasingly recognised that young drivers are particularly vulnerable to impairment at low BACs. Thus, some states have established lower BAC limits for young drivers – usually at zero or 0.02 per cent. In addition, these states have seen the importance of supporting minimum drinking age laws with other related policies. Evaluations of these laws indicate that they have significantly reduced alcohol-related traffic deaths in the affected age groups. Hingson (1992) found a 42 per cent decrease in fatalities for teenagers in states with the lower limits while fatalities in comparison states declined 29 per cent. Campaigns to promote public awareness were found to be important in maximising the effectiveness of the laws. In Maryland, a change in the law coupled with a vigorous public awareness campaign resulted in a 50 per cent decrease in alcohol-related crashes among the affected age group (Blomberg 1992).

The movement to reduce the legal BAC limit for youth is sometimes part of a larger effort to limit the driving privileges of young drivers. Reductions in traffic crashes, both alcohol-related and non-alcohol-related, have been measured as a result of night-time driving curfews, increased age of licensure and graduated driving privileges (in which a variety of driving restrictions are gradually lifted as the driver gains experience and maturity) (Sweedler 1990). Such licensing systems have been found to be very effective in New Zealand and Australia (National Transportation Safety Board 1993).

Enforcement

It is important to note, in any discussion of enforcement, that in terms of traffic safety, detecting impaired drivers and removing them from the road can have only a small effect. No matter how effective the police are and how many impaired drivers they arrest and take off the highway, they can never hope to catch more than a tiny proportion of the impaired drivers on the road. Currently, officials estimate that the chances that a drinking driver will be arrested are as low as 1 in 1000 (Sweedler 1991). Inevitably, many of these drivers will be involved in crashes before they are caught by police. By far the most effective way of preventing crashes is to prevent drinking and driving before it occurs. One way of doing this is to convince the driving public that if they drink and drive, they are likely to be caught and promptly punished in a significant way. Some changes in enforcement policy have both increased the likelihood of apprehension and the public's perception of the likelihood.

The most well-known enforcement approach in increasing deterrence is random breath-testing. The experience of the Australian states of New South Wales and Victoria provides the most dramatic examples of its effectiveness. Random breath-testing was introduced in New South Wales in 1982. There was an immediate 36 per cent drop in alcohol-related fatal crashes, as compared to the previous three years (Homel et al. 1988), with a sustained 24 per cent decrease in single-vehicle night-time accidents over the next five years (Homel et al. 1995). In Victoria, the proportion of drivers killed over the legal blood alcohol limit (0.05 per cent) declined from 49 per cent in 1977 (when random breath testing was introduced) to 21 per cent in 1992 (Moloney 1995).

The success of random breath-testing in these Australian states is attributed to the principles laid out by Homel and colleagues (1988). They found that in order to be maximally effective, the campaign should be highly visible, conducted as often as possible, rigorously enforced so as to ensure credibility and well publicised. For example, in Victoria it was found that when random breath-testing was carried out by officers in normal police vehicles in combination with their other duties it was not nearly as effective as when it was carried out using highly conspicuous special purpose vehicles. Testing is carried out at times and in places designed to attract public and media attention and is combined with saturation advertising (Moloney 1995).

Random breath-testing efforts in Sweden and in New Zealand have had less dramatic results, perhaps because the campaigns were not carried out with the vigour and persistence that characterises the efforts in New South Wales and Victoria (Bailey 1995, Törnros 1995).

In the United States, random breath-testing is not constitutionally permissible. Instead, some jurisdictions use sobriety checkpoints. The key difference between random breath-testing and sobriety checkpoints is that in a sobriety checkpoint, the enforcement officer cannot ask for a breath sample unless there is probable cause to believe that the driver has been drinking. Research has indicated that officers do not detect a substantial portion of drinking drivers under these circumstances (Jones and Lund 1985). The use of passive breath-sensors substantially increases the effectiveness of sobriety checkpoints (Voas et al. 1985).

Researchers have observed that aggressiveness and the conspicuous nature of the sobriety checkpoints and widespread publicity surrounding them are important to their full success as deterrents (Hurst 1991). A study by Ross indicated that communities that used sobriety checkpoints experienced significant decreases in alcohol-related traffic crashes. The programmes tended to be short-lived, however, as police turned to other crime problems, such as drugs (Ross 1992b). Unfortunately, the harm-reduction potential of sobriety checkpoints was likely to be much greater than that of the other police priorities.

Penalties

Generally, the severity of punishment is not as important as its swiftness and certainty. For example, jail terms for first offenders do appear to have a deterrent effect. These penalties are expensive, however, and, in many jurisdictions, impractical. Evaluations have found that their impact on safety is not as great as that of more easily imposed sanctions, for example licence penalties (Zador et al. 1989). Following is a discussion of some policies regarding penalties for impaired driving, including administrative licence revocation, rehabilitative programmes and other sanctions.

Administrative Licence Revocation

Administrative licence revocation has been adopted in thirty-nine states in the US and parts of Canada. This penalty allows for the immediate confiscation of the driving licence by the arresting officer if a person is arrested with an illegal blood alcohol level or if the driver refuses to be tested. In most states, the arresting officer issues a temporary driving permit good for a prescribed length of time (usually thirty days). During this time, the offender has the right to appeal the revocation in an administrative process. If the offender does not appeal or if the appeal is not upheld, the driver loses his or her licence for a prescribed period (ninety days for a first offence in most states; longer for subsequent offences). This licence revocation occurs regardless of the outcome of a court trial. In most states without administrative revocation, drinking drivers can lose their licences, but only after being convicted in court. The judicial process is lengthy and uncertain. Often, the licence is never suspended at all. Plea bargaining, diversion programmes and systems failures may allow many offenders to keep their licences.

Administrative revocation has been shown to be effective in discouraging the public from driving after drinking. In one study (Zador et al. 1989) the number of traffic crashes in states with administrative revocation laws were compared to those in states without such laws. The study concluded that these laws reduced fatal night-time crashes (which are likely to involve alcohol) by about 9 per cent. These findings were supported by another study of seventeen states with administrative revocation laws (Sigmastat Inc. 1989) which found an average reduction in fatal crashes of 7 per cent. In a recent study in three states in the US, administrative revocation was found to reduce both night-time fatal crashes and the proportion of drivers involved in fatal crashes with a significant amount of alcohol in their blood (Ross 1991). Administrative licence revocation has also been found to be effective in reducing recidivism among offenders (Stewart et al. 1989) and can be implemented with little or no net cost to states (Lacey et al. 1991).

Rehabilitative Programmes

The Alcohol Safety Action Projects (ASAPs) funded by the US National Highway Traffic Safety Administration in the 1970s introduced rehabilitation modalities as part of an integrated set of alcohol/traffic safety countermeasures. ASAP rehabilitation countermeasures were conceived as a bridge between the traffic court systems that adjudicated drink-driving offences and various community health and mental health resources that provided alcohol treatment. Currently, most states in the US and a number of other countries have some sort of education/rehabilitative programme as part of the package of sanctions applied to impaired driving offenders. Rehabilitative programmes are not, technically, a form of punishment. They are widely viewed as such, however, both by the courts that include them in sentences for drinking and driving offences and by the offenders. The programmes differ in content, intensity and delivery mechanism, but usually focus primarily on educating offenders regarding the effects of alcohol, legal consequences of drinking and driving, symptoms of alcoholism and so forth.

Evaluations of a wide variety of rehabilitative programmes based on a variety of theoretical models, delivered in a variety of settings, have never measured more than modest effects on recidivism (Stewart and Ellingstad 1989). A recent meta-analysis indicated that overall, rehabilitative programmes decrease recidivism by 8–9 per cent (Wells-Parker et al. 1995). The impact of these programmes on alcohol-related traffic crashes would be much smaller. Rehabilitative programmes may be seen to serve other purposes, such as to provide an additional, appropriate and acceptable form of punishment to offenders, to enforce a general societal message that drinking and driving is unacceptable behaviour and to provide a mechanism for intervention into the drinking problems of individuals. While benefits to individuals are possible, it must also be recognised that these beneficial effects have not been thoroughly evaluated. A number of evaluations report attitude changes in offenders (Foon 1988). In evaluations measuring drinking levels or improvements in other life areas, however, very few effects have been found (Stewart et al. 1987, Reis 1982). The possibility that some poorly designed or monitored programmes may actually have harmful effects cannot be ignored.

In contrast to the meagre success of standard rehabilitative programmes, more intensive treatment and monitoring programmes have shown more promise. Voas and Tippetts (1990) found marked decreases in recidivism among offenders who were sentenced to an in-patient facility followed by weekly monitoring or to weekly monitoring alone.

Closely related to rehabilitative programmes is the system for recertifying drivers for licensure after an impaired driving conviction. In most countries, the driver's licence of a person convicted of drinking and driving is suspended or revoked. The licence is generally automatically eligible for reinstatement when the suspension period is over. A number of countries, however, including Switzerland, Sweden and the United Kingdom, have programmes that require some offenders to provide medical certification that they have their problem with alcohol under control before they can have their licence returned. These programmes vary from country to country. The type of rehabilitative programme is generally not specified, only the results are measured (International Council on Alcohol, Drugs and Traffic Safety 1995). The effectiveness of this type of approach has not been established.

Penalties and Strategies for Persistent Drinking Drivers

The progress that has been made in reducing drinking and driving means that most people who are more easily deterred from impaired driving have already changed their behaviour. Thus, more attention is being paid to repeat offenders and other 'persistent' drinking drivers. A good definition of this group includes persons who repeatedly drive after drinking, especially with high blood alcohol concentrations, as well as repeat offenders. Using this broad definition, persistent drinking drivers represent an estimated 65 per cent of fatally injured drinking drivers, or about 30–35 per cent of all drivers killed in the United States each year (Simpson 1995).

Several practical, cost-effective steps have been proposed to deal with the persistent drinking driver (Transportation Research Board 1995). The cornerstone of any programme to address the problem of the persistent drinking driver is a comprehensive and efficient system for imposing and enforcing licence penalties. Such a system includes (1) administrative licence revocation to ensure prompt and certain punishment; (2) improvement in traffic records and the delivery system for information to the courts and the police officers on the road so that police, prosecutors and judges will have access to the complete prior record of the offender at the time of arrest and when charging and sentencing; (3) the imposition of serious penalties for driving while a licence is suspended or revoked because of impaired driving or a related offence; and (4) the elimination of programmes that permit drivers arrested for impaired driving to avoid losing their licences by entering a treatment or education programme.

A variety of sanctions can be imposed on drivers who persist in driving while impaired or driving while their licence is suspended for drinking and driving. These sanctions are designed to separate them from the vehicle they were driving when caught driving illegally and possibly from any other vehicle to which they might have access. As has been proven effective with the licensing sanction, this vehicle sanction should be applied administratively, although it may take a number of forms. For example, the vehicle can be impounded, immobilised or confiscated, or the licence plates can be seized. Evaluations of many of these vehicle sanctions have not yet been completed, but initial indications of their effectiveness are promising (Transportation Research Board 1995).

Changes in the Transportation Environment

The characteristics of the transportation environment can affect the degree to which consumption of alcohol results in traffic crashes. Many people depend on private automobiles, making driving after drinking more likely. Approaches have been tried based on providing alternative means of transportation. Efforts have also been made to improve the safety of roads so that crashes are avoided or minimised. The safety of the vehicle itself is critical once a crash has already occurred.

Transportation Policy

Changes in transportation policy have not been widely considered as a way of decreasing impaired driving in the US, nor has the nature of the transportation environment usually been a part of the examination of alcohol availability. For example, many bars are located in places where the only possible transportation is private automobiles. Similarly, public transportation in most US cities stops running hours before bars close. In many European countries, public transportation is more available and more widely used.

Strategies to provide alternative means of transportation include designated driver programmes and 'safe rides' programmes that provide free or reduced-price taxi rides or other forms of transportation. In Scandinavian countries, the use of designated drivers who do not drink or who drink very little has been widespread for many years. In the United States, such practices (especially the designated driver) are frequently not used appropriately (Stewart et al. 1995).

Concerns have been raised that the provision of transportation alternatives may encourage drinking to the point of serious impairment, thus leading to other negative effects of alcohol, including crime, violence and non-traffic accidental injury (DeJong and Wallack 1992). Recent research indicates that among a college student sample, 22 per cent of students who use a designated driver drank more than their usual amount the last time they were the passenger of a designated driver (DeJong et al. (forthcoming)).

Improved Roadway and Vehicle Safety

Roadway and vehicle safety policies have not received widespread attention as a way of decreasing alcohol-related traffic injuries. Unsafe driving will always occur and in many cases will involve alcohol. Thus, reducing the hazards on roadways and improving the crash worthiness of vehicles can make a life-or-death difference when prevention and deterrence efforts have failed.

The modification of roadside hazards provides one example of how roads can be made safer. A frequent type of alcohol-related fatal crash involves hitting a roadside hazard, such as a tree or utility pole. Perchonok et al. (1978) found that the frequency of collisions with utility poles declined by about 5 per cent for every six feet of distance between the poles and the roadway.

Another important strategy for decreasing alcohol-related injuries is to increase safety belt use. Mandatory seat belt use laws have been shown to decrease traffic fatalities by between 5 and 15 per cent (Lund et al. 1987, Skinner and Hoxie 1988). This percentage is lower than might be hoped because the vehicle occupants who are most likely to be involved in crashes, including impaired drivers, are least likely to wear safety belts (Williams and Lund 1988). It can be assumed, however, that as safety belt usage increases to very high levels (as seen, for example, in the United Kingdom where use rates approach 90 per cent) even impaired drivers are more likely to buckle up.

Because of the low safety belt use rate by those drivers most likely to crash, the importance of passive restraints, in particular air bags, is even greater. The Insurance Institute for Highway Safety reported in 1991 that driver deaths in frontal crashes were 28 per cent lower in air bag-equipped cars and moderate to severe injury was 25–29 per cent lower. Even when drivers were wearing seat belts, fatalities were reduced 15 per cent by the air bags.

Discussion

Of course, no analysis of a complex phenomenon such as impaired driving can be simple. In addition, there must certainly be important differences from country to country and culture to culture. Thus, the strategies that can reduce harm will also vary from country to country. What is acceptable and highly successful in one country may not be in another. For example, random breath-testing has been highly successful in Australia and has been enthusiastically implemented there. Other countries find this enforcement technique not to be politically or socially feasible. Similarly, the imposition of a higher minimum drinking age has proved to be a very successful technique for reducing alcohol-related crashes and deaths among young people in the United States. Other countries find the idea of such restrictions until the age of twenty-one culturally unacceptable. The fact that effective strategies cannot be shipped intact across national borders, however, does not reduce their significance. Their effectiveness in their own countries cannot be disputed. Moreover, more generalised lessons can be inferred. For example, random breath-testing shows the importance of deterrence as compared to detection in impaired driving enforcement; the minimum drinking age in the US shows the importance of special attention to young drivers who seem especially vulnerable to alcohol and to traffic crashes. These lessons can transcend borders.

We must be alert, however, to the differences that economic and social forces can have in altering drinking and driving behaviour and the effectiveness of countermeasures. Dramatic increases in impaired driving in former communist countries following the collapse of communism indicate the importance of the particular economic, social and political climate and public expectations about enforcement and punishment. For example, in the German Democratic Republic (East Germany), prior to reunification the legal BAC limit was 0.00 per cent while in the Federal Republic of Germany (West Germany) the limit was 0.08 per cent. For more than two years following reunification, the legal limit remained unchanged in the eastern part of Germany. Despite the fact that the law was unchanged, however, there was a sharp increase in alcohol-related crashes in the former East Germany, but no similar increase in the former West Germany. During the transition period, driving exposure also increased, as did non-alcohol-related crashes. It appears, however, that a variety of forces led to changes in the behaviour of drivers from the former East Germany in addition to the legal and exposure factors that might typically be expected to play a role (Krüger 1995, Vingilis and Fischer 1995).

The reductions in alcohol-related traffic fatalities that have been achieved in the last decade have prevented great suffering and have demonstrated the power of social and policy change to address social problems. The problem of impaired driving is still immense and many thousands of people die or are seriously injured in traffic crashes in which alcohol plays a part. If further progress is to be made, the effective strategies described above must be applied even more vigorously. Additional efforts must be made in other areas that have received less attention. These include changes in the social environment regarding alcohol, including controls on alcohol pricing and availability and the use of responsible service practices. Changes in the transportation environment may also have an impact on impaired driving fatalities.

On the whole, it appears that a partnership of citizens and government has been effective in reducing impaired driving. Citizen outrage and concern led to changes in policies and laws, which together led to changes in attitudes and behaviour in the general public. The progress we have witnessed in impaired driving in the last decade is not necessarily permanent, however. If public concern shifts to other issues, if laws and policies are weakened or are not enforced, we may see progress eroded. The evidence of the last decade, indicating that our efforts can be effective, should serve as a motivation to continue and expand them with vigour and determination.

Note

1   In order for a 160 pound man to reach 0.10, he would have to drink 5 US standard drinks of 1.5 centilitres in one hour.

References

Bailey, J. (1995) 'An Evaluation of Compulsory Breath Testing in New Zealand', in Kloeden, C.N. and McLean, A.J. (eds) *Alcohol, Drugs and Traffic Safety, Volume 2*, Australia, NHMRC Road Accident Research Unit, pp. 834–9.

Blomberg, R. (1992) *Lower BAC Limits For Youth: Evaluation of the Maryland 0.02 Law*, National Highway Transport Safety Administration, US Department of Transportation.

Borkenstein, R., Crowther, P., Shumate, R., Ziel, W. and Zylman, R. (1964) *The Role of the Drinking Driver in Traffic Accidents*, Indiana, Indiana University.

DeJong, W. and Wallack, L. (1992) 'The role of designated driver programmes in the prevention of alcohol-impaired driving: A critical reassessment', *Health Education Quarterly*, 19: 429–42.

DeJong, W., Wechsler, H. and Winsten, J. (forthcoming) 'The use of designated drivers by US college students: A national study'.

Evans, L. (1991) *Traffic Safety and the Driver*, New York, Van Nostrand Reinhold.

Foon, A.E. (1988) 'The effectiveness of drinking-driving treatment programmes: A critical review', *International Journal of the Addictions*, 23: 151–74.

Hingson, R. (1992) 'Effects of lower BAC Levels on Teenage Crash Involvement', Paper presented at the 71st Annual Meeting of the Transportation Research Board.

Homel, R., Carseldine, D. and Kearns, I. (1988) 'Drink-driving countermeasures in Australia', *Alcohol, Drugs and Driving*, 4: 113–44.

Homel, R., McKay, P. and Henstridge, J. (1995) 'The impact on accidents of random breath testing in New South Wales: 1982–1992', in Kloeden, C.N. and McLean, A.J. (eds) *Alcohol, Drugs and Traffic Safety Volume 2*, Australia: NHMRC Road Accident Research Unit, pp. 849–55.

Hurst, P. (1991) 'Impaired driving countermeasures in New Zealand', *The ICADTS Reporter*, 2: 2.

Insurance Institute for Highway Safety (1991) 'Studies quantify effectiveness of air bags in cars', *Status Report*, 26: 1–3.

International Council on Alcohol, Drugs and Traffic Safety (1995) *Regranting of Driving Licences*, University of Limburg, Maastricht, The Netherlands, The Institute for Human Psychopharmacology, Publication No. IHP 95–53.

Johnson, D.M. (1995) *Preliminary Assessment of the Impact of Lowering the illegal BAC Per Se Limit to 0.08*, Washington, D.C., National Highway Traffic Safety Administration, February.

Jones, I. and Lund, A. (1985) 'Detection of alcohol-impaired drivers using a passive alcohol sensor', *Journal of Police Science and Administration*, 14. Insurance Institute for Highway Safety, Arlington, Virginia.

Kloeden, C. and McLean, A.J. (1995) 'Late night drink driving in Adelaide two years after the introduction of the 0.05 limit', *Alcohol, Drugs and Traffic Safety*, 13: 80.

Krüger, H.P. (1995) 'Differential effects of deterrence – What can be learned from raising a BAC limit', in Kloeden, C.N. and McLean, A.J. (eds) *Alcohol, Drugs and Traffic Safety Volume 1*, Australia, NHMRC Road Accident Research Unit, pp. 386–96.

Lacey, J., Jones, R. and Stewart, J. (1991) *Cost–Benefit Analysis of Administrative License Suspensions*, Chapel Hill, N.C., UNC Highway Safety Research Center.

Lund, A., Zador, P. and Pollner, J. (1987) 'Motor vehicle occupant fatalities in four states with seat belt use laws', in *Restraint Technologies: Front Seat Occupant Protection*, Warendale, PA, Society of Automotive Engineers.

Moloney, M. (1995) 'Random Breath Testing in the State of Victoria, Australia', in Kloeden, C.N. and McLean, A.J. (eds) *Alcohol, Drugs and Traffic Safety Volume 2*, Australia, NHMRC Road Accident Research Unit, pp. 823–7.

Moore, D. (1992) *Has the Emperor No Clothes?: The NHTSA Report on Lowering the BAC Limit in California*, Washington, D.C., The American Beverage Institute.

Moskowitz, H. and Burns, M. (1990) 'Effects of alcohol on driving performance', *Alcohol, Health and Research World*, 14: 12–14.

National Highway Traffic Safety Administration (1995) *Monthly Traffic Fatality Report*, December, Washington, D.C., US Department of Transportation.

National Transportation Safety Board (1993) *Special Report to the States on Reducing the Incidence of Youth Involvement in Highway Crashes*, Washington, D.C.

Perchonok, K., Ranney, T., Baum, A., Morris, D. and Eppich, J. (1978) *Hazardous Effects of Highway Features and Roadside Objects*, Technical Report, Washington, D.C., Federal Highway Administration.

Reis, R.E. Jr (1982) *The Traffic Safety Effectiveness of Education Programs for First Offense Drunk Drivers. Final Report, Comprehensive Driving Under the Influence of Alcohol Offender Treatment Demonstration Program*, California, County of Sacramento Health Department.

Ross, H. (1991) *Administrative License Revocation for Drunk Drivers: Options and Choices in Three States*, Washington, D.C., AAA Foundation for Traffic Safety.

Ross, H. (1992a) *Confronting Drunk Driving: Social Policy for Saving Lives*, New Haven, CT: Yale University Press.

Ross, H. (1992b) 'Effectiveness of sobriety checkpoints as an impaired driving deterrent', Paper presented at the 71st Annual Meeting of the Transportation Research Board.

Sigmastat Inc. (1989) *Changes in Alcohol-Involved Fatal Crashes Associated with Tougher State Alcohol Legislation*, Washington, D.C., National Highway Traffic Safety Administration.

Simpson, H. (1995) *Who is the Persistent Drinking Driver? Part II: Canada and Elsewhere*, Transportation Research Circular, Number 437, *Strategies for Dealing with the Persistent Drinking Driver*, Washington, D.C., Transportation Research Board, National Research Council.

Simpson, H., Mayhew, D. and Bierness, D. (1995) 'The decline in drinking-driving fatalities in Canada: A decade of progress comes to an end?' in Kloeden, C.N. and McLean, A.J. (eds) *Alcohol, Drugs and Traffic Safety Volume 1*, Australia, NHMRC Road Accident Research Unit, pp. 508–12.

Skinner, D. and Hoxie, P. (1988) *Effects of Seatbelt Laws on Highway Fatalities: Update – April 1988*, Technical Report, Washington, D.C., National Highway Traffic Safety Administration.

Stewart, K., Cohen, A., Taylor, E. and Solé, C. (1995) 'Values and motivations of young drivers: Key components of impaired driving countermeasures', in Kloeden, C.N. and McLean, A.J. (eds) *Alcohol, Drugs and Traffic Safety Volume 1*, Australia, NHMRC Road Accident Research Unit, pp. 148–52.

Stewart, K. and Ellingstad, V. (1989) 'Rehabilitation countermeasures for drinking drivers', in *Surgeon General's Workshop on Drunk Driving Background Papers*, Rockville, MD, US Department of Health and Human Services, Public Health Service, Office of the Surgeon General, pp. 234–46.

Stewart, K., Epstein, L., Gruenewald, P., Laurence, S. and Roth, T. (1987) *The California First DUI Offender Evaluation Project Final Report*, Walnut Creek, CA, Pacific Institute for Research and Evaluation.

Stewart, K., Gruenewald, P. and Roth, T. (1989) *An Evaluation of Administrative Per Se Laws*, Bethesda, MD, Pacific Institute for Research and Evaluation.

Stewart, K., Voas, R. and Fell, J. (1995) 'The nature of and reasons for the decline in drinking and driving in the United States: An update', in Kloeden, C.N. and McLean, A.J. (eds) *Alcohol, Drugs and Traffic Safety Volume 1*, Australia, NHMRC Road Accident Research Unit, pp. 517–22.

Sweedler, B. (1990) 'Strategies to reduce youth drinking and driving', *Alcohol Health and Research World*, 14: 76–80.

Sweedler, B. (1991) 'The case for administrative licence revocation', Paper presented at Lifesavers 9, Charlotte, N.C., May.

Törnros, J. (1995) 'Effects of a random breath testing campaign in southern Sweden', in Kloeden, C.N. and McLean, A.J. (eds) *Alcohol, Drugs and Traffic Safety, Volume 2*, Australia, NHMRC Road Accident Research Unit, pp. 828–33.

Transportation Research Board (1994) *The Nature of and the Reasons for the Worldwide Decline in Drinking and Driving*, Transportation Research Circular Number 422, April 1994.

Transportation Research Board (1995) *Strategies for Dealing with the Persistent Drinking Driver*, Transportation Research Circular Number 437, February 1995.

Vingilis, E. and Fischer, B. (1995) 'The effect of German unification on alcohol-related traffic crashes', in Kloeden, C.N. and McLean, A.J. (eds) *Alcohol, Drugs and Traffic Safety, Volume 1*, Australia, NHMRC Road Accident Research Unit, pp. 378-85.

Voas, R., Rhodenizer, A. and Lynn, C. (1985) *Evaluation of Charlottesville Checkpoint Operations*, Technical Report, Contract No. DTNH 22 83 C 05088. Washington, D.C., National Highway Traffic Safety Administration.

Voas, R. and Tippetts, A. (1990) 'Evaluation of treatment and monitoring programmes for drunken drivers', *Journal of Traffic Medicine*, 18: 15-26.

Wells-Parker, E., Bangert-Drowns, R., McMillen, R. and Williams, M. (1995) 'Final results from a meta-analysis of remedial interventions with drink-drive offenders', *Addiction*, 90: 907-26.

Williams, A. and Lund, A. (1988) 'Mandatory seat-belt use laws and occupant crash protection in the United States', in Graham, J. (ed.) *Preventing Automobile Injury: New Findings from Evaluation Research*, Dover, MA, Auburn House, pp. 51-89.

Zador, P., Lund, A., Fields, M. and Weinberg, K. (1989) 'Fatal crash involvement and laws against alcohol-impaired driving', *Journal of Public Health Policy*, 10: 467-85.

9 Interventions to Reduce College Student Drinking and Related Health and Social Problems

Ralph Hingson, James Berson and Katie Dowley

Introduction: The Legal Drinking Age in the United States

The United States has a unique policy towards drinking by young people. In all 50 states it is illegal to sell alcohol to persons under 21 years of age. Because a very high proportion of young persons are licensed to drive, raising the drinking age to 21 has prevented numerous traffic deaths (General Accounting Office 1987). The National Highway Traffic Safety Administration (NHTSA) estimates that raising the drinking age to 21, done by all states by 1988, produced a 13% decline in traffic fatalities involving drivers 18 to 20. That translates into 700–1000 fewer teenage deaths each year – 14,816 fewer deaths since 1975 (NHTSA 1995).

Because of their inexperience in driving, young persons are at greater risk per miles driven of fatal crash involvement than older drivers (Mayhew et al. 1986). Furthermore, each alcoholic drink consumed before driving increases the fatal crash risk for younger drivers under 21 even more than for older drivers (Zador 1991).

To further reduce the alcohol-related fatal crashes among younger drivers in June 1995 President Clinton called on all states to adopt 'zero tolerance' laws, that would make it illegal for young persons to drive with any measurable blood alcohol in their body. In November 1995 the US Congress passed legislation that would withhold Federal Highway Funds from states that do not adopt zero tolerance laws. As of July 1996, 37 states have passed this legislation. An analysis comparing the first eight states to adopt zero tolerance laws with eight nearby states that did not, revealed the law was accompanied by a 20% decline in the proportion of fatal crashes among drivers under 21 that involved single vehicles at night, the type of fatal crash most likely to involve alcohol (Hingson et al. 1994). That study projected that if all states adopted the zero tolerance legislation for drivers under 21 400 fewer fatal crashes involving drivers under 21 would occur each year. In part because of the drinking age of 21 and zero tolerance laws, alcohol-related traffic fatalities among 15–20 year olds dropped from 5380 in 1982 to 2343 in 1994, a 56% reduction. The proportion of youth fatalities that were alcohol-related dropped from 63% to 38%, more than a 40% decline. This compared to a 26% decline among adult drivers from 58% to 43% (NHTSA 1995).

The legal drinking age of 21 and zero tolerance laws place unique responsibilities on US colleges and universities with regards to alcohol because many, but not all, of their students are younger than 21.

College-age Drinking and Associated Problems

Despite progress to reduce drinking by persons under age 21, drinking by college and university students remains a persistent problem. While the proportion of college students who used marijuana (cannabis) has dropped from 51% to 28% since 1980 and the proportion using other illicit drugs was decreased from 32% to 13%, the percentages who use alcohol and consume 5+ drinks per occasion have remained remarkably constant (Johnston et al. 1994). According to the 1993 *Monitoring the Future* study, 87% of college students consumed alcohol in the past year, 72% in the past month and 40% had consumed 5 or more drinks at a single occasion in the past two weeks. That is more than same-age non-college students (36%) or graduating high school seniors (28%).

Drinking by college students has been associated with numerous health and social problems, including automobile crash injury and death, suicide and depression, missed classes and decreased academic performance, loss of memory, blackouts, fighting, property damage, peer criticism and broken friendships, date rape, and unprotected sexual intercourse that places persons at risk for sexually transmitted diseases, HIV infection and unplanned pregnancy (Williams and Knox 1987).

In a national survey of a random sample of college students (Weschler 1994) 41% of students reported binge drinking in the previous two weeks, 5+ drinks at a single time for men, 4+ for women. In that study nearly half of those studied were under 21. Yet, the rate of binge drinking did not differ between students under 21 and those 21–23 years of age. As a group, binge drinkers were significantly more likely to report having hangovers, done things they regretted, missed classes, forgotten where they were or what they did, lagged behind in school work, argued with friends, had unplanned sexual activity, been hurt or injured, not used protection when having sex, damaged property and been in trouble with the police.

Further, non-bingeing students at schools with high binge levels were more likely than similar students at schools with low binge levels to experience assaults, property damage, interrupted sleep, unwanted sexual advances, serious quarrels and having to take care of a drunken student. Binge drinking by college students not only poses health risks to the drinking students, their alcohol consumption also imposes health and social problems on other students.

There is clearly a need for public health officials and college and university administrators to learn more about how to reduce drinking and related health and social problems on college campuses. This chapter will review available literature on interventions to reduce college-age drinking and related social and health problems, offer suggestions for additional research into the topic, and recommend potential interventions to address the problem.

Individually Oriented Prevention Programmes

The authors located 24 experimental or quasi-intervention studies that had targeted individual knowledge, attitude and drinking changes. Ten studies identified 14 interventions that produced significant reductions in drinking or drinking problems. This is elaborated in Table 9.1 overleaf.

It should be noted that of the 14 interventions that reduced drinking or related problems, four had cognitive education components, but only the cognitive behavioural skills training module produced replicated reductions.

The studies that produced these conclusions varied widely in their methodological rigour. Six of the studies used a random assignment procedure: Rozelle (1980), Garvin et al. (1990) (assignment of groups), Kivlahan et al. (1990), Baer et al. (1992) and Darkes and Goldman (1993). All but one of the studies used self-administered questionnaires preventing interviewer biases. However, some had methodological flaws so serious as to render their conclusions speculative at best. For example, two studies of educational interventions did not have comparison or control groups (Caleekal-John and Pletsch 1984, McLaran 1985).

Moreover, only one of the studies used objective non-self-report

Table 9.1: Individually oriented prevented interventions found to reduce college drinking

Intervention	Study Author
Behavioural Self Management	Garvin et al. 1990
Self Monitoring of Drinking Behaviour	Garvin et al. 1990
6 Week Cognitive Behavioural Skills Training	Baer et al. 1992
Single Session of Individualised Feedback and Professional Advice	Baer et al. 1992
Cognitive Behavioural Skills Training	Kivlahan et al. 1990
Didactic Alcohol Information Programme	Kivlahan et al. 1990
Content Oriented Alcohol Education	Rozelle 1980
Experiential Peer Facilitated Approach	Rozelle 1980
2 Week Alcohol Education Module Focused on Medical Effects of Alcohol Abuse	Caleekal-John and Pletsch 1984
One Credit Course on Lifestyle	McLaran and Sarris 1985
Cognitive Information and Affective Instruction and Selected Field Experiences	Dennison 1977
Psychosocial Aspects of Alcoholism Class Combined with Contracted Abstinence	Blum et al. 1980
Semester Long Lecture Drug Education Course	Bailey 1990
Drinking Expectancy Challenge Intervention	Darkes and Goldman 1993

measures such as motor vehicle crashes or attendance records or grade point average. Further, none of the studies randomly selected students. Students were either recruited, or were enrolled in particular classes. This can pose bias to the internal validity because of the motivational level of the subjects and it limits generalisability of the results.

Table 9.2: Behavioural interventions not found to reduce college drinking

Intervention	Study Author
Alcohol Awareness Courses	Meacci 1990
Assertiveness Training	Williams et al. 1983
Designated Driver Programmes	Shore et al. 1991
Direct Mail Campaigns	McCarty et al. 1983
15 Week Physical Activity Programme	Engs and Mulhall 1981
Cognitive Information and Selected Field Activities	Dennison 1977
5 Week Psycho-educational Module on Substance Abuse	Robinson et al. 1993
Teaching Specific Guidelines for Alcohol Consumption	Jackson et al. 1989
Peer Counsellor Alcohol Awareness Programme Developed by Staff and Students	Engs 1977
Peer Directed Alcohol Awareness Programme	Schall et al. 1991
Implicit Instruction	
Explicit Instruction	Robinson 1981
Values Clarification	
Substance Abuse Workshops to Develop Assertiveness Skills, Self Awareness, Resistance Refusal Skills, Stress Reduction	Ametrano 1992
4 Hour Module Using Peer Leaders Audio Visuals, Values Clarification	Gonzalez 1982
Controlled Alcohol Use Programme Based on the Health Belief Model	Portnoy 1980

In contrast to the ten studies of individually oriented interventions that found significant post-programme alcohol use reductions, 14 other studies reported on 16 different approaches that did not reduce drinking (Table 9.2 above). Of note, two separate studies found peer counsellor programmes ineffective and one cognitive information and selected field activities produced a conflicting negative result compared to a study using a similar approach that found reductions in consumption.

These studies did not appear to be methodologically more rigorous than the studies which identified significant reductions. For example, none of these 14 studies used random allocation to groups and one, Shore et al. (1991), had no comparison group.

It should be noted that six other studies – Sawyer (1978), Eckert (1980), McKillip et al. (1985), Gay et al. (1990), Gonzalez (1990a), Grossman et al. (1994) – did not measure the effects of their interventions on behaviour, but rather on knowledge, attitudes and perceived levels of risk. Two other studies, by Chen et al. (1982) and Chen and Dosch (1987), compared participants in voluntary educational programmes to persons not motivated to participate. Predictably, participants drank less than non-participants.

Treatment Studies

Several studies described treatments for college students with alcohol problems but did not assess their impact. Only three treatment studies were identified that assessed treatment effects. Results were mixed: Guydish and Greenfield (1990) randomly assigned 56 heavily drinking volunteer fraternity men to one of three intensities of a self-control training intervention minimally involving self-monitoring of drinking with some participants also involved in guided reading or training experiences. No differences in outcomes between the three treatments were observed. Flynn and Brown (1991) studied the effectiveness of a seven-hour classroom experience required for university students involved in conduct violations while using alcohol (focus on driving while intoxicated). Three months following completion, alcohol-related problems, quantity consumed, and frequency of consumption were all reduced among seven students who were followed. Initially 31 students were in the experimental group and a control was selected matching for gender, age and residence type. The very large loss to follow up renders the findings of this study suggestive at best. O'Connell and Beck (1984) described an 8-session programme for violators of campus no-alcohol policy, which included self-reports on drinking history and the nature of their violation, lectures on the effects of alcohol, emotions, filling out drink log forms and reasons for drinking, stress management and developing a plan to avoid future alcohol use. Twenty-two of 36 students enrolled were followed. Of these 41% reported a reduction in alcohol use. However, no comparison group was included in the design.

At this point a large literature on alcoholism/alcohol problems treatment clearly indicates that it reduces drinking particularly if those with drinking problems voluntarily enrol in treatment (Institute of Medicine 1990a). However, despite high levels of heavy drinking, less than 1% of college students or binge drinkers believe they have drinking problems or have ever sought help for those problems (Weschler 1994). Currently, there is no evidence that treatment programmes uniquely tailored to college populations are more effective than conventional treatment programmes. Even if they were highly effective, if less than 1% of college students have contact with treatment then the effect of treatment on the overall college drinking problem can only be small. (Clinical issues are considered further in Chapter 13, this volume.)

Efforts are needed to explore ways to help problem drinking college students recognise their problems and seek help to reduce these problems.

Environmental Interventions to Reduce College-age Drinking

Drinking-age Changes
Ten studies were identified that explored the effects of raising the legal drinking age. Five of those studies identified reductions in drinking or related problems: Engs and Hanson (1986, 1988), Davis and Reynolds (1990) and Gonzalez (1991). Four studies found no decline in problems: Hughes and Dodder (1986), Kraft (1988), Williams et al. (1990) and Gonzalez (1990b) and one study found declines in drinking in the targeted age group but did not attribute them to the drinking-age change: Perkins and Berkowitz (1989). Among the 10 studies of legal drinking-age increases, four of the seven that explored consumption reported declines either in the proportion of students who drank or in their frequency/quantity of consumption. All three that explored driving after drinking reported post-law declines, and in contrast two reported post-law increases in violence while only one reported a post-law decrease.

Findings from the college literature are only partially consistent with general population studies which look at all persons targeted by the law, not just college students. The National Highway Traffic

Safety Administration (1991) estimates that on average, raising the Minimum Legal Drinking Age (MLDA) to 21, done by all the states by 1988, produced a 13% decline in traffic fatalities involving 18–20-year-old drivers and that since 1975 14,816 teenage traffic deaths have been prevented. An evaluation using the National High School Senior Survey (O'Malley and Wagenaar 1991) found that an MLDA of 21 not only reduced consumption for persons under 21, it reduced subsequent consumption for persons aged 20–25 who grew up in states where 21 was the MLDA, as compared with those who were teenagers in other states. A comparison of nine states that raised the MLDA to nine states that did not (Williams et al. 1983) found that increased MLDA decreased night-time fatal crash involvement of youth in eight of the nine states.

Several factors, however, reduce the ability to draw as strong conclusions about the benefits of increased MLDA in the college population as in the overall group of drivers under 21. First, none of the college-age studies looked at traffic fatalities as an outcome. Second, none of the college-age studies used both comparison groups and pre- and post-law designs. Third, none of the college studies (with the possible exception of Kraft) evaluated enforcement and education about the law. Fourth, all of the drinking-age studies with college students relied exclusively on self-report outcome data. (None used other measures, such as attendance records, disciplinary records, grade point average, arrest records, and so on.) Finally, sample sizes in most of the drinking-age studies were rather small, and often response rates and comparisons of participants to non-participants were not provided.

Nonetheless, a majority of studies on college students indicate that raising the drinking age was associated with declines in drinking and driving after drinking. These are benefits which are consistent with the larger body of literature on the topic. However, a minority of these studies found post-law increases in violence, non-motor vehicle injury and other problems. This is not consistent with research on general populations of youth.

Research on Other Environmental Approaches to Reduce College-age Drinking

Low alcohol beer
Geller et al. (1991) compared serving low alcohol beer at one party to serving regular alcohol level beer. At the first party 64 males and 43 females received standard 7% alcohol while 70 males and 48 females received low alcohol beer. At a third party 53 males and 41 females

were randomly assigned to receive regular and low alcohol content beer. In both situations those receiving low alcohol beer did not drink more than those receiving regular beer. Consequently the blood alcohol content (BAC) of low alcohol beer drinkers was lower than the standard alcohol drinkers at exit from the party. Subjects in the regular alcohol had mean BACs of 0.06 while low alcohol beer drinkers had exit BACs of 0.045. Thus, on campuses that allow beer to be served, allowing only low alcohol beer to be served would probably result in some reduction in drunkenness and related untoward events.

Alcohol ban at a college stadium

Spaite et al. (1990) examined the impact of banning alcohol at the University of Arizona stadium with a seating capacity of 58,000 persons. The authors reviewed four years of medical incident reports on injuries and illnesses for two years preceding and two following the ban. Of the 13 illnesses and injuries measured, only heat-related illness declined significantly after the ban; extremity strains and fractures actually increased from 8 to 20.

The study did not specifically look at alcohol involvement in illnesses and there was no comparison stadium, nor was information collected that was specific to college students.

Residence hall tavern

Mills et al. (1983) studied the installation of an experimental university residence hall tavern to increase resident participation in alcohol abuse prevention activities. Upperclass students enrolled in a course in alcohol abuse prevention activities. Baseline and follow-up self-report surveys were conducted with 425 students in the programme and 404 in the comparison group. The baseline was completed by 471 students, the follow-up by 361 and 161 completed both. Posters and educational sessions at the bar were also conducted. Programme intervention focused on high-risk parties and drinking and driving after parties.

After the programme service area respondents were more likely than controls to report disapproval of heavy drinking and more likely to expect moderate consumption before driving. Changes were not found in levels of alcohol use, frequency of alcohol-related problems, noise, property damage or concern with alcohol use.

Multi-component university-based programmes

Conyne (1984) described a comprehensive programme at the University of Cincinnati that included: environmental policies (1) prohibiting drinking by persons under 19 according to the Ohio law, and (2) requiring equal availability of beer and non-alcoholic beverages, formation of a campus BACCHUS organisation, and a multi-media campaign on responsible drinking, single sessions. Four two-hour group-designed sessions on knowledge about alcohol as a substance, awareness of responsible and irresponsible alcohol and promoting constructive house-drinking norms among fraternity members were evaluated. Comparison groups were not analysed. Little impact on drinking among fraternity groups was detected as a result of the project.

Kraft (1988) reported on a comprehensive Alcohol Demonstration from 1975 to 1980 at the University of Massachusetts. At a cost of $90-130,000 per year, eight full-time staff targeted interventions to a campus of 22,000 students. Extensive dissemination of student-produced posters (4300/year) and pamphlets was coupled with 23 hours of university radio station programming per year. Intensive individual education programmes were offered to 5-10% of students, student leaders, staff, faculty and administration regarding campus alcohol policies. Public transportation schedules were continued at late hours to prevent alcohol-related traffic injuries. The campus pub was required to make non-alcoholic beverages equally available and all party sponsors were required to attend educational sessions prior to giving parties. Credit courses about alcohol use and abuse were also offered. Student-run colloquia and staff training were undertaken. Annual student self-administered surveys (response rate 61%) revealed alcohol use increased over the five project years. Alcohol-related visits to the student health centre remained unchanged, as did alcohol-related arrests. Sales of alcohol at the campus pub also remained unchanged.

It should be noted that this was a time when drinking and alcohol-related traffic deaths were increasing nation-wide and state-wide in Massachusetts. No comparison area or university was studied.

Research on other Environmental Interventions in the General Population

Several studies of general populations (not just college students) have found positive effects from environmental interventions in reducing drinking and related health problems among youth, such as traffic crashes. A number of these are reviewed elsewhere in this book, so only brief reference is made to these in this chapter.

Taxes

Between 1975 and 1990 the real prices declined for distilled spirits by 32%, wine by 28% and beer by 20%. Chaloupka (1993) has recently summarised the work of Cook (1981) and Saffer and Grossman (1987a, 1987b), which consistently found that alcohol tax increases can reduce alcohol-related traffic fatalities. Grossman and colleagues (1991) examined motor vehicle fatalities using a time series of annual state cross-sections covering the 48 contiguous states from 1982 to 1988. Three different fatality rates were examined, both for the overall population and for young people aged 18–20. The effect of the recent 1991 tax increase on alcohol was simulated. They reported that had the 32¢ per six-pack tax been present throughout the period, an estimated 1744 fewer people might have died each year and 671 of those each year would have been 18–20 year olds. They further estimated that if beer tax had been set at 81¢ per six-pack from 1982 to 1988 (based on a tax of 25¢ per ounce of pure alcohol) an estimated 7142 fewer people of all ages would have been killed annually, 2187 of whom would be youth and young adults, a considerably greater life saving in the 18–20-year-old age group than has been attributed to the minimum legal drinking age of 21. (See Chapter 3, this volume, for further discussion of economic issues.)

Server Intervention

(This theme is considered in detail in Chapters 5 and 12 of this volume.) The largest single point of departure of alcohol impaired drivers in the US is bars and restaurants (McKnight and Streff 1993). Between one-third and one-half of intoxicated drivers consumed their last alcohol at these locations based on drivers given alcohol tests in roadside surveys (Palmer 1988, Foss et al. 1990) and drivers injured in automobile crashes (Santana and Martinez 1992). Breath tests given to patrons leaving bars have revealed that approximately one-third have blood alcohol levels (BALs) above the legal limit (Werch et al. 1988, Stockwell et al. 1992). Yet servers rarely refuse drinks to intoxicated patrons. McKnight (1991) reported that in more than 1000 visits to 238 drinking establishments in eight states research personnel simulating obvious signs of intoxication were refused a drink only 5% of the time.

Curfews for Young Drivers

Driving under the influence of alcohol has been reviewed in detail in the previous chapter. The following section considers evidence specifically related to college students. One-third of young people in the United States grow up in jurisdictions where there are night-time driving curfews for youth. McKnight and colleagues (1990) reported no declines in night-time fatal crashes after Maryland imposed a provisional licensing law for young drivers that included night curfews. However, Preusser and colleagues (1990) reported that such curfews in Detroit, Cleveland and Columbus produced a 23% reduction in motor vehicle injuries in the targeted age groups during curfew hours, underscoring the potential of this approach.

Lower Legal Blood Alcohol Limits

Four types of studies have identified impairment on a variety of physiological responses that in turn impair driver performance at blood alcohol concentration below the 0.10% legal standard in most states.

First, experimental laboratory studies have shown that at 0.08%, a level reached by a 150 pound person consuming four drinks in an hour on an empty stomach, there is:

- reduced peripheral vision;
- poorer recovery from glare;
- poor performance in complex visual tracking;
- reduced divided attention performance. (Moskowitz and Burns 1990)

Second, driver simulation and road course studies have revealed poorer parking performance, driver performance at slow speeds and steering inaccuracy (Mortimer and Sturgis 1975). Third, roadside observational studies have identified increased speeding and breaking performance deterioration (Damkot et al. 1975). Fourth, Zador (1991) obtained breath alcohol samples from 2850 drivers stopped in a national probability sample survey of 34 localities in 1986 – 92% of the drivers stopped provided samples. Their breath-test results were compared to the blood-test results of drivers killed in single vehicle traffic crashes in 1986 in the US Department of Transportation's Fatal Accident Reporting System. Data were taken only from 29 states that test at least 80% of fatally injured drivers. To match driver fatalities to the roadside breath-testing exposure, crash times, days and roadway types were restricted to those used in the survey. They found that each 0.02% increase in BAC limit of a driver nearly doubles the risk of being in a single-vehicle fatal crash. For each 0.02% increase in BAC the fatal-crash risk rises even more for younger drivers and for female drivers, a finding also reported by Mayhew et al. (1986). For drivers under 21, impairment begins with the first drink.

Effects of Lowering Blood Alcohol Limits

Lower BALs for Minors

Thirty-seven states and the District of Columbia have set lower legal blood alcohol limits for young drivers under the age of 21 than for adults. An analysis of the first 12 states to lower legal blood alcohol limits for youth revealed that during the post-law period the proportion of fatal crashes that involved single vehicles at night declined 16% among young drivers targeted by those laws, while it rose 1% among drivers in nearby comparison states. Lowering BALs to 0.00% or 0.02% (zero tolerance laws) produced a 20% greater decline than in comparison states, but no significant reduction occurred in states that lowered to 0.04–0.06% relative to comparison states. Based on the magnitude of results observed one can estimate that if all states adopted 0.00% or 0.02% BAL limits for drivers aged 15–20, at least 400 single-vehicle night-time fatal crashes involving teenage drivers would be prevented each year (Hingson et al. 1994).

The effects of lower BAL limits for youth can be enhanced by educational programmes to inform young drivers about the laws. Blomberg (1992) examined the impact of intensive education to inform drivers under 21 in Maryland of a new 0.02% legal limit targeting their age group. Four counties on the eastern shore of Maryland and four in western Maryland received an informational programme on the new law including TV and radio public service announcements (PSAs) and brochures and posters for local distribution. The proportion of teenage drivers surveyed before and after the educational campaign who knew it was illegal to drive with a BAL of 0.02% or higher jumped from 41% to 71% in the experimental counties but remained at 47% throughout in the comparison counties. The proportion of crash-involved drivers who had been drinking declined 44% in the experimental counties relative to 30% in the comparison counties, St Mary's and Charles.

0.08% Limits for Adult Drivers

In the US 13 states have lowered the legal blood alcohol limits from 0.10% to 0.08%, while the limit is 0.08% in the UK and Canada. Australia, New Zealand and many European nations have adopted 0.05% as the legal standard. Evidence is beginning to emerge in the US that lowering BAL among adults from 0.10% to 0.08% will also have some beneficial effect.

Untested Environmental Intervention at the Community Level

As described in Chapter 4, this volume, Wittman (1993) has identified several other environmental interventions that several communities are currently implementing that can plausibly reduce drinking and drink-driving but for which a body of scientific empirical data has not been collected. These include: alcohol-free public events; local public ordinance, such as beer keg regulation; local general ordinances that allow localities to manage drinking in public places or events and to use nuisance abatement procedures against owners of private property who permit alcohol and other drug (AOD) use/sales on their property in ways that violate civil and criminal laws; and informal voluntary agreements – informal agreements to resolve differences between parties directly involved in an alcohol or other drug availability problem.

Comprehensive Community Interventions

An approach to reduce alcohol and other drug-related problems widely used in the general population is comprehensive community interventions. The National Academy of Sciences has recommended multi-strategy community interventions to reduce alcohol-related health problems, citing their long-term success with other public health problems (Institute of Medicine 1989). Two of three major community interventions in the cardiovascular risk-reduction area have identified significantly greater improvements in the programme communities in reduced fatalities, blood pressure, cholesterol, smoking and mortality. However, examination of blood cholesterol levels, smoking prevalence, blood pressure, body mass index, regular physical activity and overall coronary heart disease risk, revealed improvements in the desired direction in both Minnesota Heart Health programme. intervention and comparison communities.

Two studies of comprehensive community interventions to reduce alcohol consumption or alcohol-related problems have yielded positive results: Pentz et al. (1989) studied the Midwestern Prevention Project in Kansas City to reduce cigarette, alcohol and marijuana use in adolescents. The project included mass media programming, a school-based educational programme for youth, parent education and organisation, community organisation and other health policy changes over a six-year period. Adolescents aged 10–14 were the target of the intervention. When students in 24 programme schools were compared at one year follow-up to students in 18 delayed intervention schools, prevalence of use of all three drugs was lower in the intervention schools: 17% versus 24% for cigarette use; 11% versus 16% for alcohol use, and 7% versus 16% for marijuana use. This reflects a decline in drug use onset in the programme schools.

In six Massachusetts cities, community taskforces of private citizens and public officials from multiple city departments organised school-based and public education about alcohol-impaired driving and safety belts, publicity about police enforcement, alcohol-server training programmes, beer keg registration, liquor outlet surveillance, speedwatch telephone hot-lines and pedestrian safety initiatives. Education programmes on college campuses were conducted including mock trials and crashes and educating college students about community police enforcement and liquor outlet surveillance. During the five programme years, compared to the previous five, fatal crashes declined from 178 to 120 in programme cities, a statistically significant 25% reduction relative to the rest of Massachusetts. Fatal crashes involving alcohol had a 42% relative decline from 69 to 36 in programme cities. The greatest declines in fatal crashes were among drivers aged 15–25. Fatal crashes in that age group dropped from 98 to 45, a 39% drop relative to the rest of Massachusetts. Visible traffic injuries/100 crashes had a relative 6% decline from 21.5 to 16.6. In programme cities, self-reported driving after drinking declined from 19% per month to 9% among teenage drivers, and from 36% to 14% among college students in programme cities while there was no change in driving after drinking among young drivers and college students in the rest of Massachusetts (Hingson et al. 1996).

Over 2000 community substance-abuse prevention programmes that include a public–private partnership and community coalition have been identified nation-wide (Rosenbloom et al. 1993).

Discussion

Inadequacies of Interventions and Research

The literature on interventions to reduce college-age drinking indicates that both interventions aimed to change individual beliefs, knowledge, attitudes and behaviours as well as environmental changes, such as increases in the minimum alcohol purchase age and alcohol content levels of beer, can reduce drinking. However, no intervention examined in more than one study produced reductions in college student drinking in every study that explored the intervention.

Several improvements are needed to upgrade the quality of research on this topic.

1 Almost all the studies on this topic rely exclusively on self-report (usually self-administered questionnaires). Rarely are other data included, such as observational data or university or other records on academic performance, attendance, arrests, traffic crashes or other encounters with the police.

2 The majority of studies on individually targeted interventions use convenience samples that are unlikely to be representative of the college population.

3 Random assignment to different interventions was conducted in only a minority of studies.

4 Most studies did not include process measures that assess the implementation of interventions.

5 Virtually none of the studies of environmental interventions such as drinking-age changes used comparison areas and hence are not able to control for secular trends in use.

6 Assessment of the means by which college students obtain alcohol was not explored. None of the studies explored provision of alcohol to minors, even though a considerable amount of college-age drinking occurs in settings that include both underage individuals and persons above the age of 21.

7 None of the studies explored drinking practices and consequences in minority populations.

Although some of the individually oriented interventions have been rigorously studied and found to yield reductions in drinking and related problems, their feasibility on a broad scale is not clear. The expense of widespread application may be prohibitive and has not been calculated.

Environmental interventions probably have the greatest potential to reduce drinking at the lowest cost. However, research on environmental interventions with college students has been very narrow, focusing primarily on legal drinking-age studies. A host of alternative interventions have not been considered, such as increased taxes on alcohol, changes in hours and location of outlets; licensing actions on outlets for sales to minors; dram shop and social host liability; or changes in drinking and driving laws, such as use-lose laws, changes in legal blood alcohol limits, provisional licensing for young drivers, night curfews or efforts to close loopholes in drinking-age laws through penalties for use of false-age ID, possession of alcohol, and attempting to purchase. As we have noted, most of these interventions have been found to reduce drinking or related problems in general populations.

With the exception of the Kraft study (1988), the use of community organising bringing students, faculty, staff and members of different departments (for example, police, health, athletics, fraternities, sororities and other student groups) together on campus to formulate environmental policies and programmes, was not pursued. Further, none of the studies involved collaboration between college or university administration, students, staff, faculty and non-university community officials and private citizens in the surrounding communities. None of the educational interventions focused on providing students with information on existing community ordinances or state laws or community law enforcement efforts, even though research on general youth populations indicates such educational efforts can reduce harm associated with alcohol (Blomberg 1992).

Proposed Intervention

The use of multi-target, multi-strategy community-generated interventions that develop co-operation between city government and universities to reduce college student drinking has not been tested. Nonetheless, the preponderance of data on comprehensive community interventions suggests that such an approach including individual preventive education, could reduce college-age drinking and related problems.

The following steps should be taken in developing such initiatives:

(1) *Develop a community/university task force* comprised of officials from:

(a) various city departments: health, education, police, parks and recreation, alcohol and restaurant licensing boards;
(b) concerned private organisations and citizens, local TV, radio and newspapers;
(c) a cross-section of university students, staff, faculty, fraternity, sorority, and student government officials as well as members of student papers, radio, TV, members of various school departments (for example, athletics, healthy police).

It is important that university officials and city officials as well as students be involved in the development of plans to identify problems associated with college drinking and to reduce college-age drinking and its consequences. Often alcohol use restrictions by universities shift drinking from college campuses into the community. On the other hand, city officials are often concerned that campus officials shield students on campus from local law enforcement. Students need to be involved in policy formation so that they will not dismiss educational messages and regulation as paternalistic interventions.

Examination of university alcohol policies should not only consider students but should recognise heavy drinking by alumni, staff and faculty can cause problems as well. Students will be more likely to participate if they are not singled out as the sole source of alcohol problems.

(2) *Undertake an assessment of college drinking on their campus and in their community.* This can be used as:

(a) a needs assessment;
(b) a benchmark against which to measure subsequent progress; and
(c) as a report to stimulate community and college concern about the problem.

A survey of college students about their personal drinking, smoking, drug use and related health and social problems accompanying their drinking, and that they have experienced because of drinking among their peers, should be included in the baseline assessment.

However, the evaluation should go well beyond mere survey data collection. Community and university alcohol use and problem indicator data should be collected. This should include:

- trends in fatal and injury crashes involving college-age drivers;
- hospital and student health service admissions for alcohol-related diagnoses (for example, assaults, unintentional injuries, suicide attempts, sexually transmitted diseases);
- number of alcohol outlets;
- alcohol sales;
- alcohol-related police arrests involving students;
- complaints to police about alcohol-related disorderly conduct;
- college records of alcohol-related disciplinary action;
- attendance and academic records where available; and
- surveys of alcohol purchase attempts by underage college students within each community should be undertaken.

Within each community and college/university an inventory of current policies and programmes to address substance use should be examined, as should key state laws regarding sales to minors, purchase, sales, possession of alcohol, consumption of alcohol, provision to minors, possession and attempted use of false identification, DWI laws, and so on. A review of resources and facilities for recreation opportunities in the absence of alcohol should be monitored. In short, the review should identify not only risks but also potential resources to address the problem.

(3) *Develop strategies to reduce alcohol use and related problems within the community and on the campuses.* In developing the strategies the taskforces should provide a rationale for the selection of that strategy based on existing demonstrated effects in other locations or an assessment of its plausibility within that particular setting. Strategies can include:

- education about adverse health and social consequences of alcohol;
- resistance skills training and some of the individually oriented behavioural techniques that have shown promise in the literature;

- education about city ordinances, campus regulations and state laws regarding alcohol use, drink-driving, and so on;
- counselling or treatment programmes;
- reviewing policies regarding university admission and disciplinary actions and making changes as needed;
- reviewing other city or university policies and efforts to enforce those policies.

Potential policies could include:

- taxes on alcohol with revenue earmarked for education and treatment;
- zoning to reduce outlet density;
- licensing requirements for server training;
- beer keg registration;
- reviews of alcohol advertising in university publications;
- alcohol-free dormitories and sporting events;
- changes in laws regarding serving or providing alcohol to minors, possession of fake-age identification, attempted alcohol purchase (closing loopholes in age 21 drinking laws);
- strengthened drink-driving laws, and so on.

University policies, city ordinances, and state laws should all be considered. In developing strategies, community hearings or policy panels that collect information from diverse community groups and prepare reports with specific recommendations should be encouraged. A particularly important issue that university and city officials will need to address is enforcement of laws pertaining to alcohol use, violence, traffic violations, and so on, and whether city police should engage in active enforcement on campus.

(4) *Review alcohol problem diagnostic procedures of clinicians in their universities and communities, and offer brief intervention referral, treatment and aftercare services for persons with problems posed by alcohol should be expanded as needed.* Training of professionals and required sections on alcohol problems in clinical records should be considered. Employee assistance programmes that hold loss of job as a consequence of failure to receive treatment or reduce problematic drinking have been shown to markedly reduce drinking and alcohol problems (Walsh et al. 1991). Similar models with continued university enrolment as an incentive could be applied on campuses. As noted earlier, while undoubtedly many students engage in problem drinking behaviours, few perceive their own drinking to be problem-

atic. Development and implementation of problem identification procedures and instruments as well as treatment and referral options should be a focus of campus activities.

(5) *Develop a plan to evaluate the proposed intervention,* including:

- a process evaluation of what was implemented, by whom, who was contacted, in what setting, with what message or strategy;
- an impact evaluation of the programme's effects on knowledge, attitudes and drinking behaviour; and also
- an outcome monitoring of trends in many of the community indicators collected at baseline.

Including objective indicators like single-vehicle night-time fatal and injury traffic crashes will enhance the credibility of the evaluation. Repeating surveys and monitoring of official indicators on an annual or otherwise specified periodic basis will be important.

In the development of the evaluation plan it is imperative that data be collected from comparison areas, preferably communities with similar colleges or universities, population size and demographic characteristics. Failure to have comparison areas is the most serious shortcoming of previous studies of environmental drinking interventions in college populations. If comparison communities are selected within the same state, that will permit the evaluators to control for differences in state laws concerning alcohol, drinking and driving, as well as economic and other state-level policies that may influence drinking.

It is important that plans be developed for an evaluator to be involved as early as possible in the planning process. Each community should complete annual reports documenting programme organisation, planning strategies, implementation and outcomes and action plans to further reduce college-age alcohol use/problems in future years.

(6) *At the very beginning of the programme develop plans to institutionalise the programme.* Annual reports to the university/community from the taskforce, a permanent line of funding at the university or in a City Hall department, plans for transfer of programme initiatives to city departments and university departments, would be helpful, as would development of plans to raise needed resources for post-programme operations (for example, membership drives and grant applications to other sources). It might also be important to

consider at the outset developing a college interest-group programme to further control college drinking over time.

The type of comprehensive community/university intervention discussed above to reduce college student drinking has never been tried before. Previous efforts to reduce college-age drinking have focused within the university community or involved environmental policies in jurisdictions that happened to have universities within their borders (for example, state-level legal drinking-age changes).

The type of comprehensive, multi-target intervention we are recommending has shown sufficient effects in cardiovascular risk reduction and preventing some alcohol problems to warrant a test evaluation as an effort to reduce college drinking and the harm that results from it.

Acknowledgement

This chapter is based on a review that was funded by a grant from the Robert Wood Johnson Foundation.

References

Ametrano, I.M. (1992) 'An evaluation of the effectiveness of a substance abuse prevention program', *Journal of College Student Development*, 33: 507–15.

Baer, J., Marlatt, A., Kivlahan, D., Fromme, K., Larimer, M. and Williams, E. (1992) 'An experimental test of three methods of alcohol risk reduction with young adults', *Journal of Clinical and Consulting Psychology*, 60: 974–9.

Bailey, W.J. (1990) 'Affecting alcohol and other drug use via large lecture drug education course: The Indiana University experience', *The Eta Sigma Gamman*, 22: 23–6.

Blackburn, H. (1984) 'The Minnesota Heart Health Program: A Research and Demonstration Project in Cardiovascular Disease Prevention', in Matarazo, J.D., Miller, N.E., Weiss, S.M. and Herd, J.A. (eds) *Behavioral Health: A Handbook of Health Enhancement and Disease Prevention*, Silver Spring, MD, Wiley.

Blomberg, R. (1992) *Lower BAC Limits for Youth: Evaluation of the Maryland 0.02% Law*, DOT HS, pp. 807–60.

Blum, S.B., Rivers, P.C., Horvat, J. and Bellows, D. (1980) 'The effect of contracted abstinence on college students' behavior toward alcohol use', *Journal of Alcohol and Drug Education*, 25: 70–8.

Caleekal-John, A. and Pletsch, D. (1984) 'An interdisciplinary approach to alcohol education in the university curriculum', *Journal of Alcohol and Drug Education*, 30: 50–60.

Chaloupka, F. (1993) 'Effects of price on alcohol-related problems', *Alcohol, Health and Research World*, 17: 46–54.

Chen, W. and Dosch, M. (1987) 'Comparison of drinking attitudes and behaviors between participating and non-participating students in a voluntary alcohol education program', *Journal of Alcohol and Drug Education*, 32: 7–13.

Chen, W., Dosch, M. and Cychosz, C. (1982) 'The impact of a voluntary educational program – Tip it Lightly, Alcohol Awareness Week – On the drinking attitudes and behaviors of college students', *Journal of Drug Education*, 12: 125–35.

Conyne, R.K. (1984) 'Primary prevention through a campus alcohol education project', *The Personnel and Guidance Journal*, May, pp. 524–8.

Cook, P.J. (1981) 'The effect of liquor taxes on drinking, cirrhosis and auto accidents', in Moore, M.H. and Gerstein, D.R. (eds) *Alcohol and Public Policy: Beyond the Shadow of Prohibition*, Washington, D.C., National Academy of Sciences, pp. 225–85.

Damkot, D.K., Perrine, M.W., Whitmore, D.G., Todissie, S.R. and Geller, H.A. (1975) *On the Road: Driving Behavior and Breath Alcohol Concentration*, Vols. I and II (Technical Report), DOT HS 364 37567.

Darkes, J. and Goldman, M. (1993) 'Expectancy challenge and drinking reduction experimental evidence for a mediational process', *Journal of Clinical and Consulting Psychology*, 61: 344–53.

Davis, J.E. and Reynolds, N.C. (1990) 'Alcohol use among college students: Responses to raising the purchase age', *Journal of American College Health*, 38: 263–9.

Dennison, D. (1977) 'The effects of selected field experiences upon the drinking behavior of university students', *Journal of School Health*, pp. 38–41.

Dennison, D., Prevet, T. and Affleck, M. (1977) 'Does alcohol instruction affect student drinking behavior?' *Health Education*, November/December, pp. 28–30.

Eckert, P.S. (1980) 'Bottoms up: An alcohol abuse prevention model for college campuses', *Health Values*, 4: 222–8.

Engs, R. (1977) 'Let's look before we leap: The cognitive and behavioral evaluation of a university alcohol education program', *Journal of Alcohol and Drug Education*, 22: 39–45.

Engs, R.G. and Hanson, D.J. (1986) 'Age-specific alcohol prohibition and college students' drinking problems', *Psychological Reports*, 59: 979–84.

Engs, R.G. and Hanson, D.J. (1988) 'University students' drinking patterns and problems: Examining the effects of raising the purchase age', *Public Health Reports*, 103: 667–73.

Engs, R. and Mulhall, P. (1981) 'Again – let's look before we leap: The effects on physical activity on smoking and drinking patterns', *Journal of Alcohol and Drug Education*, 26: 65–74.

Flynn, C. and Brown, W. (1991) 'The effects of a mandatory alcohol education program on college student problem drinkers', *Journal of Alcohol and Drug Education*, 37: 15–24.

Foss, R.D., Voas, R.B., Bierness, D.J. and Wolfe, A.C. (1990) *Minnesota 1990 Statewide Drinking and Driving Roadside Survey*, Contract No. 525493, St Paul, Minnesota, Office of Traffic Safety, Minnesota Dept. of Public Safety.

Garvin, R.B., Alcorn, J.D. and Faulkner, K.K. (1990) 'Behavioral strategies for alcohol abuse prevention with high risk college males', *Journal of Alcohol and Drug Education*, 36: 23–34.

Gay, J., Minelli, M., Tripp, D. and Keilitz, D. (1990) 'Alcohol and the athlete: A university's response', *Journal of Alcohol and Drug Education*, 35: 81–6.

Geller, E.S., Kalsher, M.J. and Clarke, S.W. (1991) 'Beer versus mixed-drink consumption at fraternity parties: A time and place for low-alcohol alternatives', *Journal of Studies on Alcohol*, 52: 197–203.

General Accounting Office (1987) *Drinking Age Laws: An Evaluation Synthesis of Their Impact on Highway Safety*, GAO/PEMD, 87-100, March.

Gliksman, L. and Single, E. (1988) 'A field evaluation of a server intervention program: Accommodating reality', Paper presented at the Canadian Evaluation Society Meeting, Montreal, Canada, May.

Gonzalez, G. (1982) 'Alcohol education can prevent alcohol problems: A summary of some unique research findings', *Journal of Alcohol and Drug Education*, 27: 2–12.

Gonzalez, G. (1990a) 'Effects of a theory-based peer-focused drug education course', *Journal of Counseling and Development*, 68: 446–9.

Gonzalez, G. (1990b) 'Effects of raising the drinking age and related campus initiatives on student alcohol consumption and alcohol-related problems', *Journal of College Student Development*, 31: 181–3.

Gonzalez, G. (1990c) 'Effects of drinking age on reduced consumption of alcohol reported by college students: 1981–1986', *Journal of Drug Issues*, 20: 67–73.

Gonzalez, G. (1991) 'Five-year changes in alcohol knowledge, consumption and problems among students exposed to a campus-wide alcohol awareness program and a rise in the legal drinking age', *Journal of Alcohol and Drug Education*, 37: 81–91.

Grossman, M., Saffer, H. and Chaloupka, F. (1991) *Alcohol Regulation and Motor Vehicle Mortality*, Final Report for Grant No. SRO1AA07593, Rockville, MD, National Institute on Alcohol Abuse and Alcoholism.

Grossman, S., Canterbury, R.J., Lloyd, E. and McDowell, M. (1994) 'A model approach to peer-based alcohol and other drug prevention in a college population', *Journal of Alcohol and Drug Education*, 39: 50–61.

Guydish, J. and Greenfield, T. (1990) 'Alcohol-related cognitions: Do they predict treatment outcome?' *Addictive Behaviors*, 15: 423–30.

Hennessy, M. and Seltz, R.F. (1990) 'The situational riskiness of alcoholic beverages', *Journal of Studies on Alcohol*, 51: 422–7.

Hingson, R. et al. (forthcoming) 'Impact of the Saving Lives Program on alcohol-related traffic injuries and deaths'.

Hingson, R., Heeren, T. and Winter, M. (1994) 'Lower legal blood alcohol limits for young drivers', *Public Health Reports*, 109: 738–44.

Hingson, R., Heeren, T. and Winter, M. (1996) 'Lowering state legal blood alcohol units to 0.08%: the effects of fatal motor vehicle crashes', *American Journal of Public Health* 86: 1297–99.

Hingson, R., McGovern, T., Howland, J., Heeren, T., Winter, M. and Zakocs, R. (1996) 'Reducing alcohol impaired driving in Massachusetts: The Saving Lives Program', *American Journal of Public Health*, 86: 791–7.

Holder, H.D. and Wagenaar, A. (1994) 'Mandated server training and reduced alcohol involved traffic crashes: A time series analysis of the Oregon experiences', *Accident Analysis and Prevention*, 26: 89–97.

Hughes, S.P. and Dodder, R.A. (1986) 'Raising the legal minimum drinking age: short-term effects with college student samples', *Journal of Drug Issues*, 16: 609–20.

Institute of Medicine (1990a) *Broadening the Base of Treatment for Alcohol Problems*, Washington, D.C., National Academy Press, pp. 148–9.

Institute of Medicine (1990b) *Prevention and Treatment of Alcohol Problems Research Opportunities*, Washington, D.C., National Academy Press.

Jackson, V., Dorman, S., Tennant, K. and Chen, W. (1989) 'Effects of teaching specific guidelines for alcohol consumption on alcohol knowledge and behavioral intent of college students', *Health Education*, 20: 51–4.

Johnston, L., O'Malley, P. and Bachman, J. (1994) *National Survey Results on Drug Use from the Monitoring the Future Study, Volume III, College Students and Young Adults*, National Institute on Drug Abuse, NIH Publication No. 94-3810.

Kivlahan, D., Marlatt, A., Fromme, K., Coppel, D. and Williams, E. (1990) 'Secondary prevention with college drinkers: Evaluation of an alcohol skills training program', *Journal of Clinical and Consulting Psychology*, 58: 805–10.

Kraft, D.P. (1988) 'The prevention and treatment of alcohol problems on a college campus', *Journal of Alcohol and Drug Education*, 34: 37–51.

Luepher, R., Murray, D., Jacks, D. et al. (1994) 'Community education for cardiovascular disease prevention: Risk factor changes in the Minnesota Heart Health Program', *American Journal of Public Health*, 84: 1383–92.

Mayhew, D.R., Donelson, A.C., Bierness, D.J. and Simpson, H.M. (1986) 'Youth, alcohol and relative risk of crash involvement', *Accident Analysis and Prevention*, 18: 273–87.

McCarty, D., Poore, M., Mills, K. and Morrison, S. (1983) 'Direct-mail techniques and the prevention of alcohol-related problems among college students', *Journal of Studies on Alcohol*, 44: 162–70.

McKillip, J., Lockhart, D., Eckert, P. and Phillips, J. (1985) 'Evaluation of a responsive alcohol use media campaign on a college campus', *Journal of Alcohol and Drug Education*, 30: 88–97.

McKnight, A.J. (1990) 'Factors influencing the effectiveness of server intervention education', *Journal of Studies on Alcohol*, 52: 389–97.

McKnight, A.J. and Streff, F.M. (1993) 'The effect of enforcement upon serving of alcohol to intoxicated patrons of bars and restaurants', *Alcohol, Drugs and Traffic Safety*, T92: Proceedings of the 12th International Conference on Alcohol, Drugs and Traffic Safety, Cologne, Germany Varlog TUV, Rheinland, pp. 1296–302.

McKnight, A.J., Tippetts, M.S. and Marguis, P.R. (1990) *Provisional Drivers Licences System for Follow Up: Evaluation of Maryland's Youth License Demonstration Control Project, Final Report*, DTNH 22-88-POS-102, Washington, D.C., National Highway Traffic Safety Administration.

McLaran, D.M. and Sarris, R. (1985) 'Attitudes, knowledge and behavior before and after an undergraduate health and lifestyle course', *Journal of American College Health*, 33: 220–2.

Meacci, W. (1990) 'An evaluation of the effects of college alcohol education on the prevention of negative consequences', *Journal of Alcohol and Drug Education*, 35: 66–72.

Mills, K.C., McCarty, D., Ward, J., Minuto, L. and Patzynski, J. (1983) 'A residence hall tavern as a collegiate alcohol abuse prevention activity', *Addictive Behaviors*, 8: 105–8.

Mortimer, R.G. and Sturgis, S.P. (1975) 'Effects of low and moderate levels of alcohol on steering performance', in Israelstam, S. and Lambert, S. (eds) *Alcohol, Drugs and Traffic Safety*, Toronto, Addiction Research Foundation, pp. 329–45.

Moskowitz, H. and Burns, M. (1990) 'Effects of alcohol on driving performance', *Alcohol, Health and Research World*, 14: 12–14.

National Highway Traffic Safety Administration (1991) *Fatal Accident Reporting System 1990: A Review of Information on Fatal Traffic Crashes in the US*, Washington, D.C.

National Highway Traffic Safety Administration (1993) *Traffic Safety Facts 1992*, DOT HS 808 022.

National Highway Traffic Safety Administration (1994) *Traffic Safety Facts 1994*, US Department of Transportation, Washington, D.C.

National Highway Traffic Safety Administration (1995) *Youth Fatal Crashes and Alcohol Facts, 1994*, US Department of Transportation.

National Institute on Alcohol Abuse and Alcoholism (1983) *Eighth Special Report to the US Congress on Alcohol and Health*, From the Secretary of Health and Human Services. Washington, D.C., US Department of Health and Human Services, September.

O'Connell, D.F. and Beck, T. (1984) 'An involuntary therapeutic group for alcohol abusers', *Journal of College Student Personnel*, November, pp. 547–8.

O'Malley, P. and Wagenaar, A.C. (1991) 'Effects of minimum drinking age laws on alcohol use, related behaviors and traffic crash involvement among American youth', *Journal of Studies on Alcohol*, 52: 478–91.

Palmer, J.W. (1988) 'Minnesota roadside survey alcohol positive drivers', *Journal of Traffic Safety Education*, 35: 10–13.

Pentz, M.A., Dwyer, J., McKinnon, D., Flay, B., Hansen, W., Wang, E. and Johnson, A. (1989) 'A multi community trial for primary prevention of adolescent drug abuse', *Journal of the American Medical Association*, 261: 3259–66.

Perkins, H.W. and Berkowitz, A.D. (1989) 'Stability and contradiction in college students' drinking following a drinking law change', *Journal of Drug and Alcohol Education*, 35: 60–77.

Portnoy, B. (1980) 'Effects of a controlled usage alcohol education program based on the Health Belief Model', *Journal of Drug Education*, 10: 181–95.

Preusser, D., Williams, A., Lund, A. and Zador, P. (1990) 'Curfew ordinances and teenage motor vehicle injury', *Accident Analysis and Prevention*, 22: 391–7.

Robinson J. (1981) 'A comparison of three alcohol instruction programs on the knowledge, attitudes and drinking behaviors of college students', *Journal of Drug Education*, 11: 157–66.

Robinson, S., Roth, S., Gloria, A., Keim, J. and Sattler, H. (1993) 'Influence of substance abuse education on undergraduates' knowledge, attitudes and behaviors', *Journal of Alcohol and Drug Education*, 39: 123–30.

Rogers, P. (1993) *The Long Term Effectiveness of California's Administrative Per Se Law, Second Interim Report*, OTS Project #AL9101, Research and Development Section Program Policy Administration, California Department of Motor Vehicles, December.

Rosenbloom, D.L., Hingson, R. and Dawkins, C. (1993) *1993 Report to the Nation, Community Leaders Speak Out Against Substance Abuse, Join Together: A National Resource for Communities Fighting Substance Abuse.*

Rozelle, G. (1980) 'Experiential and cognitive small group approaches to alcohol education for college students', *Journal of Alcohol and Drug Education*, 26: 40–54.

Saffer, H. and Grossman, M. (1987a) 'Beer taxes, the legal drinking age and youth motor vehicle fatalities', *Journal of Legal Studies*, 16: 351–74.

Saffer, H. and Grossman, M. (1987b) 'Drinking age laws and highway mortality rates: Cause and effect', *Economic Inquiry*, 25: 403–17.

Santana, J.R. and Martinez, R. (1992) 'Alcohol purchase and consumption site prior to an automobile collision', 4th Proceeding of the Association for the Advancement of Automotive Medicine, Des Plaines, IL: The Association for the Advancement of Automotive Medicine.

Sawyer, C. (1978) 'Methodology in measuring attitude change: Problems and alternatives', *Journal of Alcohol Education*, 8: 289–97.

Schall, M., Kemeney, A. and Maltzman, I. (1991) 'Drinking by university dormitory residents: Its prediction and amelioration', *Journal of Alcohol and Drug Education*, 36: 75–86.

Shore, E., Gregory, T. and Tatlock, L. (1991) 'College students' reactions to a designated driver program: An exploratory study', *Journal of Alcohol and Drug Education*, 37: 1–6.

Spaite, D.W., Meislin, H.W., Valenzuala, T.D., Criss, E.A., Smith, R. and Nelson, A. (1990) 'Banning alcohol in a major college stadium: Impact on the incidence and pattern of injury and illness', *Journal of American College Health*, 39: 125–8.

Stockwell, T., Rydon, P., Giannette, S., Jankis, E., Ovendar, C. and Syed, D. (1992) 'Levels of drunkenness of customers leaving licensed premises in Perth Western Australia: A comparison of high and low risk premises', *British Journal of Addiction*, 87: 873–81.

Stunkard, A.J., Felix, M.R.J. and Cohen, R.Y. (1977) 'Mobilizing a community to promote health: The Pennsylvania County Health Improvement Program (CHIP)', in Rosen, J.C. and Solomon, L.J. (eds) *Prevention in Health Psychology*, Hanover, N.H., University Press of New England.

Walsh, D., Hingson, R., Merrigan, D., Levenson, S. et al. (1991) 'A randomized trial of treatment options for alcohol-abusing workers', *New England Journal of Medicine*, 325: 775–82.

Werch, C.E., Bakema, D., Ball, M. and Lee, D. (1988) 'Categorizing blood alcohol level and alcohol consumption data in field settings feasibility and findings', *Journal of Studies on Alcohol*, 49: 561–6.

Weschler, H., Davenport, A., Dowdall, G., Moeykens, B. and Castillo, S. (1994) 'Health and behavioral consequences of binge drinking in college', *Journal of the American Medical Association*, 272: 1672–7.

Williams, A., Zador, P., Harris, S. and Karpf, R. (1983) 'The effects of raising the minimum drinking age on involvement in fatal crashes', *Journal of Legal Studies*, 12: 169–79.

Williams, J., Hadden, K. and Marcavage, E. (1983) 'Experimental study of assertion training as a drug prevention strategy to use with college students', *Journal of College Student Personnel*, pp. 201–6.

Williams, F.G., Kirkman-Liff, B.L. and Szivek, P.H. (1990) 'College student drinking behaviors before and after changes in state policy', *Journal of Drug and Alcohol Education*, 3: 12–25.

Williams, F.G. and Knox, R. (1987) 'Alcohol abuse intervention in a university setting', *Journal of American College Health*, 36: 97–102.

Wittman, F. (1993) 'Environmental approaches to community level prevention of alcohol and drug problems', Presentation to the Center for Substance Abuse Prevention, PEPS Advisory Panel, 15 December.

Zador, P. (1991) 'Alcohol-related relative risk of fatal driver injuries in relation to driver age and sex', *Journal of Studies on Alcohol*, 52: 301–10.

10 Creating Safer Bars

Kathryn Graham and Ross Homel

Bars are places where patrons go primarily to socialise (Ratcliffe and Nutter 1979), and public drinking is perceived as a positive social activity for many people across many cultures (Clark 1981). At the same time certain harms are associated with public drinking, the most well known being bar-room aggression. Several studies have shown that in some cultures, greater violence is associated with drinking in bars than in other drinking settings (Homel et al. 1991, Ireland and Thommeny, 1993, Stockwell et al. 1993).

Although other risks are associated with drinking in bars such as a heavier drinking generally (Cosper et al. 1987; see also review by Single 1993) and greater likelihood of drink-driving (O'Donnell 1985), in this present chapter, bar safety is discussed primarily with reference to bar-room aggression. The focus of the chapter is on the ways that aggressive behaviour in bars can be prevented, managed and made less harmful by changing the bar environment.

The importance of the environment in channelling behaviour has been recognised for some time (Sommer 1969, Stokols 1992). Increasingly, researchers are recognising the role of situational factors in the occurrence of aggression generally (Goldstein 1994). Moreover, the effects of situational factors may be even greater for alcohol-related aggression than for aggression that does not involve alcohol. Studies of violent crimes have found that crimes involving alcohol use by the assailant are less likely to involve premeditation (Virkkunen 1974, Myers 1986), more likely to involve personal disputes (Welte and Abel 1989), and more likely to involve drinking by the victim (Mayfield 1976, Lindqvist 1991). Thus, the lack of premeditation and the presence of an escalation process, especially with an intoxicated other person, highlight the important role of the situation in the occurrence of alcohol-related violence.

Further evidence for the crucial role of situational factors in the genesis of violent behaviour comes from the experimental literature on alcohol and aggression. In neutral situations, alcohol does not increase the probability of aggression; on the other hand, alcohol use combined with specific situational circumstances such as frustration or provocation (see reviews by Bushman and Cooper 1990, Gustafson 1993, Graham et al. 1996) consistently results in increased aggression. Given the large role of situational factors in alcohol-related aggression, there is considerable opportunity to make drinking environments safer both in terms of reducing the frequency of harmful behaviour as well as by minimising the consequences of such behaviour. It is surprising that so little research and policy have been directed towards this goal.

This chapter is divided into two sections. The first section describes the implications of existing research for creating bar environments that minimise aggression as well as the harmfulness of aggression when it occurs. The organisation of the review shows the specific aspects of bar environments that seem to be related to aggression. It should be noted, however, that much of the available data come from naturalistic observation where it was usually not possible to examine specific features in isolation from other features. For example, crowded bars also tend to be noisy and smoky or stuffy. Therefore, the structure adopted for the chapter is not intended to imply that changes in aggressive behaviour can necessarily be obtained by changing a single aspect of the bar environment. Increasing safety in bars seems likely to be a function of systemic change rather than changing isolated features of the environment, and these descriptions of individual features should be seen in that context.

The second section of this chapter focuses on the political/ policy side of making bars safer. Reducing violence associated with public drinking has been accomplished successfully by focusing on bar policies and procedures as well as on training of bar staff. In this part of the chapter general issues in changes in the bar environment are reviewed and an example of a successful project to increase bar safety is described.

Bar Characteristics Associated with Aggression

The bar has both a physical and a social environment, that can influence the frequency of aggressive behaviour, as well as the harm resulting from incidents of aggression.

The Physical Environment

Although the physical environment probably plays a lesser role in the occurrence of bar-room aggression than social atmosphere and patron characteristics, the physical characteristics of the bar environment offer great potential for making safer bars because these aspects are easily controlled or modified by the bar owner as well as society generally (in the form of policies and enforcement). The importance of bar-room design, in particular the relationship of design and licensing regulations, was first noted by Sommer in his 1969 book (Chapter 8, 'Designed for Drinking': 120–31). As will be described in the following, the physical environment can influence behaviour in a variety of ways. Specific safety measures in the environment can also reduce the harm resulting from aggression, much in the way that a home is 'child-proofed' (for example, storing household poisons in inaccessible places) to ensure the safety of small children.

Using the Environment to Create Expectations About Behaviour

Attractive, nicely furnished, well-maintained bars may give a message to the patron that the managers do not anticipate physical violence and associated damage to furnishings. Indeed, a study of bars in Vancouver, Canada (Graham et al. 1980), found that aggression was significantly correlated with poorly maintained, unclean, unattractive bar environments. Similarly, an Australian study (Homel, Clark et al. 1994) found a relationship between bar cleanliness and aggression, although earlier qualitative research suggested that the key causal factors probably had more to do with comfort, roominess and ventilation than the actual state of cleanliness or degree of renovation (Homel et al. 1992).

These correlational data do not necessarily demonstrate an effect of the environment per se. It is possible that different types of bars attract more or less aggressive patrons. However, given the importance of expectations in the occurrence of alcohol-related aggression – MacAndrew and Edgerton 1969 (the role of cultural expectations); George et al. 1989, Leonard and Senchak 1993 (the role of individual expectations regarding the effects of alcohol on behaviour); see also Pernanen's discussion of the role of the stereotype of bar-room brawls (1991: 92–3) – it is a reasonable hypothesis that the first clue the patron has as to what kinds of behaviour will be tolerated is the care and maintenance of the bar.

Nevertheless, expectations are governed by various factors, and there appear to be situations where run-down bars do not necessarily convey high tolerance of aggressive behaviour. MCM Research (1993) concluded, on the basis of their study of best practices in Britain, that aggression was most likely in 'moderately uncomfortable' bars rather than in the most uncomfortable bars (p. 24). There are also situations where the run-down nature of the bar is part of a highly esteemed 'decor'. A well-known dance bar in Austin, Texas, is extremely run down (including solving a leaky roof by using rain drainage guttering on the *interior* of the building), and the owner has proudly proclaimed on numerous occasions that the bar will never become a 'fernie bar' (that is, a 'yuppified' bar with green plants) as long as he owns it. While the bar is truly decrepit and the owner's sentiments no doubt genuine, the fact that the bar was featured in a story on Austin in *National Geographic* (Moize 1990) suggests that the run-down state of the bar is misleading, for it is essentially a respectable drinking establishment.

Avoiding Physical Environment Features that Irritate or Frustrate People

Aggression in bars has been found to be associated with poor ventilation and smoky air (Graham et al. 1980, Homel, Clark et al. 1994), inconvenient bar access and inadequate seating (Homel, Clark et al. 1994), high noise level (Graham et al. 1980), and crowding (Graham 1985, Homel, Clark et al. 1994). Because these relationships were identified in observational studies, it is not known whether these factors actually caused or contributed to aggression in some way, or whether these attributes are simply more common in bars where aggression occurs due to other causes. However, it is known from the experimental literature on alcohol and aggression that drinking increases the likelihood of aggression in situations where there is frustration or provocation. Therefore, a plausible link between these aspects of the environment and aggressive behaviour is the role of these factors in irritating, frustrating or otherwise provoking bar patrons, particularly highly intoxicated bar patrons.

Poor air quality would constitute a direct irritant for the person, as would noise levels that hurt the ears. High noise level and crowding might also be expected to have a physiological impact on the person that would make aggression more likely. Geen (1990) concluded that a number of environmental stressors were related to aggression, including excessive heat, noise, and air pollution, especially smoke. Crowding was also related to aggression but the relationship is complex because the effects of crowding vary according to the social context (Geen 1990).

With regards to crowding in the bar environment, the effects of crowding and inconvenient bar access may be dependent on perceived violations of 'personal space' (personal space has been described by Geen as the 'invisible "envelope" of space around each person that is felt to be off-limits to other people' (p. 72)). This space has been found to vary from person to person, situation to situation and culture to culture. Knowledge regarding personal space would suggest that crowding on the dance floor might be less stressful (because this is expected, even welcomed, in some dance settings), while being bumped or otherwise interfered with by others when one's objective is to buy a drink would be considerably more of a violation of personal space.

The importance of the subjective experience of crowding in the occurrence of bar-room aggression was strongly supported by research by Macintyre and Homel (forthcoming). Their study utilised observational techniques to assess the links between patron density, crowding, and aggression in six night clubs in Australia. Density was defined as the number of people per unit of area, in contrast to crowding which was conceptualised as a subjective experience of sensory and social overload and was measured indirectly by counting low level and unintended bumps in a defined area. It was found that, for a given density level, high aggression night clubs had higher crowding levels than low aggression clubs. Moreover, crowding across both groups of clubs was a strong predictor of aggression, controlling for male drunkenness and a number of other risk factors. The key feature of high aggression night clubs that appeared to contribute to higher crowding and aggression levels was intersecting traffic flows created by inappropriate design, especially poor location of toilets and bars, and the use of the same door as both entrance and exit. Thus, while setting limits on the number of people allowed in a bar may be important to reduce the impact of crowding on aggression, traffic flow may be an even more important consideration.

Even the aggression-promoting effects of noise may be socially mediated. Homel et al. (1992) concluded from their qualitative research that it was not the high noise level of bands, per se, that stimulated aggression, but rather bad bands – good bands held patrons' interest and seemed to prevent aggressive diversions. Similarly, bad music may contribute to heavier drinking generally. In comparing rates of drinking at different experimental drinking parties, Geller and Kalsher (1990: 88) noted that 'the sound quality of the dance music was clearly the worst at the party with the highest BACs'.

Minimising Provocation Related to Games and Entertainment

The role of games and entertainment was a major focus of research commissioned by the Liquor Licensing Board of Alberta, Canada, in the 1970s (Ratcliffe and Nutter 1979). In particular, they were interested in the effects of social activities of bars on drinking in order to provide a research basis for liquor licensing changes. Ratcliffe and Nutter found that people who engaged in these activities tended to drink more slowly; however, they also tended to stay in the bar longer, ultimately consuming more alcohol than the non-players. Therefore, the implications regarding the effects of the presence or absence of these activities on aggression are not clear.

However, another study (Graham et al. 1980), specifically focused on aggression and found that aggression was more likely in bars where there was dancing and pool playing (no relationship with aggression was found for other games such as darts and shuffleboard). This relationship may simply have been an artefact of the kinds of bars that tended to have dancing and pool tables (for example, more likely to be frequented by young males). But, activities might also have an independent role in creating circumstances where aggression is more likely. Gibbs (1986) in his review article used the example of pool playing to demonstrate how formal and informal rules can be used to structure bar environments in order to reduce both frequency and severity of aggression. His suggestions included limits on betting, establishing protocols regarding appropriate behaviour around pool games, and keeping observers of the game out of disputes that arise between players.

Safer Glassware and Other Harm Reduction Strategies

Shepherd (see discussion of this issue 1994) observed that some of the more severe injuries resulting from bar fights were caused by using broken glasses or bottles as weapons, and suggested the substitution of tempered glass. Consistent with this recommendation, Plant et al. (1994) found that bar managers tended to believe that tempered glass was less dangerous; however, Plant et al. also concluded that there were risks from all forms of glassware, and that attention should be focused on the more general issue of bar artefacts being used as weapons. The recent research on glassware illustrates the potential for increasing bar safety through environmental means.

Encouraging Eating with Drinking

The availability of food (especially full meals) has been associated with reduced risk of aggression in bars (Graham 1985, Homel, Clark et al. 1994). There are several possible explanations for this relationship, including the explanation that the types of bars that serve food are less likely to have aggressive patrons. However, some explanations include a larger contributing role of food. For example, eating while drinking is known to slow absorption of alcohol and thereby reduce the blood alcohol level the drinker reaches (Wedel et al. 1991). In addition there may be a social impact, with bars where meals are consumed even by only a few people taking on a different atmosphere from bars where the focus is solely on drinking.

The Social Environment and Social Control

In bar observation studies, the social environment tends to be a more powerful predictor of aggression than the physical environment (Graham et al. 1980, Homel, Clark et al. 1994). Although these factors tend to be more difficult to change than aspects of the physical environment, they may be more important to address because of this powerful relationship with aggressive behaviour.

Creating a Social Atmosphere with Clear Limits

As described in an earlier section, the physical environment provides patrons with the first indication of expected behaviour. In addition, a number of social variables reflecting the permissiveness of the environment have been shown to be associated with aggressive behaviour (Graham et al. 1980, Homel, Clark et al. 1994), including: overall decorum expectations (rated from restrictive to 'anything goes'), swearing (especially abusive swearing), sexual activity among patrons, sexual competition, prostitution, drug use and dealing, male rowdiness, and male roughness and bumping.

In addition, direct measures of the permissiveness of bar staff have been shown to be related to aggression, including greater aggression where bar staff were very permissive and did not engage in responsible serving practices (for example, serving underage patrons) (Homel, Clark et al. 1994), and where bar staff appeared to exercise little control over patrons' behaviour (Graham et al. 1980). Aggression has also been found to be more likely in bars where drunkenness is frequent (Graham et al. 1980, Homel et al. 1994) and where there are discounted drinks and other drink promotions (Homel et al. 1992).

Factors associated with permissive environments can be grouped into three categories: (1) subaggressive behaviour (for example, swearing), (2) deviant behaviour (for example, drug dealing), and (3) a lack of control of drinking behaviour (such as extreme intoxication). Server intervention training, new licensing policies and better enforcement of existing policies can address (2) and (3) (Stockwell et al. 1995), but there is little research on creating an atmosphere that is free of subaggressive behaviour, with the exception of the recent Surfers Paradise Safety Action project (described in the second section of this chapter – Homel, Hauritz et al. (forthcoming)) in which male swearing and other 'rowdy' behaviours were substantially reduced as part of a concerted effort to make bars safer.

There is also evidence from experimental research that people (such as bar workers) in the drinker's environment can influence aggressive behaviour. In particular, encouraging non-aggressive responses to provocation have been shown to reduce aggressiveness among persons who have been drinking (Taylor and Gammon 1976, Jeavons and Taylor 1985). These and other data suggest that the ease and availability of non-aggressive responses may be an important factor in preventing alcohol-related aggression (see review by Graham et al. 1995) and might be an aspect of the bar environment that is amenable to control through informal or formal bar social rules.

Fostering a Positive Social Atmosphere

As described by Pernanen (1991: 200–1), social interactions in drinking settings are far more likely to be positive than negative or aggressive. And, in general, bar-room observational studies have found that positive atmospheres (an atmosphere that is friendly rather than tense and hostile, that includes quiet laughter and small talk rather than hostile talk, and where patron boredom is low) are associated with a lower risk of aggression (Graham et al. 1980, Homel, Clark et al. 1994).

There are no data available focused specifically on how to create a more positive atmosphere. It seems likely, however, that factors already discussed, such as the presence of interesting activities and high-quality entertainment, an environment with firm limits that feels safe, and discouraging subaggressive behaviour would contribute to such an environment. In addition, it is well known that the pharmacological effects of alcohol are highly variable depending on the context of drinking. Therefore, positive, pleasant atmospheres may have an additive effect in reducing aggression, over that which can be achieved solely by reducing the risk factors associated with negative atmospheres.

Discouraging Drinking to Intoxication

As described in the previous section, the presence of highly intoxicated patrons is a good predictor of bar-room aggression. Intoxication not only signals a permissive environment, but there is evidence across studies that the likelihood of aggression increases with higher blood alcohol levels (see review by Graham et al. 1996). Moreover, higher levels of drunkenness have been associated with greater severity of aggression (Graves et al. 1981). The issue of controlling levels of intoxication is discussed in more detail in the second section of this chapter.

Employing Trained Peace-loving Bar Workers

Aggression has been found to occur in response to bar staff exercising social control such as refusing service and otherwise intervening with intoxicated patrons (Graves et al. 1981, Felson et al. 1986, Homel, Clark et al. 1994). Bouncers, in particular, who have largely a social control role, have been identified across studies as sometimes *increasing* the harm associated with bar-room aggression (Homel et al. 1992, Marsh and Kibby 1992). Waring and Sperr (1982) found considerable variability in the way bar workers respond to problem behaviours. Clearly, hiring and training practices are controllable elements of the bar environment that are relevant to bar safety.

Keeping Aggressive People Out

Unlike some other environmental factors, bar operators have little control over the personality of their patrons. Nevertheless, one fairly convincing explanation of some of the variability of aggressiveness of bars is that certain bars are aggressive *because* they are frequented by aggressive people. This possibility is worth noting in developing safer bars. It is quite clear from many years of research that aggression is not randomly distributed in the general population; nor is it randomly distributed among drinkers. Therefore, a necessary feature of safer bars is the capability to recognise and ban, if necessary, major troublemakers. Obviously, it is not feasible to exclude large groups of people because they might become aggressive; however, it is possible to isolate the rare individual who causes an unusual amount of trouble.

Dealing with high-risk groups also deserves special consideration. Surprisingly, most observable patron characteristics (for example, age and gender) do not appear to predict aggression. The characteristics that have been observed to be linked with a greater likelihood or greater severity of aggression include: marginalised populations, especially skid row and First Nations/aboriginal patrons (Graham et al. 1980, Graves et al. 1981, Pernanen 1991, Homel, Clark et al. 1994), the presence of underage females (Homel, Clark et al. 1994), and the presence of groups of males who are strangers to each other (Homel et al. 1992).

Since the safety of disadvantaged groups in bars is as important as the safety of more advantaged public drinkers, the risks for marginalised subgroups deserve particular attention. While certain risks may be a function of cultural norms of particular groups, there is also evidence that bar operators do not offer the same safety considerations for some groups as for others. For example, Graham et al. (1980) observed that many skid row bar workers were quite abusive and exploitive of patrons. Commercial interests may provide the incentive for bar owners to improve bar safety in high tourist areas (as described in the second section of this chapter), but public health issues, including the medical costs of alcohol-related violence (for example, Buss et al. 1995), may need to be the driving force in promoting safety in bars frequented by marginalised subgroups.

Similarly, bars with other high-risk patronage (for example, groups of males) may need specially targeted prevention efforts. Graves et al. (1981) found that the strongest predictor of the number of people who will become involved in a bar-room incident was the size of the initiator's immediate drinking group. Consistent with the observation by Homel et al. (1992) that there is an increased probability of aggression in situations in which there are groups of males drinking together where the members of groups do not know members of other groups, Pernanen (1991: 91) and Prus (1978) have suggested that in-group/out-group perceptions particularly among males in drinking settings may lead to aggression. Other patron behaviours associated with aggression, such as a high rate of interactions among strangers, table hopping and milling about (Graham et al. 1980), may be related to this phenomenon. Bar environments characterised by these patron behaviours might require special vigilance on the part of bar staff to spot potentially problematic situations and prevent such situations from escalating.

The first section of this chapter described bar-room characteristics that have been found to be associated with a higher probability of aggressive behaviour. In the second section, a community-based model for regulating safety in public drinking settings is described, including some of the political processes involved in bringing about systematic changes in bar-room environments through regulation.

Increasing Bar Safety: The Politics of Change

In general, the public, including bar patrons, appear to support measures that would make public drinking safer. Although Cavan (1966) noted that bars tended to be very permissive environments, Ratcliffe and Nutter (1979) found that the majority of bar patrons endorsed stricter enforcement of refusal of service to intoxicated patrons. General public support has also been found for many measures that would increase the safety of bars, especially in terms of preventing service to intoxicated patrons and reducing drinking and driving (Hawks et al. 1993).

On the other hand, a number of recent articles have argued that bar owners have little incentive to adopt more responsible serving practices (McLean et al. 1994) and that there is a general perception that adopting certain practices that would increase bar safety might result in decreased profits or at least considerable inconvenience (Stockwell 1992, Stockwell et al. 1995). Maximising profit by selling as many drinks as possible (as described by Prus 1983) may run counter to adopting measures that would increase bar safety. Other measures, such as keeping the bar well maintained, also involve expenditures. The main way in which society has balanced health and safety considerations regarding public drinking with business interests of bars has been through regulations. The effectiveness of these regulations in achieving desired outcomes, however, has varied among different jurisdictions. Moreover, this is a very complex area of research, with models of effective legislation and regulation only now beginning to emerge from work in a number of settings. Australia is a country that historically has had particular problems in coming to terms with alcohol and its control (Stockwell 1994), and may therefore be useful as a case study for other jurisdictions facing similar difficulties. In order to illustrate that safety need not be sought solely through the traditional model of 'command regulation with non discretionary punishment' (Ayres and Braithwaite 1992), a description is provided of a community-based project in a popular tourist area in Queensland that was based as much on persuasion as on punishment.

A Community-based Model for Regulating Public Drinking

Criminological research on compliance by business with government regulations provides many ideas that can be applied directly to the regulation of licensed premises. The work of Ayres and Braithwaite (1992) is especially useful in this regard. These authors begin with the assumption that there is an urgent need to transcend the intellectual stalemate between those who favour strong state regulation of business and those who advocate deregulation. They propose the following regulatory approaches which are responsive to industry context and structure, regulatory culture, and history, and which incorporate, as key ideas, 'tit-for-tat' strategies that combine punishment and persuasion in an optimum mix; 'tripartism' (empowering citizen associations) as a way of solving the dilemma of regulatory capture and corruption; and 'enforced self-regulation', in which private sets of rules written by business are publicly ratified and, when there is a failure of private enforcement, are publicly enforced. Central to their model is an 'enforcement pyramid' of penalties, from the frequently used techniques of persuasion and warning letters through to the infrequently used techniques of licence suspension or revocation.

The ideological basis of Ayres and Braithwaite's ideas is 'a replacement of the liberal conception of the atomized free individual with a republican conception of communitarian empowerment' (1992: 17). In particular, tripartism fosters the participation of public interest or community groups by giving them full access to all the information available to the regulator; by giving them a seat at the negotiating table; and by giving them the same standing to sue or prosecute as the regulator. Thus they propose a model in which no one element, whether it be self-regulation, formal enforcement or citizen involvement, can operate effectively without the others.

These constitute a rich tapestry of ideas with direct and obvious application to reducing risks associated with public drinking. In addition, there is a growing body of data on what does and does not work in the regulation of licensed premises to forge a new general approach. The tit-for-tat model and the enforcement pyramid provide a framework for determining, in specific contexts, optimum mixes of punishment and persuasion; Codes of Practice developed by night clubs and industry associations provide a starting point for enforced self-regulation, although legal issues may require resolution; and the experiences of community-based safety action projects provide strong leads on who the key community or interest groups may be in different communities and how they may be empowered to be at least 'credible watchdogs', if not equal partners.

Finally, the assumed financial disincentives for bar owners to create safer bars may not be valid. Changes made in bar environments to increase safety may not result in the expected reductions in profit if savings are achieved in other ways. The Surfers Paradise Project (described below) demonstrates a situation where improving bar safety was seen as a positive financial strategy.

The Surfers Paradise Safety Action Project

Although responsible hospitality practices and stricter enforcement may command public support, the problem in many jurisdictions is that there are few legislative or economic reasons for the alcohol industry to embrace such measures. This means that different kinds of 'levers' must be found to move the industry. One possible approach that appears to be effective is illustrated by the Surfers Paradise Safety Action Project, an Australian initiative that commenced in April 1993 and concluded (for evaluation purposes) in December 1993 (see Homel, Hauritz et al. 1994, Homel (forthcoming); Homel et al. (forthcoming); McIlwain 1994). This project had as its major aim the reduction of alcohol-related violence in a major international tourist area with approximately twenty night clubs surrounding a single mall.

The project was shaped partly by an emerging public panic about safety and security in and around Cavill Mall, Surfers Paradise. During 1992 media stories about 'Surfers sleaze' and crime and violence in the mall were so frequent and strident in their tone that the Gold Coast City Council and local business people became seriously concerned that tourists would abandon Surfers altogether as a holiday destination. Surveys of residents, the business community and patrons conducted for evaluation purposes prior to the project confirmed popular impressions that there were high levels of direct and indirect contact with crime in Surfers Paradise and correspondingly high levels of concern and pessimism about the crime situation.

Community groups and the process of change
A key element of the project was that it provided a structure for focusing the community militancy about safety and security by channelling energy into a Steering Committee, three major task groups, and a Monitoring Committee responsible for overseeing adherence to a Code of Practice developed by night club managers. All aspects of the project were designed in such a way that the local community – business people, residents, community groups, representatives of Council, taxi operators, police, security operatives, and licensees themselves – had 'ownership' of the project and therefore responsibility for developing solutions appropriate to the local situation.

The interagency Steering Committee appointed a Project Officer who was responsible for co-ordinating all elements of the project; facilitating development of a Community Forum as an essential support vehicle for the project; liaising with Liquor Licensing investigators and the police to develop programmes of awareness, surveillance and compliance with the Queensland Liquor Act; incorporating the use of a Risk Assessment Policy Checklist in identifying the degree of compliance with Model House Policies; working co-operatively with licensees to promote responsible hospitality practices; and co-ordinating any training required.

From the Community Forum, three task groups were formed: the Public Spaces Task Group, the Security and Policing Task Group, and the Venue Management Task Group. The Public Spaces Task Group conducted a Safety Audit of the Cavill Mall area to examine the physical environment of Surfers Paradise and to determine the role each identified environmental factor played either individually or interactively in preventing Surfers Paradise from being a safe recreational area for a broad cross-section of people.

The Security and Policing Task Group oversaw the implementation of the recommendation of the safety audit, and, more generally, aimed to develop co-ordinated strategies involving police and security personnel to ensure safety and security in the areas around the venues; to monitor levels of violence in public places; and to examine strategies to enhance public transport systems to ensure safe and reliable routes into and out of the area.

The primary focus of the Venue Management Task Group was to encourage the responsible delivery of alcohol to the community, and to establish a positive working relationship between the Surfers Paradise Licensees, the Surfers Paradise Police and Queensland Liquor Licensing Division.

Because the focus of the project was not solely on irresponsible serving practices, the licensees for the first time were not the focus of blame. Instead they were asked to outline their perception of the problem of rising violence and public disorder in Surfers Paradise and to identify those factors which they thought were significant. It appeared that at no time previously had the licensees been involved in the process of problem identification in their own community, or in decision making regarding solutions. Despite the fact that they operated million-dollar businesses, they were something of a pariah group in need of a sense of identity and a recognised place within the community.

In essence, the project aimed to achieve a commitment from licensees to self-regulation by shifting the broad context of the licensed venues from being alcohol oriented to being entertainment oriented, with emphasis on sound responsible hospitality practices. This shift was achieved in part through the administration of the Risk Assessment Policy Checklist. This Checklist is a tool devised to assess, amongst other things, how well management deal with the provision of liquor and pricing; what responsible practices are being used; and how venues promote entertainment as well as liquor (Stockwell, Rydon et al. 1993).

A Code of Practice developed by the licensees themselves was another major tool designed to bring about change in licensed premises. The Code of Practice focused on such things as security, safety inside and outside the venue, staff responsibilities, the responsible use of alcohol, quality service and entertainment, and honest and accurate advertising. Under the security heading, the Code committed management to ensuring that all security staff were trained, registered and identifiable, and gave priority to the well-being of patrons; physical violence, harassment or threat were prohibited; it was made clear that the police would be called immediately if any act of serious violence occurred; and that any patron who felt threatened or harassed should immediately inform security staff. These good intentions were supported by training for security staff conducted by a professional group.

A regulatory measure which was implemented and which turned out to be of critical importance was the establishment by the Venue Management Task Group of a Monitoring Committee, consisting of local community and some external representatives, but (deliberately) not police or the liquor licensing authorities. The committee represented the culmination of the local community's attempts at self-regulation, and oversaw, regulated and arbitrated the Code of Practice. Essentially, the committee, as an informal regulatory body, attempted to fill the gap created by the withdrawal of both police and the Liquor Licensing Division from the collection of evidentiary information which could result in successful legal action against deviant licensees. The committee also applied 'peer pressure' to some licensees in a partially successful attempt to persuade them to comply with the Code of Practice.

Evaluation

The impact of the project was assessed using four data sets: the Risk Assessment Policy Checklists based on interviews with managers and staff in licensed venues; direct structured observation of staff and patron behaviours in licensed premises by teams of students posing as patrons; street incidents recorded by security staff employed to patrol the mall and adjoining areas; and criminal incidents occurring in the Surfers district recorded by police in occurrence sheets held at Surfers Paradise Police Station. Risk assessments and direct observations were carried out twice: once before the main part of the project commenced (that is, before the implementation of the Code of Practice) and once after the major part of the project had been completed.

Results from the Risk Assessment Policy Checklist showed statistically significant and marked improvements on all aspects except staff drinking policies and aspects of personnel style and recruitment. The patron observation study, based on unobtrusive late-night two-hour visits by trained university students, confirmed that the changes reported in the risk assessments actually took place. For example, the number of incidents of physical violence inside venues dropped from a rate of 9.8 per 100 hours observation to 4.7 per 100 hours observation after the project.

Corresponding to these declines in observed aggression and violence, there was a significant reduction in binge drinking by men and in rates of intoxication. Given the results of Homel, Clark et al. (1994), this reduction in acute levels of drinking is the best internal evidence from the evaluation that the project itself, rather than some unknown exogenous factor, caused the reduction in violence. The reductions in intoxication were in turn the result of major improvements in management and serving practices, evidenced by the reduced use of gimmicks, lower use of drink promotions and happy hours, and a reduction in the unsolicited topping up of patrons' drinks.

Future Research Directions Related to Increasing Bar Safety

The first section of this chapter described the kinds of environmental changes that might be expected to increase bar safety by reducing the frequency and severity of aggression. The recommendations were based on bar observational studies that showed considerable convergence in identifying the attributes of aggressive bars. In addition, relevant findings from other types of research were cited in support of the rationale supporting specific recommendations. These recommendations provide a suitable starting framework for making environmental changes to create safer bars. The second section of the chapter demonstrated that environmental and regulatory changes could indeed make bars safer. The community action process described as part of the Surfers Paradise Project provides a useful model for implementing changes in bar environments in order to increase safety.

There have been very few studies directly examining the relationship between bar-room aggression and environmental characteristics. While existing studies have shown considerable convergence, there is a need for more research in this area in order to develop a greater understanding of the environmental controls of aggression in public drinking settings. There is also a need for more intervention studies related to public drinking and aggression. This may include replications of the safety action model on which the Surfers Paradise Project was based, utilising a wide variety of motivational techniques, including the purely commercial but also appealing to feelings of social responsibility and to the desire to be well regarded in the community. A variety of intervention studies would have the further benefit of pointing to regulatory systems that might be more effective than current practices in reducing alcohol-related harm.

A focus on regulatory systems highlights the need for research on bar safety to place more emphasis generally on the wider social environment. It is known that bar-room aggression is not solely determined by the bar environment. The pharmacological effects of alcohol, the characteristics of bar patrons and the broader cultural context of drinking are likely to have a role as well. In particular, part of the broader cultural context relating to public drinking is the positive value placed on aggressive bars in some cultures. This has been observed in Canadian bars by Dyck

(1980) whose research identified fighting or 'scrapping' as an important social function of bars (supported by Stompin' Tom Connors' song 'Sudbury Saturday Night', where the success of the drinking occasion is conveyed in the line, 'We had a good fight!'). Burns' US study (1980) also described males intentionally seeking out aggressive locales as part of the 'fun' of the drinking event. This phenomenon needs further study, particularly with respect to minimising harm associated with behaviours that might have been intended to be harmless 'rowdiness'.

The existence of aggression-seeking drinkers raises the possibility that reducing aggression in one environment will cause it to be displaced to other environments. As part of the Surfers Paradise study, Homel, Hauritz et al. (1994) examined police statistics for the entire Gold Coast area and concluded that displacement could not account for the extent of changes observed in Surfers Paradise following the interventions. Their conclusion is consistent with more current thinking on aggression in which 'hydraulic' models of aggression are no longer assumed; in fact, 'contagion' models are considered more likely. Therefore, community-based approaches to reducing aggression in public drinking environments may not only be affected by the broader social context but may actually help to change this context by reducing the expectations that drinking and aggression are inextricably linked. Historical analyses might provide some insight on this issue.

In addition, some consideration needs to be given to the social environments of bars as distinct from other environments. In his review, Fagan (1993) identified a number of defining characteristics of many bars that increase the probability of aggression (for example, drunken people with money, time-out atmosphere, close proximity to strangers, and so on). Some of these attributes define the function of public drinking and are, therefore, not necessarily aspects of the environment to be changed. In fact, the success of changes and the optimal strategies for change will depend on respecting the legitimate social functions of public drinking and harmonising safety considerations with these functions.

Finally, there is a greater need for qualitative and quantitative studies focused on understanding the process of bar aggression in order to identify further measures for increasing safety. It is known that 'violence is typically the culmination of multi-stage interactions between two or more persons that involves moves and counter-moves of an escalatory nature' (Gibbs 1986: 137). Basic data on aggressive incidents are needed to address the manner in which situational or environmental factors influence the initiation of aggression (for example, provocation such as crowding) and the escalation of minor incidents into severe violence. More information is also needed regarding the interaction of attitudes and personality with situational factors and the effects of alcohol in violent episodes.

References

Ayres, I. and Braithwaite, J. (1992) *Responsive Regulation: Transcending the Deregulation Debate*, New York, Oxford University Press.

Burns, T.F. (1980) 'Getting rowdy with the boys', *Journal of Drug Issues*, Spring, pp. 273–86.

Bushman, B.J. and Cooper, H.M. (1990) 'Effects of alcohol on human aggression: An integrative research review', *Psychological Bulletin*, 107: 341–54.

Buss, T.F., Abdu, R. and Walker, J.R. (1995) 'Alcohol, drugs, and urban violence in a small city trauma center', *Journal of Substance Abuse Treatment*, 12: 75–83.

Cavan, S. (1966) *Liquor license, An ethnography of a bar*, Chicago, IL, Aldine.

Clark, W.B. (1981) 'Public drinking contexts: Bars and taverns', in Harford, T.C. and Gaines, L.S. (eds) Research Monographs No. 7. *Social Drinking Contexts*, Rockville, MD, NIAAA, pp. 8–33.

Cosper, R.L., Okraku, I.O. and Neumann, B. (1987) 'Tavern going in Canada: A national survey of regulars at public drinking establishments', *Journal of Studies on Alcohol*, 48: 252–9.

Dyck, N. (1980) 'Booze, barrooms and scrapping: Masculinity and violence in a western Canadian town', *Canadian Journal of Anthropology*, 1: 191–8.

Fagan, J. (1993) 'Set and setting revisited: Influences of alcohol and illicit drugs on the social context of violent events', in Martin, S.E. (ed.) *Alcohol and Interpersonal Violence: Fostering Multidisciplinary Perspectives*, Rockville, MD, National Institute of Health, 224: 160–92.

Felson, R.B., Baccaglini, W. and Gmelch, G. (1986) 'Bar-room brawls: Aggression and violence in Irish and American bars', in Campbell, A. and Gibbs, J.J. (eds) *Violent Transactions: The Limits of Personality*, New York, Basil Blackwell, pp. 153–66.

Geen, R.G. (1990) *Human Aggression*, Milton Keynes, England, Open University Press.

Geller, E. and Kalsher, M. (1990) 'Environmental determinants of party drinking', *Environment and Behavior*, 22: 74–90.

George, W.H., Dermen, K.H. and Nochajski, T.H. (1989) 'Expectancy set, self-reported expectancies and predispositional traits: Predicting interest in violence and erotica', *Journal of Studies on Alcohol*, 50: 541–51.

Gibbs, J.J. (1986) 'Alcohol consumption, cognition and context: Examining tavern violence', in Campbell, A. and Gibbs, J.J. (eds) *Violent Transactions: The Limits of Personality*, New York, Basil Blackwell, pp. 133–51.

Goldstein, A.P. (1994) *The Ecology of Aggression*, New York, Plenum Press.

Graham, K. (1985) 'Determinants of heavy drinking and drinking problems: The contribution of the bar environment', in Single, E. and Storm, T. (eds), *Public Drinking and Public Policy*, Toronto, Canada, Addiction Research Foundation, pp. 71–84.

Graham, K., LaRocque, L., Yetman, R., Ross, T.J. and Guistra, E. (1980) 'Aggression and barroom environments', *Journal of Studies on Alcohol*, 41: 277–92.

Graham, K., Schmidt, G. and Gillis, K. (1995) 'Circumstances when drinking leads to aggression', *Contemporary Drug Problems*, 23: 493–557.

Graves, T.D., Graves, N.B., Semu, V.N. and Sam, I.A. (1981) 'The social context of drinking and violence in New Zealand's multi-ethnic pub settings', in Harford, T.C. and Gaines, L.S. (eds) Research Monograph No. 7. *Social Drinking Contexts*, Rockville, MD, NIAAA: 103–20.

Gustafson, R. (1993) 'What do experimental paradigms tell us about alcohol-related aggressive responding?' *Journal of Studies on Alcohol*, Supplement No. 11: 20–9.

Hawks, D., Lang, E., Stockwell, T., Rydon, P. and Lockwood, A. (1993) 'Public support for the prevention of alcohol-related problems', *Drug and Alcohol Review*, 12: 243–50.

Homel, R. (forthcoming) 'Preventing alcohol-related injuries', in O'Malley, P. and Sutton, A. (eds) *Crime Prevention in Australia: Current Issues and Contemporary Developments*, Sydney, Federation Press.

Homel, R. and Clark, J. et al. (1994) 'The prediction and prevention of violence in pubs and clubs', *Crime Prevention Studies*, 3: 1–46.

Homel, R., Hauritz, M., Wortley, R., Clark, J. and Carvolth, R. (1994) *The Impact of the Surfers Paradise Safety Action Project: Key Findings of the Evaluation*, Griffith University, Centre for Crime Policy and Public Safety.

Homel, R., Hauritz, M., McIlwaine, G., Carvolth, R. and Wortley, R. (forthcoming) 'Preventing alcohol-related crime through community action: The Surfers Paradise Safety Action Project', in Homel, R. (ed.) *Crime Prevention Studies*, 5.

Homel, R., Thomsen, S. and Thommeny J. (1991) 'The problem of violence in licensed premises: The Sydney Study', in Stockwell, T., Lang, E. and Rydon, P. (eds) *The Licensed Drinking Environment: Current Research in Australia and New Zealand*, Melbourne, National Centre for Research into the Prevention of Drug Abuse, pp. 33–40.

Homel, R., Tomsen, S. and Thommeny, J. (1992) 'Public drinking and violence: Not just an alcohol problem', *Journal of Drug Issues*, 22: 679–97.

Ireland, C.S. and Thommeny, J.L. (1993) 'The crime cocktail: Licensed premises, alcohol and street offences', *Drug and Alcohol Review*, 12: 143–50.

Jeavons, C.M. and Taylor, S.P. (1985) 'The control of alcohol-related aggression: Redirecting the inebriate's attention to socially appropriate conduct', *Aggressive Behavior*, 11: 93–101.

Leonard, K. and Senchak, M. (1993) 'Alcohol and premarital aggression among newlywed couples', *Journal of Studies on Alcohol*, Supplement No. 11: 96–108.

Lindqvist, P. (1991) 'Homicides committed by abusers of alcohol and illicit drugs', *British Journal of Addiction*, 86: 321–6.

MacAndrew, C. and Edgerton, R.B. (1969) *Drunken Comportment. A Social Explanation*, Chicago, Aldine.

Macintyre, S. and Homel, R. (forthcoming) 'Danger on the dance floor: A study of interior design, crowding and aggression in night-clubs', in Homel, R. (ed.) *Crime Prevention Studies*, 5.

McIlwain, G. (1994) *Report on the Surfers Paradise Safety Action Project (March–December 1993)*, Gold Coast Surfers Paradise Safety Action Project.

McLean, S., Wood, L., Montgomery, I., Davidson, J. and Jones, M. (1994) 'Promotion of responsible drinking in hotels', *Drug and Alcohol Review*, 13: 247–55.

Marsh, P. and Kibby, K. (1992) *Drinking and Public Disorder*, London, England, Portman Group.

Mayfield, D. (1976) 'Alcoholism, alcohol, intoxication and assaultive behavior', *Diseases of the Nervous System*, 3: 288–91.

MCM Research (1993) *Keeping the Peace: A Guide to the Prevention of Alcohol-Related Disorder*, London, England, Portman Group.

Moize, E.A. (1990) 'Deep in the heart of Texans Austin', *National Geographic*, 177: 50–71.

Myers, T. (1986) 'An analysis of context and alcohol consumption in a group of criminal events', *Alcohol and Alcoholism*, 21: 389–95.

O'Donnell, M. (1985) 'Research on drinking locations of alcohol-impaired drivers: Implications for prevention policies', *Journal of Public Health Policy*, 42: 972–97.

Pernanen, K. (1991) *Alcohol in Human Violence*, New York, Guilford Press.

Plant, M.A., Miller, P., Plant, M.L. and Nichol, P. (1994) 'No such thing as safe glass', *British Medical Journal*, 308: 6–7.

Prus, R. (1978) 'From barrooms to bedrooms: Towards a theory of interpersonal violence', in Beyer, M. (ed.) *Violence in Canada*, Toronto, Gammon, pp. 51–73.

Prus, R. (1983) 'Drinking as activity: An interactive analysis', *Journal of Studies on Alcohol*, 44: 460–75.

Ratcliffe, W.D. and Nutter, R.W. (1979) *Drinking in Edmonton Taverns and Lounges*, Final Report to the Alberta Liquor Licensing Board.

Shepherd, J. (1994) 'Violent Crime: The Role of Alcohol and New Approaches to the Prevention of Injury', *Alcohol and Alcoholism*, 29: 5–10.

Single, E. (1993) 'Public drinking', in Galanter, M. (ed.) *Recent Developments in the Treatment of Alcoholism, Volume 11: Ten Years of Progress*, New York: Plenum Press.

Sommer, R. (1969) *Personal space: The behavioral basis of design*, Englewood Cliffs, N.J., Prentice Hall (chapter 8, 'Designed for drinking').

Stockwell, T. (1992) 'On pseudo-patrons and pseudo-training for bar staff', *British Journal of Addiction*, 87: 677–80.

Stockwell, T. (ed.) (1994) *An Examination of the Appropriateness and Efficacy of Liquor-Licensing Laws Across Australia*, Canberra, Australian Government Publishing Service.

Stockwell, T., Lang, E. and Rydon, P. (1993) 'High risk drinking settings: the association of serving and promotional practices with harmful drinking', *Addiction*, 88: 1519–26.

Stockwell, T., Norberry, J. and Solomon, R. (1995) 'Liquor laws and the prevention of violence in and around Australian pubs and clubs', Paper presented at the International Conference on Social and Health Effects of Different Drinking Patterns, Toronto, Canada.

Stockwell, T., Rydon, P., Lang, E. and Beel, A. (1993) *An Evaluation of the 'Freo Respects You' Responsible Alcohol Service Project*, Curtin University, Perth, National Centre for Research into the Prevention of Drug Abuse.

Stokols, D. (1992) 'Establishing and maintaining healthy environments: Toward a social ecology of health promotion', *American Psychologist*, 47: 6–22.

Taylor, S. and Gammon, C. (1976) 'Aggressive behavior of intoxicated subjects: The effect of third-party intervention', *Journal of Studies on Alcohol*, 37: 917–30.

Tomsen, S., Homel, R. and Thommeny, J. (1991) 'The causes of public violence: Situational "versus" other factors in drinking related assaults', *Australian Violence: Contemporary Perspectives*, pp. 176–93.

Virkkunen, M. (1974) 'Alcohol as a factor precipitating aggression and conflict behaviour leading to homicide', *British Journal of Addiction*, 69: 149–54.

Waring, M.L. and Sperr, I. (1982) 'A comparative study of male and female bartenders: Their potential for assisting in the prevention of alcohol abuse', *Journal of Alcohol and Drug Education*, 28: 1–11.

Wedel, M., Pieters, J.E., Pikaar, N.A. and Ockhuizen, Th. (1991) 'Application of a three-compartment model to a study of the effects of sex, alcohol dose and concentration, exercise and food consumption on the pharmacokinetics of ethanol in healthy volunteers', *Alcohol and Alcoholism*, 26: 329–36.

Welte, J.W. and Abel, E.L. (1989) 'Homicide: Drinking by the victim', *Journal of Studies on Alcohol*, 50: 197–201.

© 1997 Kathryn Graham and Ross Homel

11 Alcohol Education and Harm Minimisation

Martin Plant and Moira Plant

One of the least controversial strategies in the field of alcohol control policies is that of education. While some suggested approaches to controlling alcohol problems are hotly debated, it has often been assumed that education about alcohol is productive, or at least, is important. Possibly the widespread acceptance of such education is attributable to the fact that it is a benign, relatively non-invasive activity.

This chapter seeks to review the degree to which 'alcohol education' may be regarded as an effective way of curbing alcohol problems. This objective is seriously hampered by the fact that the outcomes of much of what passes for such education have never been formally evaluated. In addition it is clearly very difficult, if not impossible, to determine what the impact might be in much later life of the provision of alcohol education to adolescents or other young people. Many of the major influences on drinking behaviours have never been evaluated. The periodic rise and fall of national drinking habits certainly reflect a host of factors. These include disposable incomes, general economic prosperity and popular culture. The reasons for the recent widespread decline in alcohol-impaired driving has not yet been explained in any satisfactory way. Driving after drinking is, in a number of countries, no longer socially acceptable, but the reasons for this have not yet been satisfactorily explained.

The Purpose of Education

'Education' has been defined as a 'process of bringing up' ... 'systematic training and development of the moral and intellectual faculties' (Garmondsway and Simpson 1965). Health education has an important role in bridging the gulf between scientific and clinical knowledge about health and public awareness of such knowledge and its implications. In many countries considerable sums of money are spent in providing the general public and specific subgroups of people with information in the hope that they will then be better equipped to make rational decisions and to avoid unnecessary health risks. The emergence of the AIDS pandemic, for example, has fostered a multiplicity of health education initiatives, funded by both public and private agencies. Health education campaigns are frequently employed in order to raise public awareness. They are also sometimes used to stress political concern or commitment. Surprisingly often, in many areas of health, even the most expensive campaigns are not assessed in any objective or credible manner. Education about alcohol-related issues may be used for a considerable number of purposes. It may also be employed in relation to a number of different target groups. Examples of these groups include children, adolescents, young people, adults, the elderly, social workers, the police, health care professionals, parents, teachers, drivers, expectant mothers, students, the general public or even policy makers.

In the context of alcohol, education has been suggested as a possible means of reducing the risk that young people or adults drink in an abusive or harmful way, either in the short term, or later in life. While it is sometimes conceded that behaviour change may be difficult to achieve, alcohol education has more commonly be used to increase knowledge or to modify attitudes. Especially in the context of adolescents or young people, health education has laid special stress on 'demand reduction', in relation to illicit drugs as well as to alcohol and tobacco. This approach has been especially popular in the US under the slogan 'just say no'. It should be noted that a considerable amount of effort in industrial countries has been devoted to producing alcohol education materials for young people, mainly those at or above the age of puberty. In the US, where the minimum legal age of alcohol consumption is twenty-one, a high proportion of such materials advocate non-use of alcohol. In many other countries, this is not the dominant message and far greater emphasis has been placed on advocating 'sensible', 'moderate' or 'harm-free' drinking. In the United Kingdom, for example, a number of influential publications have sought to familiarise health professionals, problem drinkers and the general public with the alcohol content of specific types of beverage and with guidelines for 'low-risk' and 'high-risk' alcohol consumption (Royal College of General Practitioners 1986, Royal College of Psychiatrists 1986, Royal

College of Physicians 1987, Health Education Board for Scotland 1994, Royal Colleges 1995).

The term 'alcohol education' covers a wide range of activities and processes. Such education is much broader in scope than simply the provision of information and advice in the form of leaflets and videos. It could be argued that an individual's alcohol education encompasses all of the alcohol-related experiences of a lifetime. Most of these are likely to be informal. These include personal drinking occasions as well as more general impressions formed and reformed in societies or social groups in which alcohol may or may not be widely used or abused.

Bagnall (1987) has drawn attention to a conflict between two types of activity in this field:

> Some health-related initiatives concentrate on directly influencing individual knowledge, attitudes, and behavioural intentions and skills. These could be regarded as *health education* programmes. Others involve organisational and political interventions deemed necessary to facilitate certain health-related behavioural changes. These could be regarded as *health promotion* programmes. (p. 162)

She goes on to cite Green (1979) who has maintained that the assessment of changes in health-related behaviour need to be measured in terms of the 'total intervention', both health education and health promotion. Bagnall also noted that in the 'real world' the latter ideal may not always be realised. Moreover, the distinction between health education and health promotion may not always be clear. For the purposes of this chapter, attention is focused upon 'education' as defined by Bagnall. Even so, this is considered in the broader context suggested by Green.

A mass of educational materials on alcohol have been produced. Some of these appear to have been carefully designed and have been produced to a professional standard. Others have none of these virtues and appear to have been compiled with little thought or expertise. What is striking from a researcher's perspective is that only a tiny minority of such materials have ever been subjected to any form of objective assessment or evaluation. Sadly, many of the evaluations have been poorly designed, with obvious flaws such as a lack of control group. It appears that the business of producing alcohol education materials is largely disconnected from that of gauging their possible value. There are a number of reasons for this situation. First, many agencies lack resources both to produce materials and to evaluate them. Second, it is possible that it is widely assumed that 'alcohol education' is intrinsically beneficial, or at least, harmless. Third, evaluation may be seen as threatening and because of this, avoided. A recent inspection of English-language alcohol education materials for school pupils by one of the authors of this chapter (Moira Plant) indicated that there has been considerable duplication of effort. Many rather similar packs and other resource materials exist. A considerable number of these appear to have been well designed. Even so, it would have been helpful if a higher proportion of effort in this field had been devoted not to reinventing the wheel so much as to the assessment of the usefulness of those materials that already exist.

Does it Work?

Sadly, some of the most careful appraisals of the impact of alcohol education have reached the conclusion that effectiveness is hard to demonstrate in relation to either alcohol or illicit drugs. Several authors have concluded that there is very little evidence to show that health education leads people to refrain from using alcohol or illicit drugs or to reduce the levels of their use (for example, Kalb 1975, Kinder et al. 1980, Schaps et al. 1981, Bandy and President 1983, Grant 1986, Tobler 1986, Moskowitz 1989, Bagnall 1991, May 1991, Gerstein and Green 1993, Gorman 1996). Some studies have even suggested that licit or illicit drug use may even be *increased* by such initiatives (for example, Kinder et al. 1980, De Haes 1987, Plant and Plant 1992, Hawthorne et al. 1995). Clearly, it is as important to determine whether health education does any harm as it is to discover whether it does any good.

Young People

As noted above, an enormous amount of effort has been invested in the provision of alcohol education for young people. It is widely assumed that these are a high priority target group for such education because they are either not yet drinkers or are at the beginning of their 'drinking careers'. It is further frequently accepted that the young are especially vulnerable and in need of guidance in this context. Much of the pessimism in relation to the effectiveness of alcohol education is based upon studies of the impact of alcohol education on the young (see especially Kinder et al. 1980, Bandy and President 1983, May 1991, Gorman 1996).

Botvin and Botvin (1992) have drawn the following conclusion:

> Traditional approaches to substance abuse prevention relying on the provision of factual information about the adverse consequences of substance use/abuse or attempting to foster the development of self-esteem and responsible decision making have produced disappointing results. (p. 299)

In spite of this general gloom, there have been some reports of positive outcomes. McAlistair et al. (1981) have reported that a group of high school students in the US were enabled to better withstand peer pressure to drink, smoke or use illicit drugs. Bagnall (1991) concluded that an alcohol education programme for British school students did produce a significant, if small, positive impact on alcohol-related behaviours. Gerstein and Green (1993) have reported that although there is little persuasive evidence of attitudinal or behavioural change, it does appear that some educational initiatives have increased levels of alcohol-related knowledge. Hawthorne et al. (1995) have reported that their evaluation of the large-scale Life Education Programme in Australia suggested that exposure to this scheme was associated with *increased* substance use. Their results showed that involvement with this programme had led to an increase in smoking by teenage girls, while amongst boys exposed to the programme, drinking, smoking and analgesic use had increased. The implications of these findings are considered later in this chapter.

Hansen (1992), reviewing available evidence, drew the conclusion that 'social influence' and 'comprehensive' educational programmes appear to have been the most likely to have led to reductions in the use of legal or illegal drugs by school students. This author further concluded that approaches that emphasise providing information do not appear to be very effective.

Exhortation to drink less, by itself, appears to have little, if any, effect. This view has been endorsed by a number of authors (see especially, Wodak 1994). Moreover, as stressed by Kline and Canter (1994), health education on alcohol is unlikely to have much impact if youthful drinking is influenced by

> factors beyond the influence of school-based interventions such as demographic characteristics or quality of family environment. On the other hand, educational programs would have greater

potential efficacy if teenage drinking is influenced by factors more amenable to change, such as characteristics of individual adolescents like their alcohol expectancies or social reasoning. (p. 139)

These authors concluded from their own study of white US high school students that: 'drinking varied with different types of "unchangeable" and "changeable" factors for male and female students'. Amongst males, 9 per cent of the variance of their drinking was explained by demographic family variables. A far higher proportion, 38 per cent, was explained by 'adolescent characteristic variables'. Amongst the latter, it was further noted that the most important item, accounting for 23 per cent of the variance, was 'social skills reasoning'. For both sexes, lower social reasoning skills were associated with higher levels of alcohol consumption. Amongst females, a different general pattern of results was evident. Adolescent characteristic variables explained a lower proportion of the variance of drinking, 21 per cent. Social reasoning skills only explained 9 per cent. Amongst females, demographic-family and peer approval variables were uniquely predictive. These results indicated that for both sexes, a substantial proportion of the variance of drinking patterns was not explained. Moreover, what was explained showed that a high proportion of the variance was due to 'unchangeable' factors.

Pentz et al. (1989) have described a favourable outcome from a study in which teenage drinking was slightly reduced. This intervention involved a combination of school activities and televison. This exercise attempted to involve parents through their children's homework. The possible role of the mass media in this context is discussed below.

These results certainly support the view that, while teenage drinking may be influenced by education, there are substantial limits on what might be achieved. Kline and Canter further concluded that there is evidence (see Schinke and Gilchrist 1985, Hays and Ellickson 1990, Newman et al. 1992) that there is value in teaching specific skills to resist peer pressure in relation to licit and illicit drug use. 'Although such interventions may be more beneficial for males than females, the potential for alcohol-related problems is much greater among males' (Kline and Carter 1994: 146).

Anderson (1995) concluded that active participation appears to be a key ingredient in the most effective substance education for young people. She also noted that positive outcomes have been reported from studies which take into account young people's attitudes and behaviours.

The subject of alcohol-impaired driving is discussed in detail by Stewart and Sweedler in Chapter 8 of this volume. Even so, under the heading of 'young people' one related study is cited here. Kooler and Bruvold (1992) have described an educational intervention programme for juveniles convicted of driving while under the influence of alcohol. This exercise was conducted in Contra Costa County, California. The study group of this study were more than 100 individuals who had been convicted between 1983 and 1988. These were compared with others who did not participate. This study produced the following conclusions:

> Participants demonstrated increased knowledge, stronger attitudes against driving under the influence, and less risky alcohol and automobile related behaviors. County juvenile records analyzed by the logit procedure showed that class participants had a significantly lower number of repeat offences compared to non-program participants that could not be explained by race, offense severity, age or gender. (p. 87)

The theme of alcohol-impaired driving is also discussed by Hingson, Berson and Dowley in Chapter 9 of this book.

The Use of Mass Media

A number of campaigns have been mounted using the mass media to provide information for the general public. A number of these have been assessed. Such evaluation has invariably been short term in scope, though use has sometimes been made of control group areas in which populations have not been exposed to the campaign under scrutiny (for example, Plant et al. 1979). Attempts to employ the media to persuade people to change their drinking habits appear to have generally been unsuccessful (Plant et al. 1979, Dorn and South 1983).

Edwards et al. (1994) have stated:

> In summary, efforts to assess the effect of mass media campaigns on drinking behaviour which have utilised quasi-experimental designs, have generally failed to detect significant effects on consumption as a consequence of exposure to these campaigns. When campaigns have been supplemented by other interpersonal and policy focused interventions, they may have contributed to behavioural change. (pp. 174–5)

These authors also concluded that mass media campaigns may change, or at least support change, in the 'social climate' in relation to drinking. They cite several studies to support this view. These include an investigation by Barber et al. (1989) in which self-reported drinking was reduced by the use of a combination of televison advertising and letters circulated prior to the use of this medium. Other studies are also cited in which positive effects appear to have been produced (see especially Casswell et al. 1989). Edwards et al. also draw attention to evidence that the use of mass media increased both awareness and support in relation to Ontario policy on the availablity of alcohol in recreational areas (see especially Glicksman 1986, Douglas 1990).

Some Underlying Theories

Human motivation is a never-ending topic for investigation. Drinking habits reflect an enormous number of factors: social, cultural, economic, psychological and physiological (Fazey 1977). It has been demonstrated that even very young children form clear, if sometimes transient, views of alcohol and its use by adults (Jahoda and Cramond 1972, Fossey 1994). Individual drinking habits often change markedly at different stages in a person's life or 'drinking career' (Fillmore 1988). 'Education' about alcohol begins early for many people and extends far beyond what might formally be provided or considered to constitute 'alcohol education'. Drinking is an integral part of many cultures and is featured prominently in the continuing process of socialisation to which an individual is exposed (Heath 1995).

The formal provision of health education has sometimes taken into account a number of theories. These include the *Theory of Reasoned Action* (Fishbein and Ajzen 1975), *Social Learning Theory* (Bandura 1984) and the *Health Belief Model* (Janz and Becker 1984). The *Theory of Reasoned Action* stresses that human behaviour is influenced by the desire to receive the approval of friends and significant others. *Social Learning Theory* suggests that behaviours are influenced by the outcomes of one's actions upon oneself and other people. The *Health Belief Model* suggests that people weigh the potential benefits and disadvantages of specific actions. The latter equation may be influenced by available information. Tones (1987) has described a *'Health Action Model'*. This emphasises factors that might serve as barriers to health, such as inaccurate information or unhelpful public policy.

An important barrier to health promotion is the fact that many, if not most, people enjoy engaging in pleasant activities, even if these sometimes incur risks. Elkind (1967, 1984, 1985) has described the concept of the 'Personal Fable'. This is the belief of many people – and especially, it has been argued, adolescents – that they may indulge in risky forms of behaviour without harm. Some people believe that they are invulnerable. Health warnings are unlikely to have much impact on such individuals.

May (1993) has noted that there has been a shift in the emphasis of alcohol education from that viewing target audiences as 'passive' to an approach demanding a more active participation. He further commented that newer, more sophisticated models of affective or skills-based education have become evident. These approaches are exemplified by 'Social assertiveness training (Pentz 1985), life skills training (Botvin 1985a, b) and cognitive-behavioural skills training (Schinke and Gilchrist 1984)' (p. 159).

A detailed review by Gorman (1996) examined the impact of school-based social skills to prevent alcohol use amongst young people. Gorman concluded that such programmes, though not counterproductive, had produced little effect. May (1993) had earlier noted that some recent alcohol education initiatives have been intended to develop in adolescents the skills to resist peer pressure to engage in health-risk behaviours such as heavy drinking. He takes issue with the assumption that peer pressure is either necessarily bad, or that adolescent alcohol 'misusers' are necessarily socially incompetent. He stresses that peer groups may restrain drinking patterns as well as foster heavy drinking. May also states that socialisation into drinking habits occurs mainly beyond the school. He endorses the suggestion of O'Connor and Saunders (1992) that it would be logical to attempt to teach the young to drink safely. Even so, he acknowledges that such an approach might not be generally acceptable. Bauman and Ennett (1996) have suggested that peer influence may be of less importance in shaping adolescent drug use than is widely believed. They put forward the view that this might be one reason why so many educational initiatives have led to poor or very modest, short-lived results.

Jessor and Jessor (1977) have made a major contribution to the understanding of adolescent behaviours in the form of 'Problem Behavior Theory'. This emphasises the possible importance of family background and upbringing on an individual's propensity to engage in risky or health threatening or 'deviant' behaviours. It should, however, be noted that this theory originates mainly from US urban studies. These may not be wholly applicable to other contexts. As emphasised by several commentators (for example, Plant 1979, Fillmore 1988), individual drinking patterns frequently change during different stages in life. It cannot, therefore, be assumed that people are necessarily locked upon a fixed course that is predetermined by their early life experiences, even though the latter may be important.

Conclusions and Discussion

Drinking habits, as noted above, are influenced by a multiplicity of complex factors. Different subgroups of people, if they drink at all, do so in varied and often changing ways. It is unrealistic to imagine that even the best designed alcohol education will prevent many people from sometimes drinking heavily or in a potentially damaging way. Alcohol education, in short, is no panacea for sporadic heavy or 'problem drinking'. Even so, it does have a role to play.

An inescapable conclusion from the available literature on 'alcohol education' is that there is very little evidence to indicate that it is effective in changing the behaviour of either young people or of the population in general. Current evidence is plentiful, but of generally poor quality and must mainly be discounted as being inconclusive or lacking in scientific rigour. Most of the studies that report achieving change relate to short-term attitudes or levels of knowledge. Few have demonstrated a capacity to modify behaviour in the short term and their possible longer-term impact remains unknown. As noted above, several studies have suggested that exposure to education on alcohol and other psychoactive drugs may even lead to increases, rather than decreases, in levels of their use. In this context, the study by Hawthorne et al. (1995) has important implications. These authors have put forward the following suggestion:

> These mixed findings suggest that drug education programmes should be both drug specific and matched with students' gender and drug recruitment patterns rather than generic and indiscriminately delivered. (p. 214)

A realistic comment on the role of health education in relation to the limitation of 'problem drinking' has been provided by Keeling (1994):

> the big question is how to do this: how to reshape the environment of norms and expectations, to humanise the context of

choices, to construct caring communities, and thereby to reduce the prevalence and cost of problem drinking. This is no short-term project. It will not fit neatly into the scope of 2 years of a grant. It is also not just health education. (p. 246)

It is morally right that people should be provided with the best and most accurate information about alcohol that is available. While medical and scientific opinion on a number of issues may vary, it is important to avoid unnecessary confusion. An example of the latter was provided in the United Kingdom in December 1995. Before that date, there had, for a number of years, been in use criteria for 'low-' and 'high-risk' drinking agreed by the Royal Medical Colleges. A report by the Department of Health (for England) recommended raising the weekly levels of 'low-risk' drinking for males and females from 21 and 14 'units' of alcohol to 28 and 21 units respectively: a UK 'unit' is equivalent to 7.9 grams of absolute alcohol (Department of Health 1995). This recommendation was widely criticised and lacked credibility because it did not have the support of a substantial number of influential clinicians and researchers (Marmot 1995). Extensive and largely hostile mass media coverage highlighted these differences and this situation has probably done little to increase public understanding in this context.

Existing evaluations of formally provided 'alcohol education' suggest that it is certainly not a proven or effective means of curbing general levels of 'problem drinking'. This has been clear for some time. It is unreasonable, as noted by Keeling (1994), to rely solely upon education to produce major changes in social behaviour. Drinking habits are shaped by many forces; some of these are already powerful moderators. It should be acknowledged that most people who drink generally do so in moderation and without serious adverse consequences; even though many do sometimes drink in potentially harmful ways. Peer pressure and other social factors often serve as restraining influences upon drinking behaviour.

The provision of 'alcohol education', especially for adolescents and students in schools and colleges, is politically attractive and is widespread in at least some countries. Available evidence suggests that such activity in itself may increase awareness or factual knowledge, but is unlikely in the short term at least, to reduce harmful drinking. Longer-term effects are unknown.

In view of this, what is the potential role that alcohol education could have in relation to harm minimisation? First, 'education' in this context is best defined as the total process of informing and instructing about alcohol, its use, problems and the likely means of reducing such problems. The type of information that is reviewed in this book is part of this process. Alcohol education should be conceived of as extending far beyond what might be formally provided on school or college curricula. Most people's information about and orientations to alcohol are derived, not just from formal teaching in educational institutions, but from their total socialisation, their families, friends and life experiences. The material presented in this book demonstrates that the drinking environment and patterns of drinking may exert important influences on whether or not alcohol consumption does have harmful consequences.

Following on from the recommendations of Hawthorne et al. (1995), it would appear advisable for future formal initiatives in alcohol (tobacco or drug) education to be tailored for specific subgroups of recipients. It may sometimes not be productive to expose large, mixed groups of people to general messages in view of their varied experiences and behaviours in relation to alcohol use. School-based alcohol education could usefully concentrate more on the issue of the patterns and circumstances when drinking is most likely to cause harm. The latter include drinking to intoxication and driving. Even so, it would seem that school-based initiatives have produced meagre results and only rarely have positive behavioural changes been reported (see Pentz et al. 1989).

A more fruitful approach to alcohol education would be for schools and colleges to be integrated within more general community programmes to devise and implement local harm-minimisation policies. An indispensable element in the creation and operation of such initiatives would be the diffusion of information on which strategies have been shown to work in the past. The list of options here includes the creation of safe and attractive settings in which the young and others may drink safely. The training of bar staff, the enforcement of laws on underage drinking or of serving alcohol to intoxicated persons, and the introduction of by-laws to restrict the late-night opening of licensed premises are examples of strategies which appear to have been productive in some places in the past. 'Alcohol education' in the widest sense should be a crucial and central component in the design of local as well as national or international responses designed to reduce levels of alcohol-related problems. Accordingly, it would be logical to target not only school or college students, but also local and national politicians and policy makers (such as local and national civil servants, teachers and professionals in the health and social services, the police and those engaged in the production, distribution and sale of beverage alcohol). There is a great gulf between the considerable array of information of the type reviewed in this book and awareness of 'what works'. This is paralleled in relation to the failure of much of the information about the effectiveness of clinical treatments for alcohol problems to be widely known amongst health care professionals. Another obvious priority target group for alcohol education are parents. The latter are certainly very influential in shaping the orientations towards alcohol of their children, but could they be helped to do this better?

Future research could usefully investigate whether it is possible to influence youthful drinking behaviours by modifying the settings, such as bar environments, in which drinking commonly occurs. Some of the evidence presented elsewhere in this book suggests that such strategies have been productive.

Alone, alcohol education is not a panacea for the problematic consumption of alcohol and its sequelae. Even so, education is and should remain an important, if supporting rather than primary, part of alcohol policy. It is evident that, even short term, alcohol education campaigns may increase knowledge and thereby serve to raise awareness. Changing attitudes or behaviours is a more elusive objective. In spite of this, alcohol problems need not be wholly intractable. In many countries, as already noted, rates of crimes of drunkenness and accidents involving intoxicated drivers have declined in recent years. Such changes certainly reflect a number of factors, such as overall levels of alcohol consumption. Even so, in the United Kingdom, for example, these changes have been disaggregated from the much smaller changes in per capita consumption. It is possible that the decline in alcohol-impaired driving has been at least in part a response to heightened public awareness of the seriousness of this type of behaviour.

To conclude, alcohol education has not so far emerged as a dependable or effective general means of controlling heavy or problematic drinking. It is, however, morally right that people should be provided with the most accurate relevant information about alcohol and its effects. Moreover, it should be emphasised that education about alcohol is largely informal and is imparted through socialisation and life experience. The 'alcohol field' is highly politicised and messages about alcohol frequently reflect strong ideologies or major political and economic interests. Researchers and educationalists have a duty to operate in an ethical manner in this sometimes disorderly arena (see Plant et al. 1996). Education may serve to shape popular culture and sentiment about alcohol. Accordingly, alcohol education, though not a primary arm of alcohol control policy, should be an important secondary or supporting part of such policy. It would be unfair to impose unrealistic or inflated expectations on formal 'alcohol education' of the type so commonly provided in schools and colleges. Even so, such provision should continue to be a legitimate part of the educational process, albeit with far more concern about effectiveness than has hitherto been the case.

Acknowledgements

The authors are indebted to Mrs Kellie Anderson for comments and advice on the initial draft of this chapter. The Alcohol & Health Research Group receives funding from the Portman Group. Its work is also supported by agencies such as charities, research councils and government departments. The views expressed in this chapter are solely those of the authors.

References

Anderson, K. (1995) *Young People and Alcohol, Drugs and Tobacco*, Copenhagen, World Health Organization Regional Publications European Series No. 66.

Bagnall, G. (1987) 'Alcohol education and its evaluation – some key issues', *Health Education Journal*, 46: 162–5.

Bagnall, G. (1991) *Educating Young Drinkers*, London, Tavistock/ Routledge.

Bandura, A. (1984) ' "Self Efficacy". Toward a unifying theory of behavioral change', *Psychology Review*, 84: 191–215.

Bandy, P. and President, P.A. (1983) 'Recent literature on drug abuse and prevention and mass media, focusing on youth, parents, women and the elderly', *Journal of Drug Education*, 13: 255–71.

Barber, J.G., Bradshaw, R. and Walsh, C. (1989) 'Reducing alcohol consumption through television advertising', *Journal of Consulting and Clinical Psychology*, 57: 613–18.

Bauman, K.E. and Ennett, S.T. (1996) 'On the importance of peer influence for adolescent drug use: commonly neglected considerations', *Addiction*, 91: 185–98.

Botvin, G.J. (1985a) 'The life skills training program as a health promotion strategy: theoretical issues and empirical findings', *Special Services in the Schools*, 1: 9–23.

Botvin, G.J. (1985b) 'Prevention of adolescent substance abuse through the development of personal and social competence', in Glynn, T.J., Lenkfeld, C.G. and Ludford, J.P. (eds) *Preventing Social Problems Through Life Skills Training*, Seattle, University of Washington Press.

Casswell, S., Gilmore, L., Maguire, V. and Ransome, R. (1989) 'Changes in public support for alcohol policies following a community-based campaign', *British Journal of Addiction*, 84: 515–22.

De Haes, W.F.M. (1987) 'Looking for effective drug education programmes: 15 years' exploration of the effects of different drug education programmes', *Health Education – Theory and Practice*, 2: 433–8.

Department of Health (1995) *Sensible Drinking: The Report of an Inter-Departmental Working Group*, London, Department of Health.

Dorn, N. and South, N. (1983) *Message in a Bottle: Theoretical Overview and Annotated Bibliography on the Mass Media and Alcohol*, Aldershot, Gower.

Douglas, R.R. (1990) 'Formulating alcohol policies for community recreation facilities: tactics and problems', in Giesbrecht, N., Conley, P., Denniston, R.W., Gliksman, L., Holder, H., Pederson, A., Room, R. and Shain, M. (eds) *Research, Action, and the Community: Experience in the Prevention of Alcohol and Other Drug Problems*, Rockville, MD, US Department of Health and Human Services OSAP Prevention Monograph Number 4, pp. 61–7.

Edwards, G., Anderson, P., Babor, T.F., Casswell, S., Ferrence, R., Giesbrecht, N., Godfrey, C., Holder, H., Lemmens, P., Mäkelä, K., Midanik, L., Norström, T., Österberg, E., Romelsjö, A., Room, R., Simpura, J. and Skog, Ø-J. (1994) *Alcohol Policy and the Public Good*, Oxford, Oxford University Press.

Elkind, D. (1967) 'Egocentrism in adolescence', *Child Development*, 30: 1025–34.

Elkind, D. (1984) 'Teenage thinking: implications for health care', *Pediatric Nursing*, 10: 383–5.

Elkind, D. (1985) 'Cognitive development and adolescent disabilities', *Journal of Adolescent Health Care*, 6: 84–9.

Fazey, C. (1977) *The Aetiology of Psychoactive Substance Use*, Paris, UNESCO.

Fillmore, K.M. (1988) *Alcohol Use Across the Life Course*, Toronto, Addiction Research Foundation.

Fishbein, M. and Ajzen, I. (1975) *Belief, Attitude, Intention and Behavior: An Introduction to Theory and Research*, Massachusetts, Addison-Wesley.

Fossey, E. (1994) *Growing Up With Alcohol*, London, Tavistock/Routledge.

Garmondsway, G.N. and Simpson, J. (1965) *The Penguin English Dictionary*, Harmondsworth, Penguin, p. 236.

Gerstein, D. and Green, L. (eds) (1993) *Preventing Drug Abuse, What Do We Know?* Washington, D.C., National Academy Press.

Gliksman, L. (1986) 'Alcohol management policies for municipal recreation departments: an evaluation of the Thunder Bay model', in Giesbrecht, N. and Cox, A. (eds) *Prevention and the Environment*, Toronto, Addiction Research Foundation, pp. 198–204.

Gorman, D.M. (1996) 'Do school-based skills training programs prevent alcohol use among young people', *Addiction Research*, 4: 191–210.

Grant, M. (1986) 'Comparative analysis of the impact of alcohol education in North America and Western Europe', in Babor, T. (ed.) *Alcohol and Culture - Comparative Perspectives from Europe and North America*, New York, New York Academy of Sciences, pp. 198–210.

Green, L. (1979) 'National policy in the promotion of health', *International Journal of Health Education*, 22: 161–8.

Hansen, W.B. (1992) 'School-based substance abuse prevention: a review of the state of the art in curriculum, 1980–1990', *Health Education Research*, 7: 403–30.

Hawthorne, G., Garrard, J. and Dunt, D. (1995) 'Does Life Education's drug education program have a public health benefit?' *Addiction*, 90: 205–16.

Hays, R.D. and Ellikson, P.L. (1990) 'How generalizable are adolescents' beliefs about pro-drug pressures and resistance self-efficacy?' *Journal of Applied Social Psychology*, 20: 321–40.

Health Education Board for Scotland (1994) *That's the Limit: A Guide to Sensible Drinking*, Edinburgh, Health Education Board for Scotland.

Heath, D. (1995) (ed.) *International Handbook on Alcohol and Culture*, Westport, CT, Greenwood Press.

Jahoda, G. and Cramond, J. (1972) *Children and Alcohol: A Developmental Study in Glasgow*, London, HMSO.

Janz, N.K. and Becker, M.H. (1984) 'The Health Belief Model, a decade later', *Health Education Quarterly*, 11: 1–47.

Jessor, R. and Jessor, S. (1977) *Problem Behavior and Psychological Development: A Longitudinal Study of Youth*, New York, Academic Press.

Kalb, M. (1975) 'The myth of alcoholism prevention', *Preventive Medicine*, 4: 404–16.

Keeling, R.P. (1994) 'Changing the context: The power in prevention: Alcohol awareness, caring and community', *Journal of American College Health*, 42: 243–7.

Kinder, B.N., Pape, N.E. and Walfish, S. (1980) 'Drug and alcohol education programmes: a review of outcome studies', *International Journal of the Addictions*, 15: 1035–54.

Kline, R.B. and Canter, W.A. (1994) 'Can education programs affect teenage drinking? A multivariate perspective', *Journal of Drug Education*, 24: 139–49.

Kooler, J.M. and Bruvold, W.H. (1992) 'Evaluation of an educational intervention upon knowledge, attitudes and behavior concerning drinking/drugged driving', *Journal of Drug Education*, 2: 87–100.

McAlistair, A., Perry, C., Killen, J., Simkard, L.A. and Maudsy, N. (1981) 'Pilot study of smoking, alcohol and drug abuse prevention', *American Journal of Public Health*, 70: 719–25.

Marmot, M. (1995) 'A not-so-sensible drinks policy', *Lancet*, 346: 1643–44.

May, C. (1991) 'Research on alcohol education for young people: a critical review of the literature', *Health Education Journal*, 50: 195–9.

May, C. (1993) 'Resistance to peer group pressure: an inadequate basis for alcohol education', *Health Education Research*, 8: 159–65.

Moskowitz, J. (1989) 'The primary prevention of alcohol problems: a critical review of the research literature', *Journal of Studies on Alcohol*, 50: 54–88.

Newman, I.M., Anderson, C.S. and Farrell, K.A. (1992) 'Role rehearsal and efficacy: Two 15-month evaluations of a ninth-grade alcohol education program', *Journal of Drug Education*, 22: 55–67.

O'Connor, J. and Saunders, W.M. (1992) 'Drug education: an appraisal of popular prevention', *International Journal of the Addictions*, 27: 165–83.

Owen, R. (1995) 'A comment on "just say 'no' to alcohol abuse and misuse" ', *Addiction*, 90: 133–4.

Pentz, M.A. (1985) 'Social competence skills and self-efficacy as determinants of substance abuse in adolescence', in Schiffman, M. and Wills, T.A. (eds) *Coping With Substance Use*, New York, Academic Press.

Pentz, M.A., Dwyer, J.H., Mackinnon, D.P., Flay, B.R. and Hansen, W.B. (1989) 'A multicommunity trial for primary prevention of adolescent drug abuse: effects on drug use prevalence', *Journal of the American Medical Association*, 261: 3259–66.

Plant, M.A. (1979) *Drinking Careers: Occupations, Drinking Habits and Drinking Problems*, London, Tavistock.

Plant, M.A., Pirie, F. and Kreitman, N. (1979) 'Evaluation of the Scottish Health Education Unit's 1976 campaign on alcoholism', *Social Psychiatry*, 14: 11–24.

Plant, M.A. and Plant, M.L. (1992) *Risk Takers: Alcohol, Drugs, Sex and Youth*, London, Tavistock/Routledge.

Plant, M.A., Plant, M.L. and Vernon, B. (1996) 'Ethics, funding and alcohol research', *Alcohol and Alcoholism*, 30: 1–9.

Royal Colleges (1995) *Alcohol and the Heart in Perspective*, London, Royal Colleges of Physicians, Psychiatrists and General Practitioners.

Royal College of General Practitioners (1986) *Alcohol: A Balanced View*, London, Royal College of General Practitioners.

Royal College of Physicians (1987) *A Great and Growing Evil: The Medical Consequences of Alcohol Abuse*, London, Tavistock.

Royal College of Psychiatrists (1986) *Alcohol: Our Favourite Drug*, London, Tavistock.

Schaps, E., Dibartolo, R., Moskowitz, J., Balley, C.G. and Churgin, G. (1981) 'A review of 127 drug abuse prevention programme evaluations', *Journal of Drug Issues*, 11: 17–43.

Schinke, S.P. and Gilchrist, L.D. (1984) *Life Skills Counselling With Adolescents*, Baltimore, MA, University Park Press.

Schinke, S.P. and Gilchrist, L.D. (1985) 'Preventing substance abuse with children and adolescents', *Journal of Consulting and Clinical Psychology*, 53: 596–602.

Tobler, N. (1986) 'Meta-analysis of 143 adolescent drug prevention programs, Quantitative outcome results of program participants compared to a control or comparison group', *Journal of Drug Issues*, 16: 537–67.

Tones, K. (1987) 'Role of the health action model in preventing drug abuse', *Health Education Research – Theory and Practice*, 2: 305–16.
Wodak, A. (1994) 'Just say "no" to alcohol abuse and misuse' (Editorial), *Addiction*, 89: 787–9.

12 Local Regulation and Enforcement Strategies for Licensed Premises

Philip Rydon and Tim Stockwell

Introduction

This chapter examines the major harm-minimisation strategies in the area of local liquor-licensing regulation and law enforcement. Research has highlighted that patrons attending licensed premises place themselves at increased risk of experiencing a social, medical or legal problem by becoming intoxicated. The risk of such problems may be minimised via three main regulatory approaches: responsible self-regulation by licensees; an effective law enforcement programme; and regulation by liquor-licensing and other government authorities concerned with the operation of licensed premises. While most of the data cited in this chapter are from Australia, we believe the implications are international.

Harm and Licensed Drinking Settings

While it has been estimated that only one-third of all alcohol sold in Australia is actually consumed on licensed premises (Stockwell 1996) such venues have been identified as major contributors to the burden of harm associated with alcohol intoxication. For example, Australian studies suggest that: more than half of patrons leaving hotels and night clubs have breathalyser blood alcohol readings (BALs) above 0.05mg/100ml and one in ten exceed 0.15mg/100ml (Rydon et al. 1993, McLean et al. 1994a); 40% of drink-driving accidents and 50% of drink-driving offences occur after drinking at licensed venues (Lang et al. 1990); police and hospital emergency department workloads peak on Friday and Saturday nights between 10 p.m. and 2 a.m., coinciding with the peak times patrons leave hotels and night clubs (Ireland and Thommeny 1993, Stockwell 1995); around 60% of street offences (assault, offensive behaviour, offensive language, malicious damage, domestic violence, noise complaints and drink-driving) brought to the attention of the police occur in or near licensed premises (Ireland and Thommeny 1993); and 72% of respondents in a community survey, who reported experiencing harm within three months prior to the survey were intoxicated on licensed premises on that occasion (Stockwell, Lang and Rydon 1993). Reviews of the international literature also suggest that drinking on licensed premises is associated with disproportionate amounts of harm (for example, O'Donnell 1985, Single and Wortley 1993).

Despite research demonstrating that considerable problems of intoxication arise from licensed premises, police statistics indicate that very few prosecutions are brought against licensees or their employees for serving intoxicated patrons (Craze 1995). The above data suggest that current standards of management practice on licensed premises and police levels of enforcement of liquor licensing laws and their efficacy in minimising intoxication and alcohol-related violence are unsatisfactory.

Key Variables Associated with Harm in Licensed Settings

As discussed by Graham and Homel in Chapter 10 of this volume, a wide range of variables have been identified in the literature on alcohol-related violence in licensed drinking settings. For example, observational studies, such as that conducted by Homel et al. (1992) involving 300 hours of observation in 23 licensed premises with a reputation for violence in Sydney, have suggested that violence on licensed premises is concentrated in specific places, at specific times and appears to be triggered by a number of interacting risk factors such as: cheap drinks, mostly male clientele, boring music, overcrowding and high levels of intoxication. Other major factors identified by researchers include bar design, seating, noise, ventilation, high energy live bands, sexual promotions or entertainment, low bar staff–patron ratios, and aggressive or rigid security.

Most of the variables listed above can be, and often are, directly manipulated by licensees and managers of licensed venues to position the business in order to maximise profitability. Most of the key variables are also subject in legislation, if not in practice, to the regulatory control of licensing authorities and the police (Rydon 1995).

Useful Models in Understanding the Contribution of Licensed Venues to Harm

Several conceptual models provide a framework for locating regulatory approaches and their likely efficacy. The broadest of these is the public health model (Moser 1980) which views alcohol-related harm as resulting from a complex interaction between alcohol, the individual drinker and the socio-cultural/physical environment in which alcohol is consumed. Regulatory approaches which address each of these three components of the model will be discussed in the next section.

While intoxication is in itself a legal problem for drinkers who drive whilst intoxicated, the broader range of factors which mediate alcohol-related harm are also of importance to harm minimisation efforts. Marsh and Fox-Kibby (1992) provide a useful model of the alcohol–violence connection, which has important implications for the licensed drinking environment. This model suggests that intoxication leads to cognitive and perceptual deficit which, in turn, results in reduced communication and conceptual skills, lowered tolerance to frustration and reduced ability to resolve conflict. The potential for experiencing frustration at some licensed venues may be heightened by factors such as overcrowding, slow service, aggressive security, poor entertainment, competition for females at entertainment venues catering to a mostly male crowd, noise levels preventing communication, no available seating and poor ventilation.

A simple model identifying the key licensed drinking environment regulatory levers is presented in Figure 12.1 overleaf. This model highlights the bar environment as a powerful filter which has the potential to modify consumer demand and normative behaviour. Consumer demand for alcohol in licensed settings is influenced by a wide range of external factors, such as cultural norms; individual life circumstances, personality factors and tolerance to alcohol; alcohol advertising and information campaigns; the economy; and regulatory controls such as alcohol taxation and law enforcement. The bar environment, however, may exert considerable influence over consumer demand in this setting and has the potential to decrease or enhance the probability of patrons experiencing alcohol-related harm. The nature of the bar environment is largely a function of management decisions regarding the consumer niche market targeted and the short- and longer-term profitability of the business. These decisions essentially guide other management policies which may impact on alcohol-related harm. Management has a degree of control over all

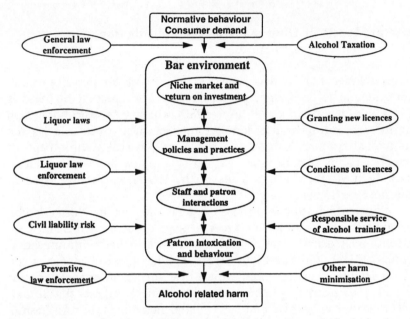

Figure 12.1: Role of regulation in the prevention of alcohol-related harm in the licensed drinking environment

three components of the public health model. For example, management can modify the physical environment to minimise patron frustration, employ staff with good social skills, price alcohol to encourage or discourage intoxication, set normative standards of behaviour in the bar environment and market the bar in such a way as to discourage individuals from causing trouble. A number of regulatory mechanisms may be exerted to place pressure on bar management to comply with a minimum standard of practice in the interests of public health. These include: the framing of liquor laws, particularly those relating to intoxication, overcrowding and underage; the effective enforcement of such laws to provide a strong deterrent to irresponsible practice; the behaviour of liquor licensing boards and authorities in granting and renewing licences which impact on marketplace competition; and in the placing of special licence restrictions and privileges concerning issues such as trading hours, discounting and the sale of packaged alcohol; a requirement for mandatory training in responsible service of alcohol for licensees, management and staff; and a pursuance of civil liability cases to highlight the potential costs of irresponsible alcohol service. Other harm-minimisation measures which may be put in place in the immediate vicinity of licensed premises include an increased visible police presence on the streets at high-risk times for violence and drink-driving; and modifications to the physical environment by local authorities, such as the provision of adequate street lighting and public transport.

A final model of value is that based on Deterrence Theory which suggests that compliance with laws or regulations proscribing socially unacceptable behaviour is best attained through creating the perception that punishment will be swift, sure and severe (Homel 1986). In the case of enforcement of the liquor licensing laws in licensed drinking settings, general deterrence appears extremely weak. Given the success of the deterrence model for random breath-testing to curb drink-driving, a strong public health argument could be made for the adoption of greater deterrence being provided to licensees to encourage more responsible management practices. The Australian police are increasingly recognising the prevention potential of making businesses accountable for problems caused by management practices. For example, the Australian police are seeking to make national trucking company executives responsible for the dangerous driving behaviour of their employees, often caused by unrealistic management demands on drivers as a result of seeking to gain a competitive edge in the marketplace ('The 7.30 report', Australian Broadcasting Corporation, 25 January 1996).

Harm Minimisation and Licensed Venues

Harm minimisation efforts in this area can be outlined under the major components of the public health model: interventions which influence the manner in which the drug alcohol is supplied; strategies focusing on patrons who consume alcohol on premises; and strategies which seek to minimise harm in and around the licensed drinking environment.

Alcohol

While the concept of harm minimisation outlined in this book focuses on strategies which can be employed without necessarily seeking to reduce consumption, we believe that control over the sale of alcohol represents a major category of harm minimisation. Patron demand for alcohol is strongly influenced by availability, price, and the manner in which high and low alcoholic beverages are promoted; factors which have, in the main, been shaped by political and market forces. Given the huge economic burden of alcohol-related harm (Collins and Lapsley 1996) a strong case can be made for minimising harm through a shift towards more healthy alcohol policies. However, there is considerable resistence to implementing any such policy changes. For example, in Australia recent efforts by public health advocates to lobby for restructuring of taxation of alcohol beverages in terms of their alcohol content have met strong resistance from vested interest groups ('Call for tax rises gets chilly response from wine makers', *The Australian*, 12 June 1995). This is the case even though such a system should modify consumer demand in terms of moderating consumption of high alcohol beverages but may not reduce the consumption of beverages containing alcohol across the board.

The Individual Drinker

With respect to patron drinking behaviour a harm-minimisation programme should recognise that a significant proportion of underage youth will seek to gain access to licensed premises (Lang et al. 1996); the majority of patrons in licensed venues at high-risk times on Friday and Saturday evenings drink enough alcohol to attain BALs considered unsafe for driving (Rydon et al. 1993); the majority of those at highest risk of harm, young adult males, view intoxication positively (Broadbent 1994); and alcohol discounting sessions which elevate levels of crowd intoxication are popular with those in attendance, as evidenced by their use by licensees to attract patronage.

Given these assumptions, a harm-minimisation approach would seek to provide patrons with information which will enable them to decide on courses of action prior to drinking which may reduce their risk of harm when intoxicated; for example, arranging safe transport from the venue and avoiding venues which are poorly managed or have a reputation for violence. While there are compelling social arguments for not issuing drinkers with legal penalties for intoxication per se (Midford 1993), effective patron deterrence programmes are needed not only for drink-driving, but for violence, sexual harassment, public disorder and other intoxication problems. Legal deterrence for such behaviour in and around licensed premises needs greater emphasis. In the absence of an effective legal deterrent for such inappropriate patron behaviour, educational attempts are unlikely to yield significant short-term shifts in harm related to intoxication.

The ability of patrons to purchase alcohol is to some extent controlled via the law prohibiting service to drunk or underage customers. That the implementation of these regulations is heavily dependent on the compliance of licensees and staff of licensed premises only underscores the necessity of further harm-minimisation efforts which focus on regulation of the licensed drinking environment.

The Licensed Drinking Environment

The available data on retail alcohol industry practices suggests the adoption of a framework which acknowledges that industry procedures to discourage the sale of alcohol to underage are inadequate (Lang et al. 1996); few bar managers actively discourage extreme levels of intoxication (Rydon et al. 1996); some managers driven by market forces actively encourage crowd levels of intoxication through discounting promotions ('Hoteliers fight bid to end happy hours', *The West Australian*, 9 July 1993); many high-risk venues for alcohol-related harm are managed by operators who do not engage in responsible serving practices and are highly resistant to change (Stockwell et al. 1993a, McLean et al. 1994); regulatory mechanisms lacking genuine industry support appear ineffective and have a minor deterrent effect on industry practice (Stockwell 1995); and, when seriously implemented, responsible service of alcohol has been demonstrated to minimise harm resulting from intoxication (McKnight and Streff 1992, Holder and Wagenaar 1994).

Harm-minimisation programmes should acknowledge that from the perspective of the retail alcohol industry, public health initiatives need to be balanced against minimising harm to the economic viability of the business. Where possible, identification of 'win-win' strategies which both increase profit and minimise harm should be exploited. Harm-minimisation initiatives should seek to inform licensees of the threats to economic viability posed by serving drunk patrons in terms of civil suits and possible revocation of licences. Licensees also need to be provided with support from regulatory bodies to facilitate responsible practice, and assisted in identifying key variables linked to patron frustration and harm. A wide range of management 'house policies' could be implemented in order to minimise problems of intoxication such as drink-driving and violent incidents. House policies should include measures such as not discounting full strength alcohol; promoting reduced and lower strength drinks; not serving beer in jugs; discouraging bulk ordering of drinks; offering reasonable low-cost food; preventing overcrowding; employing sufficient numbers of friendly staff to provide unhurried, courteous and professional service; ensuring adequate ventilation, seating, exits and standard of decor; making venues more attractive to females; and ensuring that individuals involved in violent incidents are brought to the attention of the police.

However, it would be unrealistic to expect many licensees to welcome sometimes costly changes to minimise alcohol-related harm. For example, ensuring an adequate staff–patron ratio at all times may improve the quality of service and reduce patron frustration, but also adds to personnel costs. We have also been informed of irresponsible management policies which are believed to enhance profitability, such as deliberately raising night club bar-room temperatures so as to encourage more rapid drinking, and the shedding of clothes. Side effects of these higher temperatures include elevated levels of intoxication and frustration. A requirement that bar-room temperature should not exceed a certain maximum would be readily measurable and enforceable. Licensees should be regulated to implement concrete measurable changes to practise and there is a strong argument for requiring responsible service strategies to become part of the conditions of the licence.

Effectiveness of Regulatory Approaches

As indicated in Figure 12.1, the regulation of licensed venue management practices are central to a harm-minimisation programme. This section will examine the efficacy of various regulatory approaches in terms of minimising harm associated with intoxication.

Self-regulation

The widespread existence of liquor-licensing regulations suggests that there has always been some concern that self-regulation by the retail alcohol industry may not be effective. However, the *laissez faire* approach adopted by most Australian and overseas regulatory bodies, particularly with respect to intoxication, has, by default, largely left the industry to self-regulate in response to community demand. This low-key form of regulation works best after extreme cases of irresponsible service resulting in death or injury are reported in the media. Responsible self-regulation by licensees involves the adoption of management practices which do not encourage or tolerate extreme intoxication and which also pay attention to environmental variables which can increase levels of patron frustration and aggression. Unfortunately ample evidence exists that breaches of regulations concerning intoxicated and underage patrons and overcrowding are commonplace (Rydon 1995). The retail alcohol industry associations are powerless to force their members to comply with their codes of conduct which in Australia, at least, have been very loosely worded statements of intent rather than concrete measurable outcomes.

Fierce marketplace competition is blamed for the inability of the retail alcohol industry to raise its standards of responsible service. For example, shortly after launching a statement of intent that licensed venues should not discount alcohol, the NSW president of the Australian Hotels and Hospitality Association (AHHA) conceded that his hotel would continue to discount in response to the market forces ('Hoteliers fight bid to end happy hours', *The West Australian*, 9 July 1993).

All of the above suggests that self-regulation, while desirable, is difficult to achieve and that all licensees cannot be expected to comply as long as there is (a) no effective deterrent and (b) a strong economic incentive to do otherwise.

Industry Assistance

A second level of intervention is the provision of assistance to the industry in the development and implementation of programmes which enhance industry knowledge and skill levels in the area of responsible alcohol service.

The implicit assumption in providing industry assistance is that the retail alcohol industry has a deficit in the area of knowledge and skills and needs only to be provided with education in order to effectively self-regulate.

While there have been a number of evaluations of voluntary industry responsible-service programmes which have generally reported some positive effects (Lang 1991), few have sought to look at the impact of the programme on the critical outcomes of changes in server behaviour to intoxicated patrons and patron BALs. One of the most comprehensive evaluations of an industry responsible service training programme to date was undertaken in Western Australia by Stockwell et al. (1993b). A wide range of outcome evaluation measures were examined, including over 2000 BAL tests; patron interviews; licensee and staff interviews; bar staff knowledge of responsible-service concepts; drink-driving statistics; changes to management house policies; and door and bar staff responses to youthful and drunk 'pseudo-patrons'. The outcomes from the 'Freo Respects You' responsible-service initiative suggested that industry-delivered training had only a minimal effect on management practices, staff behaviour and indicators of alcohol-related harm. Of the fourteen sites evaluated, seven of which received training, only one was found to have given active management support for the responsible service of alcohol. The manager of this lone establishment actively encouraged staff to refuse service to intoxicated patrons and implemented a number of responsible house policies. Three months after the programme's implementation this one site had increased refusal of service to drunk pseudo-patrons; reduced the numbers of patrons leaving their hotel with blood alcohol levels over 0.15; had no patrons charged with a drink-driving offence; and reported an increase in profits.

The results of this project suggest that while some licensees can implement such changes, the majority do not have the incentive to do so in the absence of a credible deterrent or a mandatory training requirement.

Partnerships Between Industry and Government Bodies

The underlying assumption of the following regulatory models is that licensees and their staff need more than additional knowledge and skills regarding low-risk alcohol service. They also require some motivation to put training on these issues into effect. One early Australian example of a collaborative community partnership is the West End Good Neighbourhood Forum which was established to address the issue of violence in and around one of Melbourne's major entertainment areas. The Forum, which is overseen by the Victorian Community Council Against Violence, consists of representatives from the liquor industry, police, local council, health agencies and community groups. The results of the project included the introduction of a responsible serving of alcohol programme; a voluntary code of practice developed in consultation with licensees, the Liquor Licensing Commission, police and local residents; and police patrols and police liaison officers who consult with the public regarding issues affecting the area. While at the time this programme was believed to be successful in minimising problems in the West End district (Lang 1991), recently there has been a recurrence of problems. This outbreak of problems perhaps serves to highlight the difficulty of sustaining such forums in the absence of a credible deterrent for irresponsible management. ('Act on violence, clubs warned', *The West Australian*, 27 December 1995).

Another Australian study worthy of mention is the Surfers Paradise Safety Action Project on Queensland's Gold Coast. This, as noted elsewhere in this book, involved licensees and managers of local night clubs co-operating with the local council, police, Queensland Health (Patron Care) and researchers, to address concerns over the levels of drunkenness and violence in the entertainment centre (Homel, Clark et al. 1994). There was strong evidence that the project had a positive impact on reducing alcohol-related violence and public disorder. The contribution of the enforcement component to the outcomes measured was difficult to separate from other interventions in the licensed settings and surrounding environment. Police also suggested during the project that earlier closing times for night clubs would be considered if the situation did not improve. This project was conducted within a climate of collaboration, but also clear threats to the profitability of licensed venues if more responsible practices were not implemented. During this project there were obvious doubts that self-regulation or assistance to the industry would be effective and that economic sanctions may be needed to achieve the desired outcomes.

A final example of this form of harm-minimisation strategy is the Geelong Accord, which sought the involvement of licensees in a semi-self-regulatory framework overseen by the police. The key elements of this and other similar accords which have followed, include: all local retailers agreeing not to discount alcohol; to charge an entry fee at the door after 11p.m.; and not permitting free readmission to patrons leaving the venue after this time. The most salient characteristic of this form of intervention programme is the strong emphasis on strategies which are both good for the industry in terms of profit and good for the community in terms of minimising harm. This assisted form of self-regulation, given the reports of increased profitability, does seem achievable. While reports of the Accord in the media have been highly favourable and the claims of increased profitability may encourage the industry to continue such practices, an evaluation of this strategy which measures outcomes including intoxication and harm has yet to be conducted.

Informal accounts suggest that another critical component of the programme is the threat of police sanctions – whatever these may be – for those licensees who break the Accord. It is unlikely, however, that such accords would be as readily embraced by the industry if they were to include changes to management practices which do not clearly have the potential to bolster profits.

Regulatory Enforcement Approaches

Studies which have evaluated the impact of regulatory enforcement have been based on the assumption that industry practices are highly resistant to change and that compliance can only be achieved through the threat of credible sanctions. Law enforcement procedures involving monitoring of serving practices by uniformed or plainclothes officers has resulted in substantial reductions in bar staff service to intoxicated customers and, in some cases, levels of harm.

In the Jeffs and Saunders (1983) study of an English seaside resort, uniformed police visited licensees of premises associated with public disorder at busy times, offered assistance with troublemakers, reminded staff of their responsibilities under the licensing legislation and publicly checked for underage drinking and intoxication. The second phase of the project involved uniformed police conducting random visits at least two to three times a week, during which they spoke to bar staff and thoroughly checked for underage and intoxicated patrons. With this intensive level of enforcement the researchers reported that in comparison to a control town which continued to use traditional policing methods, there was a 20 per cent reduction in recorded offences after the introduction of police visits.

A similar intervention trial conducted by Sussex Police (1987) also reported encouraging results, with a substantial reduction in alcohol-related arrests and recorded incidents for the intervention sites in comparison to an upward trend in such indicators within the wider area.

An attempt to replicate the Jeffs and Saunders study in Sydney by Burns et al. (1995) met with the finding that recorded assaults actually increased during the intervention phase using community policing methods. The researchers suggested that this finding may have been due to the greater opportunity for police officers to observe assaults and take action in the experimental area. An analysis of hospital admissions for assault-related injuries showed a decrease during the intervention period, but no data linking the location of the assaults to the admissions were available. The authors highlighted the need to include and examine a diverse range of outcome measures including the impact of the programme on domestic violence orders, resident perceptions and road traffic accidents.

Another landmark enforcement study conducted by McKnight and Streff (1992) in Michigan USA, has demonstrated that a very low cost enforcement programme can result in substantial reductions in the levels of intoxication permitted by bar staff. This programme involved an initial three-month period during which violations detected by plainclothes officers resulted in warnings, prior to the introduction of issuing citations for breaches of the intoxication offence. The aim of the enforcement effort was to deter rather than to punish licensees and bar staff. The rate of bar staff refusal of service to 'pseudo-patron' research staff who attempted to purchase alcohol while simulating signs of intoxication rose from 17.5 per cent to 54.3 per cent after the three-month warning phase, eventually declining to 41 per cent a year later. Drink-driving offences stemming from licensed premises declined from 32 per cent to 23 per cent. In a comparison county an increase in the refusal of service to pseudo-patrons was also observed, but to a significantly smaller effect, while the level of drink-driving related offences remained stable. Of special significance was that, based on the reported reductions in the levels of offenders whose last place of drinking was a licensed venue, it was estimated that for every dollar spent on extra enforcement, between $90 and $280 was saved by reducing alcohol-related traffic crashes.

The Rhode Island Community Alcohol Abuse/Injury Prevention Project was also based on the assumption that the police and management and staff of licensed premises are key agents in preventing death, injury, intoxication, drink-driving and other high-risk behaviours. This project employed a range of intervention strategies including increased law enforcement in the areas of liquor licensing and drink-driving; an increase in mandated penalties; the economic threat of dram shop legal liability to encourage server training and responsibility; the provision of education and information; and modifications to the socio-cultural environment. The programme goal was to increase responsible alcohol service by liquor licensees; minimise excessive or inappropriate drinking practices in high-risk situations; and lead to a decrease in harm associated with intoxication. Data were collected from an intervention and two matched control communities with the major outcome variables being hospital emergency room admission statistics ($n = 14,455$ visits) and police alcohol-related arrest statistics. A major finding was that, while police alcohol-related assault arrest rates in the intervention community increased by 27 per cent in comparison to a 7 per cent increase at the control sites, hospital emergency room statistics on assault injury rates showed a 21 per cent decline in the intervention site in comparison to a 4 per cent increase at control sites. The increase in police arrest rates at the intervention site was probably due to the increase in police attention, while the real reduction in emergency room assault injury rates reflected in hospital emergency admission statistics suggested that assaults were occurring less frequently at the intervention site.

Liquor-licensing legislation and conditions placed on licences by regulatory authorities have also proved effective harm-minimisation measures.

In a US study of the effects of the introduction of mandatory server training in Oregon, Holder and Wagenaar (1994) demonstrated a reduction in alcohol-involved single-vehicle night-time traffic crashes. Widespread concern has been expressed over alcohol promotions which fuel intoxication, and several Australian states have sought to prohibit such promotions. Restrictions have also recently been negotiated with Western Australian retailers in some country areas, on the sale of alcohol in glass bottles to prevent their use as projectiles or weapons. In one such community, the licensing authority acceded to community demands for restrictions to be placed on the sale of all take-away alcohol before 12 noon and also of cheap four-litre wine casks to between 4 and 6p.m. (Holmes 1994). There also appears to be increasing recognition that granting of hotel, tavern and night club licences, without due consideration, may lead to fierce competition for patronage and subsequent irresponsible management policies which can increase levels of intoxication and harm.

Discussion

A wide range of factors have been identified with the occurrence of alcohol-related harm, the key components of which are intoxication and facets of the drinking environment under management and regulatory control. These factors are characterised by elevated rates of patron consumption, intoxication, discomfort, frustration, impaired decision making, and high-risk behaviour. They are also characterised by irresponsible management policies which appear highly resistant to change and regulatory and enforcement practices which provide little deterrent value.

Harm-minimisation efforts should be guided by data-based assumptions regarding the drinking behaviour of patrons, the management practices of licensees, and the feasibility of modifying key risk factor variables both inside and outside licensed premises which are under the control of local government and regulatory authorities.

A number of potentially effective harm-minimisation 'levers' have been examined by researchers. Self-regulation as a strategy, while the preferred option of most key players, has very little empirical support for efficacy. The key barriers to effective self-regulation include lack of knowledge and motivation, marketplace competition and, in some sectors of the industry, a conflict of interest between short-term profits and responsible serving practices. Assistance provided to the industry in terms of bar staff training programme development has been found to have minimal impact on actual policies and serving practices where participation of industry staff is voluntary and there is a low expectation that regulations bearing on responsible practice will be monitored and enforced. Lack of management support and a focus on profit again have been identified as key barriers to the implementation of responsible serving practices. Partnerships between industry and government bodies appear to have a higher level of efficacy although a lack of good evaluation data and confounding factors hamper interpretations as to the most potent ingredients of these programmes. Such projects have actively engaged the industry and exerted pressure to gain a commitment to more responsible practices, often by creating the perception amongst licensees of a very real threat of police enforcement and restrictions on trading hours. The use of accords which benefit industry profits seem to be of value in terms of preventing discounting and public disorder problems caused by patrons seeking to gain access to multiple venues on any one evening. However, such accords have not been shown to prevent service to intoxicated patrons. Regulatory and enforcement approaches recognise that licensees have a conflict of interest in this area. Strict enforcement of the liquor laws, mandatory training requirements and the placing of conditions on licences which prohibit easily monitored irresponsible trading practices are supported by empirical data as being the most effective approaches to minimising alcohol-related harm. The available data indicate that the greater the level of deterrence, the more significant the shift towards responsible behaviour by owners of licensed premises and their staff. Effective enforcement and regulation of licensed premises needs to create the perception that there will be a swift and certain application of sanctions. The need for such regulation can be also be reduced (or supplemented) by formal or informal agreements between local 'cartels' to ban price discounting and charge door fees.

In conclusion, the available evidence suggests that, in the absence of strong community concern over alcohol-related problems, there is often a lack of political will to ensure effective regulation of licensed premises. Community action programmes and local accords between police, licensees and city councils appear to hold potential to minimise harm, particularly in the short term. Few such programmes, however, have been well evaluated. Compliance with such accords appears to require both that licensees have an opportunity to increase profits (for example, local bans on drink discounting) and that they believe lack of compliance will bring adverse consequences such as increased levels of police attention. Regulation of the existing legislation which provides a strong deterrent to some key components of irresponsible practice is long overdue. There is also a need for mechanisms to bring about change in those environmental risk factors under management control which have implications for business profitability. Controls for such factors should be written into the operational conditions of the licence with specific penalties outlined for breaches. Where licensees have no direct financial interest in complying with such regulations, an effective monitoring and enforcement programme appears critical.

References

Botvin, G.J. and Botvin, E.M. (1992) 'Adolescent, tobacco, alcohol and drug abuse: Prevention strategies, empirical findings and assessment issues', *Developmental and Behavioral Pediatrics*, 13: 290–301.

Broadbent, R. (1994) 'Young people's perceptions of their use and abuse of alcohol', *Youth Studies Australia*, Spring, 32–5.

Burns, L., Flaherty, B., Ireland, S. and Frances, M. (1995) 'Policing pubs: what happens to crime?', *Drug and Alcohol Review*, 14: 369–75.

Collins, D.J. and Lapsley, H.M. (1996) *The Social Costs of Drug Abuse in Australia in 1988 and 1992*, SO, Canberra, Australian Government Publishing Service.

Craze, L. (1995) 'An analysis of enforcement and operational information', in Stockwell, T. (ed.) *An Examination of the Appropriateness and Efficacy of Liquor Licensing Laws across Australia*, Canberra, Commonwealth Department of Human Services and Health, Reprinted 1995.

Holder, H.D. and Wagenaar, A.C. (1994) 'Mandated server training and reduced alcohol-involved traffic crashes; a time series analysis of the Oregon experience', *Accident Analysis and Prevention*, 26: 89–97.

Holmes, M. (1994) 'The Halls Creek initiative', *Pro-Ed*, 10: 21–2 (Perth, W.A. Alcohol and Drug Authority).

Homel, R. (1986) *Policing The Drinking Driver: Random Breath Testing and The Process Of Deterrence*, Report no. CR42, Canberra, Federal Department of Transport.

Homel, R., Tomsen, S. and Thommeny, J. (1992) 'Public drinking and violence; not just an alcohol problem', *Journal of Drug Issues*, 22: 679–98.

Ireland, C.S. and Thommeny, J.L. (1993) 'The crime cocktail: Licensed premises, alcohol and street offences', *Drug and Alcohol Review*, 12: 143–50.

Jeffs, B. and Saunders, B. (1983) 'Minimising alcohol-related offences by enforcement of the existing licensing legislation', *British Journal of Addiction*, 78: 67–78.

Lang, E. (1991) 'Server intervention: what chance in Australia?' *Drug and Alcohol Review*, 10: 381–93.

Lang, E., Stockwell, T. and Lo, S.K. (1990) *Drinking Locations of Drink-Driving Offenders in the Perth Metropolitan Area*, Technical Report prepared for the Western Australian Police Department, Bentley, W.A., National Centre for Research into the Prevention of Drug Abuse.

Lang, E., Stockwell, T., Rydon, P. and Gamble, C. (1992) *Drinking Settings, Alcohol-Related Harm, and Support for Prevention Policies. Results of a Survey of Persons Residing in the Perth Metropolitan Area*, Bentley, W.A., National Centre for Research into the Prevention of Drug Abuse.

Lang, E., Stockwell, T., Rydon, P. and Beel, A. (1996) 'The use of pseudo-patrons to assess compliance with licensing laws regarding underage drinking', *Australian and New Zealand Journal of Public Health*, 20: 296–300.

Marsh, P. and Fox-Kibby, K. (1992) *Drinking and Public Disorder*, London, The Portman Group.

McKnight, A.J. and Streff, F.M. (1992) *The Effect of Enforcement Upon Service of Alcohol to Intoxicated Patrons of Bars and Restaurants*, Landover, MD, National Public Services Research Institute.

McLean, S., Wood, L. and Davidson, J. (1991) 'Methodological considerations in a study of drinking by hotel patrons', in Stockwell, T., Lang, E. and Rydon, P. (eds) *The Licensed Drinking Environment: Current Research in Australia and New Zealand*, Perth, W.A., National Centre for Research into the Prevention of Drug Abuse.

McLean, S., Wood, L.J., Davidson, J., Montgomery, I.M. and Jones, M.E. (1994a) 'Alcohol consumption and driving intentions amongst hotel patrons', *Drug and Alcohol Review*, 12: 23–6.

McLean, S., Wood, L.J., Davidson, J., Montgomery, I.M. and Jones, M.E. (1994b) 'Promotion of responsible drinking in hotels', *Drug and Alcohol Review*, 13: 247–56.

Midford, R. (1993) 'Decriminalisation of public drunkenness in Western Australia; the process explained', *Australian Journal of Social Issues*, 28: 62–78.

Moser, J. (1980) *Prevention of Alcohol-Related Problems: An International Review of Preventive Measures, Policies and Programmes.* Toronto, Canada, World Health Organisation.

O'Donnell, M. (1985) 'Research on drinking locations of alcohol-impaired drivers: implications for prevention policies', *Journal of Public Health Policy*, 6: 510–25.

Putnam, S.L., Rockett, I.R. and Campbell, M.K. (1993) 'Methodological issues in community-based alcohol-related injury prevention projects: attribution of programme effects', in Greenfield, T.K. and Zimmerman, R. (eds) *Experiences with Community Action Projects: Research in the Prevention of Alcohol and Other Drug Problems*, CSAP Prevention Monograph No. 14, Rockville, MD, US Department of Health and Human Services.

Rydon, P., Stockwell, T., Lang, E. and Beel, A. (1996) 'Pseudo-drunk patron evaluation of bar-staff compliance with Western Australian liquor law', *Australian and New Zealand Journal of Public Health*, 20: 290–5.

Rydon, P. (1995) 'Alcohol industry practices relating to liquor licensing regulations', in Stockwell, T. (ed.) *An Examination of the Appropriateness and Efficacy of Liquor Licensing Laws Across Australia*, Canberra, Commonwealth Department of Human Services and Health, Reprinted 1995.

Rydon P., Stockwell T., Jenkins, E. and Syed, D. (1993) 'Blood alcohol levels of patrons leaving licensed premises in Perth, Western Australia', *Australian Journal of Public Health*, 17: 339–45.

Single, E. and Wortley, S. (1993) 'Drinking in various settings: Findings from a national survey in Canada', *Journal of Studies on Alcohol*, 54: 590–9.

Stockwell, T. (1995) 'Alcohol, violence and licensed premises: the nature of the relationship', in Stockwell, T. (ed.) *An Examination of the Appropriateness and Efficacy of Liquor Licensing Laws Across Australia*, Canberra, Canberra, Commonwealth Department of Human Services and Health, Reprinted 1995.

Stockwell, T. (1996) 'Regulation of the licensed drinking environment: a major opportunity for crime prevention', *Crime Prevention Studies* (in press).

Stockwell, T., Lang, E. and Rydon, P. (1993) 'High risk drinking settings: the association of serving and promotional practices with harmful drinking', *Addiction*, 88: 1519–26.

Stockwell, T., Lang, E., Rydon, P. and Beel, A. (1993) *An Evaluation of the 'Freo Respects You' Responsible Alcohol Service Project*, Bentley, W.A., National Centre for Research into the Prevention of Drug Abuse.

Stockwell, T., Rydon, P., Gianatti, S. and Jenkins, E. et al. (1992) 'Levels of drunkenness of customers leaving premises in Perth, Western Australia: a comparison of high and low "risk" premises', *British Journal of Addiction*, 87: 873–81.

Sussex Police (1987) *Sussex Police Liquor Licensing Project. Brighton 86/87: A Project to Identify and Reduce Alcohol-Related Crime.*

Victorian Community Council Against Violence (1990) *Inquiry into Violence in and Around Licensed Premises*, Melbourne, Victorian Community Council Against Violence.

PART III

Implications and Conclusions

13 Keeping the Customer Satisfied: Harm Minimisation and Clinical Practice

Douglas Cameron

There is in Leicester city centre (England) a public house called 'The Bricklayers' Arms'. It is a tall, narrow structure built in the last century. Its main entrance on a busy road is up three stone steps. Let us assume that a patron in 'The Brickies', for that is what the pub is called locally, consumes a large quantity of beer and, on attempting to leave the pub, stumbles down the steps and falls into the road where he is run over by a passing car. There are a number of ways in which that situation could be prevented or managed.

First, attempts could be made to reduce the probability of that patron choosing to render himself/herself so intoxicated by teaching him or her about alcohol, its use and its potentially detrimental physiological effects, so he/she may avoid getting into such a profound state of intoxication, thus minimising the chances of him/her stumbling. That is one form of primary prevention, and is covered in Chapters 5 and 12 of this book. Second, attempts could be made to ensure that the patron was not served with sufficient alcohol to enable him to get into a state where clumsiness was a notable feature. That could be done by server training and strict enforcement of the law (as exists in England) prohibiting the sale of alcohol to intoxicated persons. Such approaches are discussed in Chapter 5. Third, a barrier could be built between the pavement and the road thus ensuring that if our clumsy drunken patron did fall down the steps less harm would befall him/her. Such environmental approaches are discussed in Chapters 4 and 10. Fourth, the drinker, once patched up at the nearby Royal Infirmary, could be submitted to treatment for his/her alcohol problem. It is the fourth approach, an approach to be used when other harm minimisation and/or preventive strategies have failed, that is the concern of this chapter.

Dimensions of Intervention

There are world-wide a number of approaches to the treatment of people with alcohol problems. They operate from different ideological perspectives and in different settings with different levels of resource devoted to them. The varying approaches can be conceptualised on three dimensions:

1 Client Responsibility: What is the perceived nature of the drinking, do the staff of the agency believe that presenting drinkers are suffering from some disease which makes their drinking a behaviour beyond their control or do they believe that their drinking is a purposeful, meaningful, goal-directed behaviour?

2 Treatment Goal: Is abstinence the only acceptable goal of treatment for all attenders or does the agency staff actively help some of its clients/patients to resume drinking in a less harmful way?

3 Treatment Intensity: Is the agency providing simple advice and support or does it offer comprehensive residential interventions lasting weeks or months?

These dimensions are represented schematically in Figure 13.1.

These criteria might appear to be more categorical than dimensional, but close examination will reveal that it is not so. Dimension 1, the responsibility dimension, quantifying the degree of control over and wilfulness exhibited by people with regard to their drinking, is subject to much debate. Whilst the classical disease concept of 'alcoholism' posits that loss of control drinking is simply a symptom, perhaps the cardinal symptom, of the disease and that other explanations are unnecessary, such a view is not now widely held. Rather, it is accepted that there are degrees of intensity of the drive state towards alcohol consumption, or perhaps of the ability to refrain from making drinking decisions. The argument about will is, of course, a profound philosophical one which some authors put at the heart of the debate about the nature of 'addiction' (Heather 1994). Be that as it may, treatment agencies do vary in their perceptions of the responsibility of their clientele for their drinking and its problems (Cameron 1985).

Dimension 2, the active encouragement or acceptance of moderated drinking as a therapeutic goal, is also on a spectrum, from not

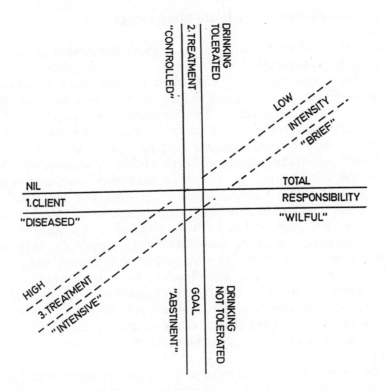

Figure 13.1: Dimensions of intervention

being tolerated for any clients through to being enabled for a selected number of clients to allowance that the client makes the decision for themselves, that is, resumed drinking is an option for everybody. The selection of people as being suitable or unsuitable for resumed drinking involves such diverse criteria as severity of 'dependence', pattern of past drinking, evidence of alcohol-related bodily or brain damage, psychiatric comorbidity, social support and partner preference (Jarvis et al. 1995).

Dimension 3, treatment intensity, has also been the subject of much debate over the past twenty years. Whereas the norm before the mid-1970s was of relatively prolonged, often in-patient-based interventions, current treatment systems vary between exceptionally brief (fifteen minute) opportunistic advice sessions in primary care settings, to up to six month's compulsory residences in concept houses or hospital units.

When is Treatment Truly Harm Minimising?

The question to be asked is where on these dimensions can treatment as harm minimisation be located. It could be argued that *any* treatment which reduces or obliterates drinking from a person's behavioural repertoire is harm minimisation. Given that the all-cause mortality curve against level of alcohol consumption is U-shaped (Anderson et al. 1993), such a claim is not tenable. For some very light drinkers, drinking cessation may be associated with increased risk of mortality, particularly of heart disease in middle-aged men. But for the vast majority of drinkers presenting to agencies with alcohol problems, cessation or even any reduction of consumption will be health beneficial, for their levels of consumption at presentation tend to be well in excess of that point where their drinking is doing no more harm than abstinence. Even so, that is harm minimisation as a by-product of treatment, not as its sole or sufficient rationale. For treatment to be *intentionally* harm minimising, it has to be towards the enabling or tolerating end of Dimension 2. In that way, it adheres to Ernst Buning's exhortation (1993) that, 'If a person is not willing to give up his/her drug use we should assist them in reducing harm to himself or herself and others.'

With regard to the other two dimensions, of perceived control over the behaviour by the drinker and intensity, harm minimisation theoretically should be neutral. But it is notable that in Buning's exhortation, it is assumed that the drug user is *capable but unwilling* to refrain from drug using. In other words, there is an explicit assumption that on Dimension 1, drinkers are towards the 'wilfully engaging in the behaviour' end of the responsibility spectrum. That suggests that ingrained in the harm-reduction philosophy is a belief about intentionality which is at variance with the 'classical' disease concept. However, it is perfectly possible to construe harm-minimisation work within a disease concept framework. Maintenance of a stable blood sugar level is a short-term and long-term harm minimisation strategy for people with diabetes mellitus. Maintaining control of blood-sugar levels is clearly beyond the ability of diabetics: telling them to will their blood sugar to stay low is simply not enough, so much pharmacological and dietary assistance is rightly given to help diabetics to stabilise their blood sugar.

Harm minimisation could also be neutral with regard to Dimension 3, treatment intensity, but as with perceived responsibility, it does not appear to be so. Less intensive interventions tend to be more likely to incorporate advocating moderated consumption of alcohol. More intensive interventions tend to be more likely to be abstinence oriented.

So, while theoretically treatment aimed at harm minimisation could be located anywhere on Dimensions 1 and 3, there tends to be a correlation between such techniques and with perceived responsibility for the drinking conduct being rested with the presenting drinker and with less intensive interventions. It is that cluster of briefly intervening, 'controlled drinking' enabling agencies which stress the client's personal responsibility for their conduct that are truly harm minimising. In other words, it is those agencies far removed from the conventional residential Alcoholism Treatment Units and from the beliefs of Alcoholics Anonymous. It is also interesting that it is for that very cluster of beliefs and treatment styles that the best evidence of efficacy of intervention resides (Miller and Hester 1980, Holder et al. 1991).

Is it simply fortuitous that the treatment modalities operating from a belief system which could embrace harm minimisation correlate with those established to be efficacious? That is unlikely. What is much more arguable is that there is efficacy *because* convergence occurs: convergence between the aims of the drinker towards wanting to continue to derive benefits from their drinking and minimising its problems and the treatment agency acknowledging those aims as appropriate and acceptable.

Everybody is Attempting to Minimise the Harms Related to their Own Drinking Behaviour

Those of us who choose to be drinkers normally do not drink to harm ourselves. We start to drink, and continue to drink, because we derive benefits from that drinking. Most of us also have some problems associated with that drinking. Learning to drink is a continuous process. From the earliest days of our drinking careers, we are learning to become skilful drinkers (McKechnie (forthcoming)). We are learning to maximise the benefits of our drinking and to minimise the problems. Acquisition of knowledge about drinking starts very early in life (Jahoda and Cramond 1972). We have to learn which beverages contain ethyl alcohol. We have to learn what effects various forms of beverage alcohol have upon us in what psychological states and in what settings. We have to learn, often by trial and error, how much is too much. We have to practise consuming some forms of beverage alcohol despite adverse initial tastes and effects until we get to like them. We have to introduce new forms of beverage alcohol into ourselves and compare the effects of one with another. We learn that some beverages upset us more than others. We have to work out the relationship between alcohol and other psychotropic drugs that we may take: whether black coffee and brandy are compatible after meals, and whether a cigarette enhances the effects of alcohol, and in what circumstances. And that is to make no mention of the relationship between alcohol and other less frequently used substances! We have to learn how to conduct ourselves when intoxicated: to learn what behaviours are acceptable and what are not. We have to work out the relationship between intoxication and a range of behaviours: socialisation, sport, sex, steering motor vehicles and so on. We have to learn that some activities mix very poorly with drinking, others mix very well.

Throughout our drinking careers, we are engaging in a constant readjustment process. We change beverage choice as a result of various influences around us, such as the company we keep, our incomes and the availability of other forms of drink. We have to learn about the new choices. We discover as we get older and less fit that we 'cannot drink like we used to', and learn to adjust our intake accordingly. We abandon some beverage choices and introduce new ones. Drinkers are living out their drinking lives actively engaged in harm minimisation.

But Aren't People who Present to Alcohol Treatment Agencies Different?

No. People who present for help with their alcohol problems are, of course, drinkers like all others, already actively personally engaged in harm minimisation. Their harm-minimisation strategies might not be serving them very well any more, and they might well be presenting for help because the harms they are inflicting on themselves and/or those around them might be massively outweighing the benefits. They might be aware that their drinking is causing problems in one or more of the areas known as the four Ls: Liver, Lover, Livelihood and Law. They might feel themselves to be caught in a vicious circle of drinking to ameliorate the ill-effects of drinking.

People do not present to treatment agencies when all is well. What presenters seek is support and help to get them out of the immediate mess they are in, and some assistance in reshaping their futures, as non-drinkers or continuing drinkers. The historical tragedy is that what many actually received, and may indeed continue to receive, on approaching a treatment agency was an immediate invalidation of all their past harm-minimisation efforts, a label 'alcoholic' that they had been avoiding having attributed to themselves for years and dire threats of the outcome of *any* resumed drinking. Understandably, denial, defaulting and disillusionment are common among presenters.

But it remains a fact that very few specialist alcohol agencies would claim that their primary motivation for intervention is harm minimisation. Most mainstream agencies would claim to be engaging in 'treatment' of or intervening in the careers of 'problem drinkers'; to be dealing with their clients' alcohol use rather than their alcohol problems. But there are agencies, a little away from that mainstream, which implicitly or explicitly engage in harm minimisation in accord with Buning's definition.

The agencies which most actively promote harm minimisation tend to be those at both ends of people's problem-drinking careers. For those early in potentially problematic drinking careers, before there are continuing and manifest problems, there has been a burgeoning of harm-minimisation strategies. Here the harm to be minimised is physical bodily damage, the Liver of the 'four Ls'. And it is done with simple advice and support related to reported level of consumption. The intervention depends upon an acceptance of the concept of there being safe limits; that it is appropriate and possible to help people who are drinking quantities of alcohol which in the long term it is suspected may be hazardous to health, to reduce their consumption to levels below such limits. Opportunistic screening and minimal intervention in primary health care settings is all the rage at present, certainly in Britain. The short-term efficacy of such techniques is reasonably high if they display the qualities incorporated in the acronym FRAMES. These are Feedback, Responsibility, Advice, Menu, Empathy and Self-efficacy (Bien et al. 1993). That is, the intervention should, in a supportive, empathetic way provide a menu of options, give clear advice and accurate feedback on performance and assist drinkers in acknowledging their responsibility for their behaviour and reassure them that they can change it if they want to. These opportunistic interventions are interestingly placed on the three dimensions above. They assume that drinkers are responsible for their behaviour; they work towards moderation rather than cessation of consumption and they are of low intensity.

At the other end of problem-drinking careers, those agencies dealing with street drunks – night shelters, Simon Community establishments and the like – also are engaged in harm minimisation. If one judges them by the narrow goal of achieved abstinence rates, they are not cost-effective (Holder et al. 1991). But that is not their function. They are explicitly attempting to keep their clientele alive. The claim in such places is that the harms to be avoided are such things as arrest for public drunkenness, mugging, hypothermia or death on the street and that the intervention is the provision of a safe environment where the individual's right to pursue the lifestyle of their choice is respected. They might also provide systems of move-on accommodation for people who wish to change their way of life. Thus, such shelters are at the tolerant end of Dimension 2: continued drinking is acknowledged as a reality. There is no declaration on the dimension of personal responsibility; the same tolerance would be expected whether the drinkers were seen to be hapless addicts or seen to be responsible, and the intervention is of moderate intensity – relatively cheap residential provision. But the harm-minimisation strategy offered is somewhat basal: it is shelter.

So, what is happening to those in the middle of problematic drinking careers? 'Early' or 'potential' problem drinkers get harm-minimisation messages. End-state, 'skid row' drinkers may be able to avail themselves of services which enable them to go on pursuing their drinking careers but which attempt to keep them alive; harm minimisation is acceptable there too. But if someone has well-developed alcohol problems and is not in skid row, harm minimisation seems to be a 'no-no'. Why should this be so? It has to be heritage, or the baggage of history: the influence of what has come to be known as 'The Alcoholism Movement'. It is in that mainstream that, predictably, there has been the least progress. The dominant see less need to mutate. That is true of family dynasties, political systems and scientific theories.

If abstinence is seen as the appropriate goal of intervention, the opposite end of Dimension 2 from the primary care minimal interventionists and the night shelters, then harm minimisation is not on the agenda. With regard to Dimension 1, it is a strange reversal. First, you are responsible for your drinking. As your career progresses, you cease being responsible. Then, if you continue drinking, you are credited with the possibility of being responsible again, or the issue of responsibility becomes irrelevant. This relates to what you are called. At the beginning of your drinking career, you are a hazardous drinker, an early problem drinker, a drinker with low alcohol dependency. In the middle phase you become an 'addict', an 'alcoholic' or someone suffering from 'the alcohol dependence syndrome'. And finally, you become a 'drunk', a word carrying with it the inference of wilful intoxication.

The social institutions which try to modify drinking careers attempt first to get people to shape up their drinking, then if drinking continues out of shape, to stop it. But if neither reshaping or cessation is sustained, the institutions stop trying. If the disease model is truly to be adhered to, then the diabetes mellitus analogy needs to be pursued. It does not matter how often the patient's blood-sugar level veers away from the normal range, corrective strategies should be instituted, regardless of what stage in his/her diabetic career the patient is, for he/she holds out the potential of delaying or preventing some of the long-term physical problems, as well as dealing with the acute problems which may or may not manifest.

It is also notable that it is predominantly those interventions which can be adapted as part of an abstinence or a non-abstinence orientated harm-minimisation approach that have been shown to be efficacious with presenting middle-career drinkers. One total list is:

1 Behavioural self-control.
2 Covert sensitisation.
3 Antabuse with assured compliance.
4 Community reinforcement.
5 Marital therapy.
6 Social skills training.
7 Stress management.

(Miller and Hester 1980)

Of those seven interventions, it is only the third, Antabuse with assured compliance, which is necessarily abstinence promoting. The other six can be used for a drinking goal placed anywhere on Dimension 2.

Harold Mulford (1994) has suggested that if alcoholism had not been invented, 'local communities nationwide [in the United States] might have taken commonsense actions to facilitate the natural rehabilitation process and provided more benefit to more alcoholics for less cost than treating alcoholism'. In other words, possibly they would opt for helping drinkers to help themselves with their harm-minimisation strategies rather than opt for trying to treat a disease – existent or not. The strategies listed by Miller and Hester, above, are notably commonsensical. They are psychological skills and community supports which would be of value to anyone attempting to resolve a wide variety of problems in their everyday lives. They are by no means alcohol-specific.

So, what would an agency working with drinkers in the 'middle phase' of their drinking career do with someone with an alcohol problem if it did not attribute some disease status to its clientele and advocate abstinence? It is very simple. It would operate a problem-orientated approach to its interventions. It would not attribute all the presenting problems to alcohol use. It would not claim that problems of living would be resolved by cessation of consumption. On the three dimensions above, it would be permissive with regard to alcohol consumption, supporting whatever decision the client makes with regard to future drinking. It would be advocating neither continued drinking nor cessation. And the intensity of intervention would also not be agency determined: ideally, it would probably be client determined. But it would maintain the client in the position of personal responsibility (and culpability) for his/her behaviour. Above all, it would respect whatever strategies the client had discovered to be efficacious with regard to minimising the harm related to his/her drinking, and would actively help the client to work out new appropriate strategies.

A Local Case Study

As it happens, the author and colleagues in Leicestershire have been attempting to operate such a system for twenty years now. It has been described in detail elsewhere (Cameron 1995). So it is entirely possible that the drinker, described in the first paragraph of this chapter, who stumbled onto the road out of 'The Brickies', would have been referred to these services. What would the agency response have been like?

We would ask the drinker simple, obvious questions: Why are you presenting now? What do you perceive your problem areas to be? What do you want to do about them? And on the basis of the responses an intervention would be constructed.

Let us speculate further about our stumbling drinker. Let us say:

His name is Malcolm. He is white, aged forty-five, separated from his wife, Joan, for one year and living in a council flat (public housing apartment) near the pub. He has always been a heavy drinker, somewhat indifferent to the requests, later demands, of Joan and the children. Eventually, Joan found someone more attentive and moved out of the family home along with the two boys. Our client, for that is what Malcolm became, gave up the tenancy of the three-bedroomed family home in favour of his new one-bedroomed flat. But it was in a tower block. He saw little of the neighbours, many of whom were also single or separated and tended to keep themselves to themselves.

He had worked as a postman for twenty years and despite the early start (5 a.m.), he enjoyed the work. He used to amaze his workmates and some householders by singing as he did his rounds! But the hours of work did mean that he saw very little of his wife and family. That, he said, rather than his drinking, was why Joan had 'gone off with someone else'. She also worked, in a local insurance office. It was there she met her new partner.

Once by himself, Malcolm tended to go to the Post Office Social Club after work, mostly for the company. He was in the club darts and pool teams. His drinking had escalated. He was consuming about six pints of strong lager per day from finishing work around noon until going to bed around 9 p.m. At weekends, he drank more. He was very lonely then and although he did have access to his two sons, he had defaulted on visiting them, quite often furnishing either before or after the intended visit a collection of lame excuses. He was having increasing difficulty getting up in the morning and had received a first written warning about erratic attendance at work. He told the personnel department that his erratic attendance was because of stress-related migraines which had started since his wife moved out. He was asked to attend his general practitioner, a kindly man, who signed him off sick with 'depression'. Because he was off sick, he felt that he could not go to the Post Office Social Club. That was why, one Saturday evening, he was drinking alone in 'The Brickies', a pub he visited infrequently. When there, he got into the company of some visiting construction workers. But they had arrived in the pub after their day's work, some hours after him. He bought a round of drinks for them, they reciprocated, and so the evening progressed. He enjoyed their company. For a while, he could forget his dismal solitary existence. It was just before 10 p.m. when he eventually decided to go home, saying that he had to go because he was taking his children out the next day. Malcolm left the pub, stumbled down the three stone steps and into the road ...

In answer to our simple questions, Malcolm said that he had presented now because he had been advised to by staff in the orthopaedic department where he had been treated for three days. He had an unpleasant time in hospital. He had a crushed ankle.

He was in considerable pain, felt sick and sweated a lot. He did not sleep well and said he would not have slept at all without pain killers and sleeping pills. He was discharged on crutches and wearing a plaster on his leg. As he had to be off sick for a few weeks, he saw this as a good opportunity to 'sort himself out'. He was really worried about losing his job. He knew he was drinking 'too much' and wanted help 'cutting it down'. He knew that his 'migraines' were hangovers but could not admit that at work. He saw his problems as being boredom and loneliness and he wanted Joan to come back to him. He was upset that since the accident, he had started drinking alone in his flat and saw that as a very bad sign: 'Alcoholics drink in secret. I might become one.'

So, his presenting problems were physical harm, which was being repaired by the orthopaedic department; loneliness, a tendency to use drinking establishments to find company; a level of alcohol consumption that interfered markedly with his work performance because of hangovers, and with his tenuous domestic relationships. In terms of a harm-minimisation approach to this man's problems, he did need help to curtail his sessional intake of alcohol. He needed help to establish non-drink-focused social networks. He needed to be equally wary about his Saturday evening drinking so that he could be a fit and proper parent on Sunday.

While he was off sick, he and his keyworker redefined and reshaped his drinking. He decided to stop all home-based drinking, in part as validation to himself that he was not 'an alcoholic'. Fortuitously, now that he was the proud possessor of a plaster on his leg, he could validly go back to the Social Club. With minimal prompting, a workmate offered to take him there twice a week. It meant Malcolm arrived later and left earlier. He changed his beverage choice back to English bitter beer. It was weaker, and he knew that if he drank too much of it, he would get diarrhoea: a real problem if one is a postman! So his consumption reduced to three pints twice per week. He said he was surprised at how little he missed his daily large dose of lager. He took the opportunity to resign from the darts and pool teams. It was when Malcolm was slowly making his way to the toilet on crutches that he saw the solution to his Saturday night problem: a poster on the staff notice board seeking new recruits to the Post Office Choir. He knew of the choir's existence but had always resisted getting involved; previously he had said he saw little enough of his family so did not want to spend one midweek evening rehearsing and Saturday night performing, but in fact, he was more concerned that it would interfere with his drinking. But now that was exactly what he wanted to do, so why not?

The service's intervention with Malcolm closed within eight weeks. His plaster had been off for four weeks and he had returned to work. His drinking remained trivial. He, rather tentatively, had joined the choir. He had reshaped his life a little but there was no sign of a reconciliation with Joan. About a year later, he sent a postcard to his keyworker in the services. It came from Copenhagen, where he was with the choir at an international festival. It was signed Malcolm and Gwen. The keyworker had no idea who Gwen was!

Conclusions

This 'factitious' story is about a service which was in a position, to use Mulford's (1994) expression, to take 'commonsense actions to facilitate the natural rehabilitation process'. Those commonsense actions are predominantly focused on harm minimisation: what are the presenting problems and what can be done to help the client remove or minimise them.

In another part of the world, or indeed of the country, a totally different package of care could have been delivered. Malcolm could have been admitted to an in-patient Alcoholism Treatment Unit. He could have been told that he was an alcoholic and that he had to cease drinking for ever. A confrontation with his family could have been set up to make entirely clear to him how his alcoholism had wrecked his marriage. He could have been 'required' to attend Alcoholics Anonymous (AA). If he resumed drinking, he could have been told that he had relapsed and that further treatment was necessary. That package might also have been effective. The fellowship of AA could have provided companionship and support as a substitute for his workmates in the Social Club. He might have met a Gwen there, but what they would initially have had in common would have been that they were both trying to overcome alcohol problems, and were vulnerable to 'relapse', not quite the same common interest as singing in a choir. However, crucially, Malcolm didn't want to stop drinking and didn't believe he was an alcoholic. So compliance would have been harder to achieve.

The main difference between that alternative (AA) package and what happens in the Leicestershire Community Alcohol Services is that the former does not facilitate that *natural rehabilitation process*, rather it works against it. The Leicestershire Services are not unique, although they might be rather extremely located on the three dimensions illustrated above. Many services do work in whole or in part in that way – more commonly in Britain than in the United States (Rosenberg et al. 1992).

But most importantly, such strategies are being implemented all the time in the general community. People are getting into bother by drinking too much. They are then tethering their consumption back, changing beverage choice, frequency, site, company. It is the 'tapping in' to those natural processes which characterises a harm-minimisation approach to treatment.

Given that both approaches have internal validity and both will have successes and failures, why should one approach or the other be adopted? There are data to suggest that the widespread availability of AA (Mann et al. 1988) and of the harm-minimisation approach as operated in Leicester (Cameron 1995) may be impacting on the overall morbidity and mortality of alcohol problems in a community. It is far too early to know whether one or other approach accrues greater benefits.

The difference is one of ideological consistency. The general population, and 'early problem drinkers', and 'alcoholics' and 'unmotivated skid row drunks' can all be helped using the same set of beliefs and strategies. The health education and promotion messages are the same as the minimal intervention messages. And they are the same as the treatment messages. The environmental manipulation messages are also consistent: drink safe quantities in a safe environment and avoid hazardous activities when intoxicated. No special deals, no hazards of inappropriate labelling (Roman and Trice 1968), just common sense.

References

Anderson, P., Cremona, A., Paton, A., Turner, C. and Wallace, P. (1993) 'The risk of alcohol', Addiction, 88: 1493–1508.

Bien, T.H., Miller, W.R. and Tonigan, J.S. (1993) 'Brief interventions for alcohol problems: a review', Addiction, 88: 315–36.

Buning, E. (1993) 'Comments at workshop on defining harm reduction', Fifth International Conference on the Reduction of Alcohol Related Harm, Toronto, Canada, March.

Cameron, D. (1985) 'Why alcohol dependence – and why now?' in Heather, N., Robertson, I. and Davies, P. (eds) on behalf of the New Directions in the Study of Alcohol, Crucial Issues in Dependence, Treatment and Prevention, London, Croom Helm.

Cameron, D. (1995) Liberating Solutions To Alcohol Problems: Treating Problem Drinkers Without Saying No, Northvale, N.J., Jason Aronson.

Heather, N. (1994) 'Weakness of will: a suitable topic for scientific study?' *Addiction Research*, 2: 135–9.

Holder, H.D., Longbaugh, T., Miller, W.R. and Rubonis, A.V. (1991) 'The cost effectiveness of treatment for alcoholism. A first approximation', *Journal of Studies on Alcohol*, 52: 517–40.

Jahoda, G. and Cramond, J. (1972) *Children and Alcohol*, London, HMSO.

Jarvis, T.J., Tebbutt, J. and Mattick, R.P. (1995) *Treatment Approaches For Alcohol and Drug Dependence, an Introductory Guide*, Chichester, John Wiley and Sons.

Mann, R.E., Smart, R.G., Anglin, L. and Rush, B.R. (1988) 'Are decreases in liver cirrhosis rates a result of increased treatment for alcoholism?' *British Journal of Addiction*, 83: 683–8.

McKechnie, R.J. (forthcoming) 'Drinking as skill', *Addiction Research*.

Miller, W.R. and Hester, R. (1980) 'Treating the problem drinker – modern approaches', in Miller, W.R. (ed.) *The Addictive Behaviours*, New York, Pergamon.

Mulford, H.A. (1994) 'What if alcoholism had not been invented? The dynamics of American alcohol mythology', *Addiction*, 89: 517–20.

Roman, P.M. and Trice, H.M. (1968) 'The sick role, labelling theory and the deviant drinker', *International Journal of Social Psychiatry*, 14: 245–51.

Rosenberg, H.A., Melville, J., Levell, D. and Hodge, J.E. (1992) 'A 10-year follow up survey of acceptability of controlled drinking in Britain', *Journal of Studies on Alcohol*, 53: 441–6.

14 Measuring Harm: Implications for Alcohol Epidemiology

Jürgen Rehm and Benedikt Fischer

If the alcohol field moves to a framework in which the minimisation of alcohol-related harm is the overarching goal (see Single 1995), we will need reliable, valid and easily available measures for alcohol-related damage. However, at the current time, such measures are in short supply and all too often harm is still inferred indirectly from alcohol consumption.[1]

To give an important example, in the early 1980s, the World Health Organization (WHO) has outlined its central philosophy, direction and goals for a global future providing a basic level of 'health for all' citizens of this planet (WHO 1981). One of the specific targets in this global framework of public health concerned people's lifestyles, and in particular the issue of harms and problems resulting from alcohol, tobacco and psychoactive substances (WHO 1981, 1994a, b). The particular concern for global public health linked to those drugs was later picked up by target 17 of the WHO-Euro goals for the year 2000, which requested that:

> By the year 2000, the health damaging consumption of dependence-producing substances such as alcohol, tobacco and psychoactive drugs should have been significantly reduced in all member states. (WHO Europe 1994)

By taking a closer look at what those goals mean to and how they have been operationalised by public health policy makers and researchers, it appears that the Europeans have been most advanced in clarifying in more detail what this goal of reduction of harm actually meant to them in more concrete terms: As the European Alcohol Action Plan states, the intention was to reduce 'alcohol consumption by 25%, with particular attention to reducing harmful use' (originally set for the year 1995; see WHO Europe 1993, 1994). Thus, while targeting harmful use and harm, the operationalisation becomes concretely defined only for consumption.

To use consumption as an indicator or surrogate measure for harm raises two main problems, however: first, the relationship between alcohol and major harm categories like mortality or morbidity is curvilinear (see, for example, English et al. 1995, Rehm, et al. (forthcoming)), and thus, an increase of consumption at very low levels of consumption decreases the mortality or morbidity risks (for limits see Maclure 1993, Ashley et al. (forthcoming)). Second, part of harm reduction is aimed at finding ways to decrease harm independent of consumption.[2]

Such a goal may not be attainable, but this cannot be decided unless we have independent measures for harm (see Stockwell et al. 1996, for an attempt to measure harmful consumption independent of total consumption).

Thus, since consumption and harm are not interchangeable concepts, independent indicators for harm have to be found and established. This does not mean that level of alcohol consumption and harm are not related. On the contrary, we know that this is the case (see Edwards et al. 1994). However, it is a big step from a – usually statistical – relation to equating one concept with another, especially if the relationship is complex.

The Measurement of Harm

How can we define and measure alcohol-related harm? Let us again turn to WHO definitions. In this agency's ICD 10 classification for 'harmful use' of a substance, there must be:

> clear evidence that the substance use was responsible for ... physical or psychological harm ... which may lead to disability or have adverse consequences for interpersonal relationships. (WHO 1993: 56; see also WHO 1992: 74–5 for an earlier, narrower, definition)

Thus, in order to establish measures for aspects or categories of harm we have to establish that (a) a consequence is perceived as harmful, as well as (b) the causal link between alcohol consumption and these harmful consequences.

The first part seems fairly simple. However, there may be cultural differences in what is generally perceived as harm in a society or on an individual level (see Mäkelä and Mustonen 1996), and this distinction will have consequences for measurement. Still, defining categories of harm that are widely and even cross-culturally accepted seems to be possible.

The second point is crucial and not as simple as the first. Definitions of causality differ between the different disciplines. Thus, causality in epidemiology (Rothman 1986, 1988) requires less strict criteria than causality in the social sciences (Gadenne 1984). Basically, causality in epidemiology is inferred from cohort or case-control studies (Rothman 1986), based on the statistical association of exposure and disease. The possibility cannot be excluded that another factor may be causal for both exposure and disease. For example, genetics may be causal for smoking behaviour as well as lung cancer. Very clearly, such an assumption is highly dubious, given the research evidence on smoking and lung cancer, especially the biochemical evidence. However, the point here is that given the usual designs of epidemiology, such a conclusion cannot be excluded because it is impossible to impose the kind of control necessary to exclude this alternative explanation (Rehm and Strack 1994). Clearly, the control necessary would imply an experimental design with randomisation of exposure (Campbell and Stanley 1966, Aronson et. al. 1990), and such a design would be highly unethical and difficult to carry out practically (Rehm and Strack 1994).

This difference in epistemological criteria becomes very apparent in the discussions about alcohol consumption and social harm. Alcohol consumption is definitely related to phenomena such as violent criminal behaviour. Even so, social scientists have argued that the involvement of alcohol may not be causal, and pointed out that adoption of a deviant way of life may constitute the underlying common cause explaining problematic alcohol consumption as well as criminality (see also the analogy to drug use and violence, for example Room 1983, McBride and McCoy 1993, Brochu 1995). On the other hand, if epidemiological criteria are applied, alcohol would clearly have to be classified as a causal factor (see English et al. 1995).

In addition, the term 'alcohol consumption' has to be specified more clearly. Dependent on the outcome, different patterns of consumption lead to different risks, even if overall consumption is constant. Walsh and Rehm (1996) found considerably reduced risk for social harm if the same weekly amount of alcohol was consumed in seven days compared to consumption in five to six days. The highest level of risk was seen if the same weekly amount of alcohol was consumed in one to four days.

Similarly, the risk for coronary heart disease is reduced if people drink very lightly but in a regular fashion (for example, one drink every day) compared to either abstention or binge drinking (Bondy 1996).

A Basic and Comprehensive Framework for Alcohol-related Harm

As outlined in Table 14.1 overleaf, a basic conceptual framework of categories of consequences of 'harm' related to the use of alcohol is suggested. This consists of two basic dimensions (see Room 1985).

First, it is suggested that it is instructive for a better understanding of alcohol-related harm potentials – as it is for most other drugs (Kendall et al. 1995) – to distinguish between different categories – single-occasion/short-term versus long-term use (columns). It seems clear that one single encounter with any drug usually entails rather different consequences for the user as well as his/her environment from the consequences of a pattern of repeated use over time – a pattern which may, in the extreme, last almost the complete span of a lifetime.

Furthermore, we are suggesting four major functional arenas in which consequences may occur from the use of alcohol. At the individual level, alcohol produces negative (as well as positive) physiological, psychophysical or mental consequences. On the physiological side, liver cirrhosis and stroke, and on the mental side, alcohol dependence are the most prevalent phenomena that have to be taken into account here (see English et al. 1995).

In addition, we propose two fundamental dimensions in which drug use can produce negative consequences, harm and costs, not only to the individual but also to others as well as to society more generally. The first category focuses on the immediate personal and social environment and the drinker's social and economic relations, especially including the environment of family, friends and peers as well as workplaces and public spaces. These can be directly and negatively affected by the short- or long-term use of alcohol through the inherent effects of drinking on the drinker and subsequently on his/her relations with the environment. However, the forms of harm and damage outlined in this dimension should be limited to alcohol's inherent effects on the user and his/her personal, social and economic environment, regardless of contingent or reactive circumstances (though a clear separation is often not easy). Violence against others or decreased productivity, it is

Table 14.1: Conceptual scheme of harm levels from alcohol for single-occasion and long-term use

	Single-occasion Use	*Long-term Use*
Physiological	Overdose	Mortality (liver cirrhosis) Morbidity (gastritis, pancreatitis)
Psychophysiological and Mental	Changed consciousness and control (hangover/suicide) injury to drinker	Dependence, depression
Immediate Personal and Social Environment (behavioural aspect)	Severe family and workplace disruption, injury to others, violence	Disruption of social and economic relations
Wider Social and Cultural Level (determined by societal reaction)	Criminal and informal sanctions	Stigmatisation; coercion to change; treatment; criminalisation of alcohol-related behaviour

argued, can be an effect of alcohol use on the social level primarily related to the drug's inherent mind-altering and other qualities, and independent of external reactions.

Finally, the last category relates to the larger societal level and the mostly institutionalised societal reactions to alcohol use and related 'harms' occurring on that level. These established societal reactions to drug use – mostly designed to prevent and control harm from alcohol-use related behaviour (that is, criminal and regulatory laws) – create part of the damage and costs that we account for in relation to alcohol use.

The category of 'reacting' variables on the societal level also produces significant harm to the alcohol user (and society), as, for example, through processes of stigmatisation or social exclusion which are the results of his/her drinking. However, these reactions, and the harm and costs attributable to them, are not primarily inherent to alcohol or its use, but are ideologically, socially and culturally dependent reactions. Examples of these include the criminalisation of alcohol use in restricted locations, under age or in correlation with violence or driving, the stigmatisation of drinkers, and also various forms of social control and pressure to change alcohol-related behaviour through (often medicalised) treatment systems.

If one considers the different principal categories of alcohol-related harm suggested, one might argue that these are not necessarily strongly linked, meaning that harm related to one category can occur without the other. On the other hand, it is evident that in practice problems in these basic conceptual categories are often related to each other. Thus loss of productivity as a form of social harm from alcohol use is largely caused by the physiological and mental effects that the use of the substance has on individuals. The harms accounted for on the 'societal level' are often a reaction to inherent social harms, for example the criminalisation of violent behaviour when it is attributed to alcohol consumption.

In aiming at a comprehensive audit of the 'harm' situation, the critical question is: which categories of alcohol-related 'harm' and 'damage' are covered by solid indicators? With further reference to Table 14.1, the most 'solid' indicators relate to the physiological consequences from alcohol use, and especially for the harms that eventually cause people's death.[3] Information about alcohol-related mortality is, at least in the industrialised world, generally quite sophisticated and mostly comparable. However, the indicators usually do not directly measure the proportion of the mortality attributable to alcohol, which varies quite widely between societies.[4] Exceptions here are disease categories that are by definition wholly alcohol-related, such as alcohol dependence or alcohol psychosis. However, the trend in constructing international classification systems for diseases tends to define diseases based on observable symptoms without taking into account their aetiology (for example, the DSM IV system).

The indicators for alcohol-related morbidity are also fairly comprehensive, again with reference to industrial countries (see Robson and Single 1995). When people suffer from negative health consequences resulting from alcohol use, they often make use of quite comprehensive health and medical services. These serve as acceptable sources of relevant information.

There are some indicators of the negative effects from changed mental states due to alcohol use on a single occasion. Such information is available from the systems which track accidents subsequent to drink-driving or other accidents, or the tracking of law-breaking in criminal justice systems. Again, usually only the criminal incidents are recorded, without taking into account the aetiology (with specific statistics for alcohol-related road accidents being the most notable exception in most industrialised countries). Knowledge about the negative contingencies of long-term drinkers' potential 'dependence' is limited. There are also cultural differences in defining and reporting information related to this subject (see Room et al. 1996).

Good indicators of the negative consequences to the direct social and personal environment from short- as well as long-term alcohol use are sparse and rather inconsistent. In both short-term and long-term use, drinking can have drastic consequences for friends, family and other social relations (Pernanen 1991). Heavy alcohol use potentially disrupts people's lifestyles as well as their personal relations but there is no evidence with which to quantify this. In terms of costs the most important category – the loss of productivity of alcohol-using individuals – can produce substantial burdens of harm and negative consequences to the community.

Finally, the use of alcohol provokes a wide array of most significant forms of 'harm' on a societal level. Many of them can be accounted for in some form of material 'cost', since they are established by some formalised societal intervention entailing a defined extent of expenses or compensation to be delivered out of public budgets (see Xie et al. 1996). On a conceptual level, harm and costs should be distinguished. However, operational cost is the major and often the only indicator for harm at this level. Economic issues have been reviewed in greater detail in Chapter 3 of this volume. These negative, socially determined consequences are, by definition, social in nature. They are a form of reaction which predominantly reflects an institutionalised system of values, actors or mechanisms intended for control of behaviour. Excessive noise after alcohol use or drinking in a public park is not inherently criminal, but its criminalisation through the legal system as the chosen mode of social control turns the drinker into a criminal. This produces harm for the individual as well as society.

Despite their obvious conceptual significance, our traditional ways of accounting for 'harm' and 'damage' from alcohol use have mostly not yet managed to find distinct and adequate ways to take into consideration the forms of 'harms' and 'costs' that occur at the personal/social/economic level or those that are due to societal reactions. Ways have not yet been devised to incorporate the disruption of families or alcohol users' social relations into the calculation of damage and costs. A conceptually solid framework for accounting for harm and damage grounded in societal responses to alcohol use has yet to be presented. The largely institutionalised responses of social control, including legal sanctions, availability control, and treatment measures, as well as social processes like labelling and the stigmatisation of alcohol users, have largely been taken for granted as processes that were directly linked to alcohol use. Instead, it becomes important to recognise that these phenomena are created as a reaction to the consumption of alcohol, in most cases evolving over a long period of time. However, these responses – as well as the harms and costs related to them – are not inherent to alcohol use, but are primarily related to societal reactions. Arrest data for 'public drunkenness' as well as the costs and damages related to such offences have also traditionally been regarded as inherently alcohol-related. Instead, we are confronted with the conceptual challenge that social systems choose to establish such societal responses to alcohol consumption, which supposedly produce some benefit ('reduced harm') on one side, but also costs and damage or negative consequences on the other side. Conceptually, alcohol-related harm epidemiology here stands at the same situation as criminology some twenty-five years ago. Labelling or reaction theory approaches to crime then indicated that the harmful property of crime was not necessarily inherent to some forms of behaviour, but may have been a result of a reaction to it (Becker 1973, Goode 1984). This issue becomes particularly crucial if we want to further our thinking in regard to how to 'reduce harm'. 'Harm reduction' on the basis of our framework will not only mean behavioural change on the side of the alcohol-consuming subject. It may equally mean modifications of the societal reaction to alcohol and alcohol-related behaviours. This brief analysis suggests that traditional concepts regarding a comprehensive account and investigation of 'harm' from alcohol are rather incomplete. There is reliance on rather rudimentary, provisional indicators of harm which omit a large array of damage and costs that should be an integral part of such an account.

Patterns of Drinking and Harm

So far, a conceptual framework for categories of harm has been introduced. At this point, further implications for alcohol epidemiology from such a framework are outlined. To achieve this, examples are drawn from some of the categories, and these are related to research questions in alcohol epidemiology. The general line of reasoning will be that the different harm categories are not linked to alcohol consumption per se but are associated with different aspects of such consumption. These aspects have usually been subsumed under the heading of drinking patterns (see also the WHO definition from 1992 cited above, where harmful use is defined by a pattern of alcohol use which is causing damage).

Clearly, patterns of drinking influence physiological consequences, and thus have to be assessed in a way which takes the aetiological knowledge into account. As already pointed out (Bondy 1996), research on coronary artery disease indicates that regularity in drinking is important for the beneficial effects of moderate drinking. Clearly, one drink per day is linked to more cardiovascular benefits than seven drinks each Friday, even though the week's average is the same in both cases. The reason for this can be found in the underlying short-term influences of alcohol, especially on the platelet function (Goldberg et al. 1995). Biochemical evidence also suggests a rebound effect for binge drinking. Thus, in trying to further explain this effect and its interactions with other variables, such as nutrition, alcohol epidemiology must use alcohol measures based on theoretical concepts that link drinking, nutrition and heart disease – the regularity of light to very light drinking, as well as the frequency of drinking occasions with meals (Veenstra et al. 1990).

On the other hand, to give a physiological example more related to single drinking occasions, there is clear evidence for a link between very heavy drinking occasions and Fetal Alcohol Syndrome (FAS) (see US Secretary of Health and Human Services 1993, Plant 1997). Again, instruments for assessing alcohol consumption related to research on FAS should very carefully try to capture binge drinking episodes and their circumstances.

The same principles should also apply to other outcome variables, on the individual as well as on the societal level. A good example would be Gruenewald and Treno's theory of drinking behaviour and injury (1996). This includes frequency, average drinks per occasion, as well as variance, as indicators of drinking patterns, on the basis of which a mathematical model to predict risk for injury is developed.

One link that is often overlooked, however, should be mentioned. Alcohol-related harm is often operationalised in surveys with questions like: 'During the last twelve months, was there a time that you felt your alcohol use had a harmful effect on your physical health?' What is often forgotten, is that these questions may measure attitudes about harm as well as harm. Thus, in a 'wet' culture like Bavaria, vomiting into the neighbour's garden during a party is nothing drastic and would surely not been taken into consideration when answering a question about alcohol-related harm. In a dry and Protestant culture like the US South, however, such a behaviour may qualify for laying a charge against somebody, and also being listed as alcohol-related harm (Cahalan and Room 1974). Unfortunately, this line of argument has not been theoretically sufficiently developed nor empirically tested.

Consequences for Alcohol Epidemiology

Unfortunately, we have had to paint a rather pessimistic picture of the state of alcohol epidemiology in terms of its current capacity to provide knowledge for harm-reduction initiatives. However, work on the relation of drinking patterns to harm is now proceeding around the world. In 1995 a conference entirely devoted to this topic was held in Toronto (International Conference on Social and Health Effects of Different Drinking Patterns, 13–17 November 1995; see Table 14.2 overleaf for a summary of the preliminary results of this conference). Further work is planned and it is hoped to establish the role of drinking patterns in harm as the standard topic of alcohol epidemiology. What is most needed at this point *are routinely collected descriptive statistics on the different harm indicators* laid out in Point 3 (see Room 1996). Such statistics are necessary for research and monitoring, as well as prevention planning and evaluation.

Second, alcohol epidemiology has to move beyond its present atheoretical phase of automatically linking average volume of drinking to different outcomes. Empirical research in the area of alcohol epidemiology needs to be securely grounded in *theories regarding patterns of drinking that are hazardous, based on growing evidence from biochemical, behavioural and social studies.* Moreover, we need to develop theoretically driven measures not only for harm indicators, but also for drinking patterns. Finally, our methodological and statistical methods have to improve dramatically to match the demands of theoretical concepts (see Rehm et al. 1996).

The leading journals in this field have a crucial responsibility for this shift. Alcohol epidemiology has always been more part of alcohol studies in general than of epidemiology. A positive consequence of this fact has been that social variables have been given more attention than in medical epidemiology. A negative consequence, however, has been a lesser attention to the biochemical evidence as well as a lack of the methodological rigour that has increasingly shaped general epidemiology or survey research. Future editorial policies should try to keep the positive aspects but should no longer accept research that does not adequately reflect the advances in other areas of science.

Table 14.2: Statements from the International Conference on Social and Health Effects of Different Drinking Patterns

Statement 1	Patterns of drinking are important influences on health and social outcomes, but epidemiological outcome should continue to include measures of volume of drinking (average quantity) as a key independent variable.
Statement 2	Patterns of drinking introduce the social element into alcohol epidemiology.
Statement 3	Social harms, benefits and casualties seem to be more closely linked than chronic health conditions to the dimension of patterns of drinking.
Statement 4	Future epidemiological research in alcohol epidemiology must develop standardised measures for the various elements encompassed by the term 'patterns of drinking' and more sophisticated methodologies and methods of analysis.
Statement 5	Variables that measure patterns of drinking are important considerations in policy and programme development. Guidelines on low-risk drinking, both from individual and population perspectives, must take these variables into account.

Source: Rehm et al., 1996.

Notes

1   Historically, the main theoretical shift in the alcohol field in this respect had been from the disease model with 'alcoholism' as an entity and the sole major problematic consequence of alcohol use to the acceptance of a wider range of alcohol-related problems including, for example, impaired driving or alcohol-related family dysfunction (Edwards et al. 1977).

2   A variant of this reasoning may focus on benefits of alcohol consumption (for example, cardiovascular, psychological) and harmful consequences, at the same time. The goal will be trying to minimise harm while keeping the maximum beneficial effects. Such a line of reasoning becomes more important as some studies indicate that alcohol overall appears to prevent more premature deaths than it causes (English et al. 1995, Single et al. 1996). However, alcohol causes much more years of

life lost and time in hospital than it prevents. While such a strategy may have consequences for the overall level of consumption, patterns of consumption play an even more crucial role to achieve this goal.

3   Mortality statistics also contribute to part of the second column (mortality from accidents and injuries; ICD 9 E-codes). In most industrialised countries the alcohol-related morbidity and mortality from accidents and injuries outweighs morbidity and mortality from more physiologically related categories such as liver cirrhosis or cancers.

4   Attributable fractions for alcohol for different causes of mortality may vary drastically for causes of death heavily influenced by the social context, such as suicide or road accidents, but there is also variation in causes such as liver cirrhosis; in some parts of the world non-alcoholic liver cirrhosis rates are quite substantial whereas in others this category is almost non-existent.

References

Aronson, E., Ellsworth, P.C., Carlsmith, J.M. and Gonzales, M.H. (1990) *Methods of Research in Social Psychology*, New York, McGraw-Hill.

Ashley, M.J., Ferrence, R., Room, R., Bondy, S., Rehm, J. and Single, E. (forthcoming). 'Moderate drinking and health: implications of recent evidence for clinical practice', *Canadian Family Physician*.

Becker, H. (1973) *Outsiders*, Glencoe, IL, Free Press.

Bondy, S.J. (1996) 'Overview of studies on drinking patterns and their reported consequences', *Addiction*, 91: 1663–74.

Brochu, S. (1995) 'Estimating the costs of drug-related crime', Paper presented at the Second International Symposium on the Social and Economic Costs of Substance Abuse, Montebello, Quebec, 2–5 October.

Cahalan, D. and Room, R. (1974) *Problem Drinking Among American Men*, New Brunswick: Rutgers Center of Alcohol Studies, Monograph No. 7.

Campbell, D.T. and Stanley, J.C. (1966) *Experimental and Quasi-Experimental Designs for Research*, Chicago, Rand McNally.

Edwards, G., Anderson, P., Babor, T.F., Caswell, S., Ferrence, R., Giesbrecht, N., Godfrey, C., Holder, H.D., Lemmens, P., Mäkelä, K., Midanik, L.T., Norström, T., Österberg, E., Romelsjö, A., Room, R., Simpura, J. and Skog, Ø-J. (1994) *Alcohol Policy and the Public Good*, Oxford, Oxford University Press.

Edwards, G., Gross, M.M., Keller, M., Moser, J. and Room, R. (eds) (1977) *Alcohol-Related Disabilities*, Geneva, WHO (WHO Offset Publication No. 32).

English, D.R., Holman, C.D.J., Milne, E., Winter, M.G., Hulse, G.K. and Codde, J.P. (1995) *The Quantification of Drug Caused Morbidity and Mortality in Australia*, Canberra, Australian Government Publishing Service.

Gadenne, V. (1984) *Theorie und Erfahrung in der psychologischen*

Forschung [Theory and experience in psychological research], Tübingen, Mohr.

Goldberg, D.M., Hahn, S.E. and Parkes, J.G. (1995) 'Beyond alcohol: Beverage consumption and cardiovascular mortality', *Acta Clinica Chimica*, 237: 155–87.

Goode, E. (1984) *Deviant Behavior*, Englewood Cliffs, N.J., Prentice Hall.

Gruenewald, P.J. and Treno, A.J. (1996) 'Drinking patterns and drinking behaviors: Theoretical models of risky acts', *Contemporary Drug Problems*, 23: 407–40.

Kendall, P., Fischer, B., Rehm, J. and Room, R. (1995) 'Charting WHO goals for the year 2000: Are we on track?', Keynote address delivered at the 37th ICAA Congress, San Diego, August.

Maclure, M. (1993) 'Demonstration of deductive meta-analysis: ethanol intake and risk of myocardial infarction', *Epidemiologic Reviews*, 15: 328–51.

McBride, D.C. and McCoy, C.B. (1993) 'The drugs–crime relationship: An analytical framework', *The Prison Journal*, 73: 257–78.

Mäkelä, K. and Mustonen, H. (1996) 'The reward structure of drinking at different stages of the drinking careers', *Contemporary Drug Problems*, 23: 479–92.

Pernanen, K. (1991) *Alcohol in Human Violence*, New York, Guilford Press.

Plant, M.L. (1997) *Women and Alcohol: Contemporary and Historical Perspectives*, London, Free Association Books.

Rehm, J., Ashley, M.J. and Dubois, G. (forthcoming) 'Alcohol and health: individual and population perspectives', *Addiction*.

Rehm, J., Ashley, M.J., Room, R., Single, E., Bondy, S., Ferrence, R. and Giesbrecht, N., in collaboration with participants in the 'International Conference on Social and Health Effects of Different Drinking Patterns' (1996) 'On the emerging paradigm of drinking patterns and their social and health consequences', *Addiction*, 91: 1615–21.

Rehm, J. and Strack, F. (1994) 'Kontrolltechniken', in Hermann, T. and Tack, W. (eds) *Methodologische Grundlagen der Psychologie*. [Methodology to control for inferring causality] *Enzyklopädie der Psychologie*, Themenbereich B, Serie 1, Band 1. Göttingen, Hogrefe, pp. 508–55.

Robson, L. and Single, E. (1995) *Literature Review of Studies on the Economic Costs*, Ottawa, Canadian Centre on Substance Abuse.

Room, R. (1983) 'Alcohol and crime: behavioral aspects', in Kadish, S. (ed.) *Encyclopedia of Crime and Justice* (Vol. 1, pp. 35–44), New York, Free Press.

Room, R. (1985) 'Alcohol as a cause: empirical links and social definitions', in Wartburg, J-P v., Magnenat, P., Müller, R. and Wyss, S. (eds) *Currents in alcohol research and the prevention of alcohol problems*, Berne, Huber, pp. 11–19.

Room, R. (1996) 'Alcohol consumption and social harm – a historical overview', *Contemporary Drug Problems*, 23: 373–88.

Room, R., Janca, A., Bennett, L.A., Schmidt, L. and Sartorius, N. (1996) 'WHO cross-cultural applicability research on diagnosis and assessment of substance use disorders: an overview of methods and selected results', *Addiction*, 91: 199–220. (With commentary series pp. 221–30.)

Rothman, K.J. (1986) *Modern Epidemiology*, Boston, MA, Little Brown and Company.

Rothman, K.J. (1988) *Causal Inference*, Chestnut Hill, Epidemiology Resources.

Single, E. (1995) 'Defining harm reduction', *Drug and Alcohol Review*, 14: 287–90.

Single, E., Robson, L., Xie, X. and Rehm, J. in collaboration with Moore, R., Choi, B., Desjardins, S. and Anderson, J. (1996) *The Costs of Substance Abuse in Canada*, Ottawa, Canadian Centre on Substance Abuse.

Stockwell, T., Daly, A., Phillips, M., Masters, L., Midford, R., Gahegan, M. and Philp, A. (1996) 'Total versus hazardous per capita alcohol consumption as predictors of acute and chronic alcohol-related harm', *Contemporary Drug Problems*, 23: 441–64.

US Secretary of Health and Human Services (1993) *Eighth Special Report to the US Congress on Alcohol and Health*, Washington, National Institute on Alcohol Abuse and Alcoholism, NIH Publication No. 94-3699.

Veenstra, J., Ockhuizen, T., Van de Pol, H., Wedel, M. and Schaafsma, G. (1990) 'Effects of a moderate dose of alcohol on blood lipids and lipoproteins postprandially and in the fasting state', *Alcohol and Alcoholism*, 25: 371–7.

Walsh, G. and Rehm, J. (1996) 'Daily drinking and harm', *Contemporary Drug Problems*, 23: 465–78.

WHO (1981) *Global Strategy for Health for All by the Year 2000*, Geneva, World Health Organization.

WHO (1992) *The ICD-10 Classification of Mental and Behavioural Disorders: Clinical Descriptions and Diagnostic Guidelines*, Geneva, World Health Organization.

WHO (1993) *The ICD-10 Classification of Mental and Behavioural Disorders. Clinical Descriptions and Diagnostic Guidelines*, Geneva, World Health Organization.

WHO (1994a) *Implementation of the Global Strategy for Health for All by the Year 2000* (Vol. 1), Geneva, World Health Organization.

WHO (1994b) *Implementation of the Global Strategy for Health for All by the Year 2000* (Vol. 5), Geneva, World Health Organization, European Region.

WHO Europe (1993) *European Alcohol Action Plan*. Copenhagen, World Health Organization, Regional Office for Europe.

WHO Europe (1994) *Health in Europe*, Copenhagen, World Health Organization, Regional Office for Europe.

Xie, X., Rehm, J., Single, E. and Robson, L. (1996) *The Economic Costs of Alcohol, Tobacco and Illicit Drug Abuse in Ontario: 1992*, Toronto, Addiction Research Foundation.

15 Implications and Priorities for the Future

Martin Plant, Eric Single and Tim Stockwell

The harmful consumption of alcohol ruins and brings to a premature end the lives of very large numbers of people. Accordingly the adoption of effective strategies to reduce the adverse consequences of drinking should receive high priority. This book has brought together a multi-disciplinary group of contributors. They have produced a collection of reviews each of which is concerned with evidence of the effectiveness of specific approaches to minimising alcohol-related problems. The approaches considered, though wide-ranging, are certainly not exhaustive, nor do the authors claim to have considered every possible example from previous experience. Indeed, most of the evidence and examples cited above have originated from the industrialised and primarily English-speaking world. Relatively little has been noted from developing countries or from Eastern Europe, for example, even though alcohol-related problems are a major cause of national concern in many countries of the latter.

Some of the major works on alcohol control have emphasised what we will call the 'public health approach' which lays great stress on the issue of controlling national per capita alcohol consumption levels (see Bruun et al. 1975, Edwards et al. 1994). Such contributions to the alcohol debate have been praiseworthy and important. In particular, such statements have done much to emphasise the complexity of the aetiology of 'problem drinking' and to highlight the social context in which such behaviours occur. There is clearly an association between overall national or community levels of alcohol consumption and levels of alcohol-related problems. Even so, this association is by no means simple or uniform. Different subgroups within each population vary greatly in relation to their patterns of drinking and their risks of incurring or inflicting upon others adverse consequences due to this behaviour. Recent evidence has, as noted above, drawn attention to the fact that the pattern of drinking is an important factor in influencing the risk of adverse consequences. Some people are at greater risk than others, even though their weekly or annual alcohol consumption may be similar.

In practical terms, the reduction of alcohol-related problems has to be negotiated within specific political and cultural contexts. There has been little sign that governments or individuals are attracted to control measures which have much effect on themselves. Less 'invasive' measures appear to have greater support. Two important points are emphasised. First, this book does present a different emphasis from works promoting the traditional public health perspective outlined above. In spite of this, it is also stressed that harm minimisation per se is neutral on the issue of controlling per capita consumption. It is the view of the editors, though not necessarily of the other contributors to this book, that alcohol control policies have to be devised in their varied local contexts. They may be adopted at different levels and in different ways. Accordingly, it is suggested that 'harm minimisation' is not incompatible with the adoption of controls on per capita consumption. The latter focuses on reducing consumption to reduce problems, while harm minimisation is designed to reduce problems. The European Alcohol Action Plan of the World Health Organization (1994) has adopted the traditional public health approach. In spite of this, one of the reports that is linked with this plan advocates the adoption of a number of practical measures of the type that has been considered in this book (Ritson 1995). As the preceding chapters have demonstrated, there appears to be a substantial and growing number of examples of attempts to implement some form of harm minimisation or reduction and that some of these have been successful.

The type of initiatives that are considered in this book could usefully be considered in a number of ways:

- Have they worked?

- Are they transferable to other contexts?

- Are they politically and/socially acceptable?

It is reasonable for each of these considerations to be applied when devising harm minimisation or any other form of strategy to curb alcohol-related problems wherever they are evident. There are major differences between political systems and national attitudes to alcohol, its use and the control of associated problems. As emphasised by Musto in Chapter 2, political orientations to alcohol have also varied at different historical periods. In view of this it is probably unrealistic to assume that any single approach to curbing alcohol-related problems will readily, if ever, be universally adopted. Responses must be socially and politically appropriate and acceptable. Because of this it is as important to consider the issue of political and social appropriateness as it is to weigh evidence related to 'effectiveness'. Some strategies may have led to reductions in some contexts, but simply be unattractive or impracticable in other settings. For example, in Chapter 9 Hingson, Berson and Dowley have described how the raising of the minimum legal age of alcohol purchase and consumption in the US has led to reductions in some measures of problems amongst college students. In spite of this, there is no sign that other countries are eager to adopt a similar policy. Some responses to alcohol problems are not readily transferable for cultural or political reasons. As discussed in Chapter 14, the European Alcohol Action Plan of the World Health Organization (1994) sets out general targets for reducing levels of per capita alcohol consumption. Such objectives may prove difficult to achieve in the context of stable or declining alcohol consumption in many western countries, and in marked contrast, escalating alcohol consumption and related problems in eastern countries. A more fundamental difficulty is likely to be the gaining of political and popular support for a programme designed to reduce total population alcohol consumption (Stockwell et al. 1996).

It is quite legitimate to commend control of per capita alcohol consumption as a means of reducing levels of alcohol-related damage. Nevertheless, it appears that this has only been attractive at particular times of national crisis or as a reflection of strong national moral or religious sentiments. In most countries and at most times, this has not been a popular approach. In view of this, it is reasonable to consider all available practical approaches to reducing what in many localities are very widespread and serious problems. It is also important to be pragmatic, hence the adoption of the subtitle of this book: 'What works?'

As the preceding chapters have demonstrated, it is possible to achieve marked reductions in levels of alcohol-related problems. Possibly the most dramatic improvement in this regard has been evident in the reduction in alcohol-impaired driving. This has been evident in a number of countries and this improvement has diverged from trends in per capita alcohol consumption. It has to be noted that the precise reasons for the fall in this particular type of problem are far from clear, since it has occurred under a number of widely divergent legal systems.

Most of the evidence considered above has related to the implementation of policies driven by the recognition that a problem was serious enough to warrant a search for a solution. Some of the policies reviewed have been implemented at a national level, but most have been local. The essential element behind all of these initiatives has been political and/or public concern. Such concern has been harnessed and channelled into action, sometimes with gratifying results. It is apparent that if within a country or a community key people are sufficiently motivated, coalitions can be formed to devise and introduce measures designed to achieve reductions in levels of specific problems. This type of targeted approach has been described by Stockwell et al. (1996) as 'sharpening the focus of alcohol policy'. The advantage of a harm-minimisation or risk-reduction approach is that it is likely to be supported by national, regional or local perception that there is a serious problem. Political and public support are essential elements in adopting effective alcohol control policies and, even more important, for sustaining those policies that prove to be effective.

From the evidence presented in preceding chapters a number of promising approaches to alcohol-related problems have emerged. These all involve introducing controls, or at least incentives, into the drinking environment. From the information that has been reviewed, it would appear worthwhile to commend the experimental adoption in new settings and jurisdictions of policies such as zoning, local by-laws to limit the opening of licensed premises, server training and responsible beverage service, standard unit labelling of alcoholic containers, warning labels or, perhaps better still, information-bearing labels, rigorous enforcement of laws relating to both alcohol-impaired driving and the operation of licensed premises. In addition, the role of access controls or fiscal controls should also be considered. As emphasised by Cameron in Chapter 13, it is also important to include treatment and counselling services and agencies such as Alcoholics Anonymous as part of any attempt to formulate a comprehensive response to alcohol-related problems.

It is emphasised that any single package of control measures is unlikely to be universally acceptable. Different national, regional and local approaches should be devised to suit specific conditions and contexts. Even so, it would be a pity if future strategies did not build upon what has already been attempted and, in some instances, achieved. It has already been stressed that some of the approaches described in this book may not be readily transferred to other settings. Others might be transferable, or at least adaptable.

Far more regional and local initiatives and experiments exist than have been described in these pages. In the United Kingdom, for example, there have for some time been a number of server training schemes and local by-laws limiting drinking in public in some urban areas. The results of many of these initiatives have not been published and the impact of much of what is done in the alcohol field remains unclear.

Accordingly, one obvious future priority is to ensure that harm-minimisation strategies should whenever possible be properly evaluated. Such evaluation should be an integral component in the design of policies. Researchers have a responsibility in this context to disseminate information about which policies appear to be productive and which do not. In addition, policy makers and key actors such as the police, those in the health and social services, city councils and those in the beverage alcohol industry need to be made aware not only of what has worked in the past, but of the importance of monitoring the effects of any major new activities. Alcohol is not at the top of every policy maker's agenda. Because of this, researchers, clinicians and others professionally concerned with the reduction in levels of alcohol problems also have a responsibility to draw to the attention of those who influence and shape public policy the facts that in many locales, alcohol-related problems are extremely widespread and serious, that such problems are often not insoluble and that a number of options exist for reducing the harm associated with the consumption of society's most popular recreational drug.

References

Bruun, K., Edwards, G., Lumio, M., Mäkelä, K., Pan, L., Popham, R.E., Room, R., Schmidt, W., Skog, Ø-J., Sulkunen, P. and Österberg, E. (1975) *Alcohol Control Policies in Public Health Perspective*, Helsinki, Finnish Foundation for Alcohol Studies.

Edwards, G., Anderson, P., Babor, T.F., Casswell, S., Ferrence, R., Giesbrecht, N., Godfrey, C., Holder, H.D., Lemmens, P., Mäkelä, K., Midanik, L., Norström, T., Österberg, E., Romelsjö, A., Room, R., Simpura, J. and Skog, Ø-J. (1994) *Alcohol Policy and the Public Good*, Oxford, Oxford University Press.

Ritson, E.B. (1995) *Community and Municipal Action on Alcohol*, Copenhagen, World Health Organization Regional Publications European Series No. 63.

Stockwell, T., Single, E., Hawks, D. and Rehm, J. (1996) 'Sharpening the focus of alcohol policy from aggregate consumption to harm and risk

reduction', Paper presented at 22nd Annual Alcohol Epidemiology Symposium, Kettil Bruun Society, Edinburgh, 7 June.
World Health Organization (1994) *European Alcohol Action Plan*, Copenhagen, World Health Organization Regional Office for Europe.

Author Index

Subject Index

Indexes by Judith Lavender